OBJECTIVE
COMMUNICATION

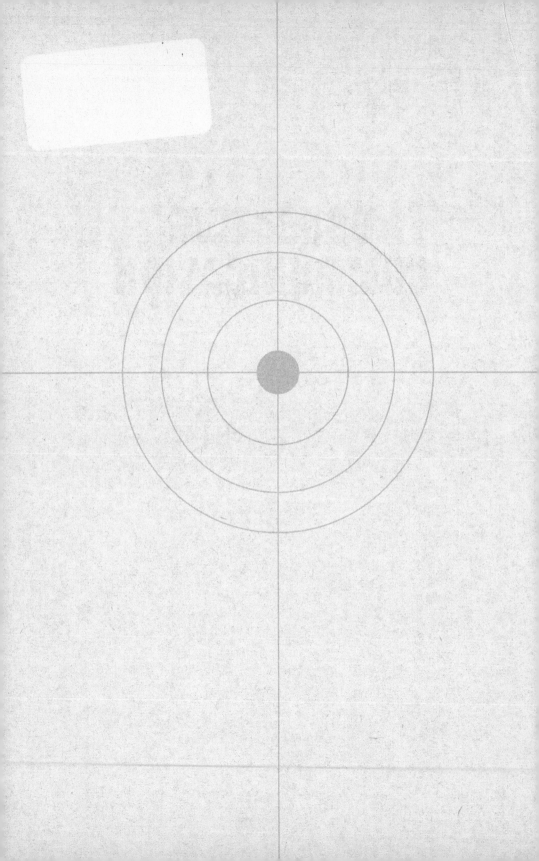

OBJECTIVE COMMUNICATION

Writing, Speaking, and Arguing

LEONARD PEIKOFF

Edited by Barry Wood

NEW AMERICAN LIBRARY

New American Library
Published by the Penguin Group
Penguin Group (USA) Inc., 375 Hudson Street,
New York, New York 10014, USA

USA | Canada | UK | Ireland | Australia | New Zealand | India | South Africa | China

Penguin Books Ltd., Registered Offices: 80 Strand, London WC2R 0RL, England
For more information about the Penguin Group visit penguin.com.

First published by New American Library,
a division of Penguin Group (USA) Inc.

First Printing, September 2013

 REGISTERED TRADEMARK—MARCA REGISTRADA

LIBRARY OF CONGRESS CATALOGING-IN-PUBLICATION DATA:
Peikoff, Leonard.
Objective communication/Leonard Peikoff; edited by Barry Wood.
p. cm.
ISBN 978-0-451-41815-9
1. Philosophy–Authorship. 2. Objectivism (Philosophy)
3. Rand, Ayn. I. Wood, Barry, 1940– editor of compilation.
II. Title.
B52.7.P45 2013
149—dc23   2013008208

Printed in the United States of America
1   3   4   7   9   10   8   6   4   2

Set in Minion Pro
Designed by Elke Sigal

PUBLISHER'S NOTE
While the author has made every effort to provide accurate telephone numbers, Internet addresses
and other contact information at the time of publication, neither the publisher nor the author assumes any responsibility for errors, or for changes that occur after publication. Further, publisher
does not have any control over and does not assume any responsibility for author or third-party
Web sites or their content.

CONTENTS

Editor's Preface   *vii*

From Leonard Peikoff   *ix*

About This Course   *xi*

1. Introductory Remarks   *1*

2. Philosophic Bases of Communication   *7*

3. Four Essential Principles   *18*

4. Keeping Material Self-contained   *49*

5. Rationalism   *71*

6. Objectivity   *84*

7. Analysis of Student Papers   *116*

8. Principles of Speaking   *173*

9. Analysis of Student Presentations   *204*

10. Principles of Arguing   *243*

11. Analysis of Student Arguments   *280*

12. Concluding Remarks   *323*

Appendices   *325*

EDITOR'S PREFACE

OBJECTIVE COMMUNICATION IS a course on how to present ideas clearly and effectively, whether in writing, speaking, or argument. Leonard Peikoff describes it in his opening remarks as "the application of Objectivist philosophic principles to the problem of achieving clear thought and communication about ideas." The material in this book was originally presented as a series of lectures in New York City in early 1980. For many years these lectures were available on tape or CD for interested listeners, and they are still used in the curriculum of the Objectivist Academic Center at the Ayn Rand Institute. A full transcript of the original lectures may be found in the Ayn Rand Archives, a special collection of the Ayn Rand Institute.

A word on the course content is in order. *Objective Communication* was not intended as a formal or methodical treatment of its subject; nor was it an attempt at original or substantial philosophic insight. Rather, it was offered as a series of informal, albeit philosophically based, observations and guidelines for students to grasp and put into practice. Thus, in addition to the lectures proper, Dr. Peikoff provided samples of writing, including writing by Ayn Rand, for the audience to analyze. He also invited volunteers to submit for critique a brief essay, oral presentation, or unscripted argument on a given topic. Finally, each lecture was followed by an extensive and wide-ranging question-and-answer period. The course thus involved a great deal of audience participation, which is reflected in the organization and contents of this book. For works offering systematic conceptual precision, coupled with integration on a broad scale, readers are referred to Dr. Peikoff's books *The Ominous Parallels*, *Objectivism: The Philosophy of Ayn Rand*, and *The DIM Hypothesis*.

In editing these lectures for publication, I have made a number of changes. I have rearranged the lecture material slightly in order to create a more orderly structure. I have eliminated repetition and colloquialisms and touched up grammar where needed. In merging the question-and-answer sessions into the text, I have eliminated some exchanges that I deemed irrelevant (however interesting), and moved others to where I thought they would be more appropriate. All punctuation is my own, as are paragraph breaks and subsection titles. Material prepared for the course by students is either integrated into the text or reproduced in the appendices.

I would like to express my profound gratitude to Leonard Peikoff for the opportunity to turn these lectures into a book. But I must also stress that while I feel confident that I have accurately rendered the original, oral material into written form, Dr. Peikoff has neither reviewed nor approved the content of this book.

Barry Wood

FROM LEONARD PEIKOFF

PEOPLE HAVE OFTEN asked for a written version of my oral lecture courses, on the premise—with which I agree—that written lectures are much more accessible to the student. Writing, however, is in this context virtually a different language from speaking; a raw transcript of an extemporaneous speech, however excellent, is almost always filled with defects and confusions of one sort or another—and so is frequently boring as well. To turn a lecture course into an accurate, clear, and valuable book, a huge amount of time-consuming editing is required, a task that can be performed only by an individual with the necessary motivation, knowledge of the subject, and editorial skills. My own age and priorities make it impossible for me to undertake such a task.

I have therefore decided to authorize several individuals who possess the necessary qualifications to edit and bring out in book form certain of my courses, and to do so entirely without my participation. Although I have confidence in these editors to the extent that I know them, I have had no part in their work at any stage—no guiding discussions, no reading of transcripts, not even a glance at early drafts or final copy. Even a glance might reveal errors, and I could not then evade the need to read more, which is precisely what is out of the question.

In my opinion, the lecture course in this book is of real value to those interested in the subject. But when you read it, please bear two things in mind: Barry Wood is an experienced editor and lecturer—and I have no idea what he has done in this book.

Leonard Peikoff
April 10, 2012

P.S. If you happen to spot and wish to point out seeming errors in the text, please e-mail Dr. Wood at the Ayn Rand Institute, c/o mail@aynrand.org. If you like this book, I may add, do not give me too much of the credit. My course provided, let us say, the spirit, but Dr. Wood gave it the flesh required to live.

ABOUT THIS COURSE

THIS COURSE STARTED as a number of small seminars that I gave to a small group. Papers or talks were presented by individual students, and then subjected to group commentary and group criticism. What I have essentially done for this series of lectures is to organize, in a more structured way, the kinds of points that came out in those early seminars, as well as some other ones. This is the beginning of a very complex field. I am not claiming that this is a comprehensive, definitive treatise on communication. But it does teach some valuable first steps.

Our concern in this course is not with style, but with content—in other words, with presenting the content clearly and interestingly. We are not concerned with literary polish, the nuances of oratory, or any such thing. We are concerned with how to present ideas objectively, logically, and convincingly. We are concerned with the communication of ideas, particularly philosophic ideas, because that is what is crucial in today's world, and, in particular, Objectivist ideas, because I want our exercises in part to serve the additional purpose of helping to refresh or expand your knowledge of Objectivism. Some of the things that we cover will obviously be more broadly applicable to any form of communication, even a declaration of love. But most of it is going to center on what is required to present ideas in writing, speaking, and arguing.

This course is titled Objective—not Objectivist—Communication. Philosophy is the base of art and science, but there is no Objectivist or Platonist physics, only physics, and the same is true of any art or science. Where then does Objectivism come in? All science and all art, including the art of communication, rests on a philosophic base. And the base of this course—not the content per se, but the base—is Objectivism. So you can regard this course as the application of Objectivist philosophic principles to the problem of achieving clear thought and communication about ideas.

OBJECTIVE COMMUNICATION

CHAPTER 1

INTRODUCTORY REMARKS

REASON, ACCORDING TO Objectivism, is man's means of achieving values. And today, we live in a very anti-reason culture. You would expect that that would affect values in every realm negatively, and if you look around you, you see that, in fact, it has. I can point to just about any realm of human existence and you see the state that it is in today. I do not even have to discuss politics, for instance, or economics; I just have to mention the price of gasoline, the presidential candidates, or Iran. I do not have to discuss the state of art, culture, and education; I just ask you to read the *New York Times Book Review*, or see the latest Hollywood movie.

The same disaster, the same total collapse, is true in the field that is the central concern of this course: communication. Communication is the act of making one's thought known to others. It presupposes the ability to think, to have thoughts that you then want to communicate. Today's anti-reason trend openly attacks and subverts both thought and its social expression, communication.

Every aspect of reason is under relentless attack, and has been for a long time. Reason begins with sensory data and integrates them into concepts, using the method of logic, in an attempt to achieve objective cognition. Just look at each of these elements. The senses are routinely attacked

1

as giving us not true reality, but merely reality as it appears to man, just the human appearance granted by our senses. Consequently, we are told that sense data are subjective. What really would give us reality? There are numerous candidates: extrasensory perception (ESP), or direct messages from the devil, or your recollection of your incarnation in a previous life, or some other nonsensory form of arrant mysticism. Concepts, we are told, are just words, mere arbitrary social conventions; there is no such thing as a right or wrong way to use words, it is said, so everybody does his own thing. Definitions, too, are said to be arbitrary. Moreover, we are told that there is nothing special about words, no reason cognition or communication requires them; the parallel to ESP, so to speak, is ECU—extraconceptual understanding—which takes the form of intuition, divine inspiration, and so on. Finally, we are told that logic, the method of reason, is a game like chess, with entirely arbitrary rules; you play whatever game you want, and anybody else can play whatever game he wants. We have a whole proliferation of alleged games—non-Aristotelian logics, many-valued logics, and so on—with the idea, therefore, that there is no objective relationship between one fact and another, or one idea and another. Anything goes, in any sequence, on any base or no base.

As a result of all this, objectivity is declared to be impossible, with regard both to facts and to values, with regard both to what is true and to what is good. We are told that every element of reason is detached from reality, and therefore that reality gives us no guidance, and therefore that we cannot be objective; we must go by our feelings, with each of us accepting what is true for him. When you are no longer guided by reason, you can be guided only by feeling—your own feeling or the feeling of your group, whether ethnic, racial, or otherwise. Therefore, we are told, each individual or group lives in a so-called private world that is inaccessible to outsiders, and we are often told, logically enough, that communication between such groups or individuals is impossible—which, of course, is true on that view of the human mind.

When all of this and much more goes through an entire culture—through its educational system, its books, its movies, and all the rest—

what will be the result in thought and communication? The obvious example of it would be what passes today for education: institutionalized illiteracy, often described as the democratic process in cognition. We see students who do not know how to spell. Nor can they define words, because words are said to have no relationship to reality; they are arbitrary. At the same time, students are told, we have to have some standard, sometimes, by which to define some things; so you have to accept an authority, which is society; and therefore, if society says that "the good" means altruism, you simply accept that. We see students who have no concept of organization, structure, or order, neither of putting words into sentences (which is grammar), nor of putting thoughts into paragraphs, nor of ordering paragraphs into a logical development. These students regard order or structure as arbitrary, of course, because they have been taught that logic is arbitrary, and therefore that you can start anywhere and go anywhere, guided by feeling and/or by the vibrations of whatever detours they expect you to take next. Students have no concept of objective methods, because they have been taught that objectivity is impossible. Therefore, when they disagree with one another, it is "I feel" versus "You feel"—which is one step away from "Aryan science" versus "Jewish science."

If cooking were taught on the same premise on which cognition and communication are taught today—that anything goes, that there are no standards, no rules, no methods, no objectivity—the result would be mass starvation. The same is true in the realm of thought and communication. We have a generation a good part of which is proudly inarticulate, who are unable to speak or state their thoughts, and who feel it is simply necessary to say, "You know, like, whatever." A mind of this sort is effectively cut off from this world cognitively, a state that often does not bother the person, because he feels he is in contact with a higher dimension. Obviously, the attacks on reason have led to a widespread deterioration, not to say collapse, of thought and communication.

There is another aspect to this problem. The widespread attacks on reason corrupt not only the tools and methods of communication, but also the content. In other words, they are attacks on ideas as such. People are bombarded by ideas that they cannot live by, ideas that are blatantly contrary to reality and to the requirements of life, ideas that would lead to immediate destruction if you took them literally. We are told, for instance, that reality is simply a social construct—a belief that would annihilate the believer if he acted on it in the face of an oncoming truck. You know, of course, what would happen if people acted on altruism literally. Given a bombardment of anti-reality, anti-reason, anti-self, anti-life ideas, people come to conclude you cannot take ideas seriously, because if you do, you cannot live. Therefore, ideas become, in people's minds, merely woozy approximations. People do not expect to take them literally, or to act on them consistently. The whole field, to them, is simply outside the realm of science, accuracy, or reason. A sentence from Galt's speech in *Atlas Shrugged* is very relevant here: "A moral code impossible to practice, a code that demands imperfection or death, has taught you to dissolve all ideas in fog, to permit no firm definitions, to regard any concept as approximate and any rule of conduct as elastic, to hedge on any principle, to compromise on any value, to take the middle of any road."* This is true of today's ideas of morality, indeed of today's ideas in all branches of philosophy. They have had the effect of engendering contempt for ideas as such. People therefore think, "Spill out something or other when you talk about ideas, some kind of verbal slop, some kind of bull session of hot air; you do not have to say anything literal, you do not have to be exact or objective. After all, this is only ideas."

The only hope to counteract all this would be a new, pro-reason philosophy. But one result of this widespread attitude is to make today's anti-reason viewpoint self-perpetuating and self-reinforcing. There are three kinds of people in this regard. One is the kind effectively wrecked by today's schools, the passive, inarticulate, "you know" type. Such people are no longer able, or at least no longer willing, to contest what is going on today, so they have no effect socially. Second, there is the kind who are better than that, but who try to preserve their sanity by escaping from

---

* *Atlas Shrugged*, p. 969; "This Is John Galt Speaking," *For the New Intellectual*, p. 172.

ideas; they drop the field of ideas more or less completely and go into a field such as engineering, business, or science, which they think is safely outside the realm of today's chaos. They try to delimit their thought to what they regard as the objective realm. But of course, by that fact, they are no threat to today's entrenched ideas; they resign from the battle without offering any challenge.

The best people are in a third category. They do accept better ideas than what exists today; they do try to fight for a pro-reason viewpoint. But most often these people, too, are undercut and hampered with regard to thought and communication, and as such, they are made comparatively ineffective. Their road is much harder; they are less clear in their own minds than they otherwise might have been, and they are less persuasive to others than is possible. This is partly because in many ways, they absorb modern subjectivity unknowingly. They have been battered throughout their formative years with so much intellectual corruption that most often, it is simply too much, too quickly for them to withstand it entirely. Partly, too, it is by sheer default. None of us, or very few of us, are taught to think or communicate. We never learned the skills or techniques involved. Yet these techniques, with regard both to thought and to communication, are neither innate nor automatic. It is a difficult, complex ability to present ideas, to deal with them, to make them clear. It is an ability that rests on definite principles that have to be defined, applied, and practiced. Thought and communication are an art that has to be learned—and it can be.

In the ancient world, this art was taught. It was called rhetoric. It was the art of how to present ideas persuasively to others, and the major philosophers all had a definite theory on the question. Aristotle wrote a whole treatise on it. Today, however, it is not effectively taught.

The future of the world depends on the spread of the right ideas. That, in turn, requires that the advocates of those ideas understand them clearly in their own minds, and then have the ability to communicate them effectively in whatever form is appropriate—whether in a cocktail party discussion (where it is called for), or to your child if he asks you whether there is a God, or to his teacher if he celebrates UN Day in grade three, or in a paper if you are a student, or to your club when it meets, or in a letter to your editor, or to Congress, or whatever. All of these are the practical, daily means by which the world is changed and saved, saved if what you present is correct. But all of this requires, on the part of the people with the right ideas, inner clarity and the ability to communicate ideas effectively.

Note for a moment the relationship between thought and communication. Communication is extremely helpful to the very process of thought itself. If you hear a new idea, it is not enough to listen passively and nod, even if it is clear to you when you hear it, because it will not really become fully clear to you that way; it will not be integrated into the rest of what you know. When you hear a new idea, you have to work with it. You have to digest it; you have to apply it; you have to make it part of your mental equipment and outlook. Communicating the idea to others is not, of course, the only way to do this. But it is extremely valuable as one method of digesting and learning ideas. It is very common to think that you understand something, to decide that you are going to present it to somebody else, and immediately to find a flood of questions triggered by this thing that you thought was so clear to you. You think, "Where should I start? What does this really rest on? What depends on it; what does it depend on?" And then, supposing you work out a presentation to an audience, you will find that your audience has questions and, sometimes, objections. Sometimes these are irrelevant, but often they are helpful. They can point out aspects or implications that you had not thought of. In my own experience, I have often found that I do not really understand something clearly until I try to give a formal presentation of it to others. The greatest selfish value of teaching, in my judgment, is the clarity that it induces in the teacher's own mind. You can get in on this particular value yourself, even if you are not a teacher, by learning something about effective communication. In other words, learning the skills of communication is a great help in learning the skills of thought as such, and therefore of clarifying your own mental contents.

CHAPTER 2

PHILOSOPHIC BASES OF COMMUNICATION

THE CRUCIAL BRANCH of philosophy that forms the base of the whole field of communication is epistemology. Epistemology is the branch of philosophy concerned with the nature and means of human knowledge. Epistemology tells us what reason is and how it operates, what objectivity is and how we can achieve it. I want to begin with some key aspects of the Objectivist epistemology as the base of understanding what communication is. This will serve as background before we plunge into our main subject.

Knowledge as Conceptual

The first point I want to stress in the philosophic base is that thought and communication require language. There is no thought without words. You can have images, emotions, percepts, or sensory data, but to know what you are perceiving, to identify the percepts, and to communicate your knowledge, you need words. Every word is the symbol of a concept, every word except proper names, such as "John Smith" or "Idaho." Every other word, like "table," "chair," "man," "red," "fish," and so on, stands for a concept. The broader point here is that all human knowledge, thought, and communication is *conceptual*. That is the base of all communication theory.

What are concepts? Ayn Rand's *Introduction to Objectivist Epistemology* gives a detailed technical account,* but as a popular, nontechnical version, we can say that a concept is an integration of percepts. It is a mental symbol that enables us to condense a vast number of percepts into a single entity, one we can thereafter hold as one unit in our minds. Consider the example of "table." How do you form that particular concept? You observe several tables; you observe that they are similar to one another in certain ways and different from other items around them, like chairs, sofas, and so on. On the basis of those differences, you isolate the tables, segregate them out from their surroundings, in your mind. You look at the tables and see that they differ in various ways, but you are able to drop, or abstract away from, the differences. That is the process that Ayn Rand describes as omitting measurements. By this process, we are able to blend or unite all of these percepts into one single mental entity, which we symbolize by a term, "table." It represents the awareness in our mind of the whole group, but it is an awareness in the form now of one symbol. The term "table" stands for an unlimited number of instances, for all the tables of the past, the present, and the future, all of them subsumed in that one word, and we are now able to deal with that vast quantity in one mental unit. That is the pattern of concept formation.

As Ayn Rand points out, concepts are a form of unit reduction. Or, to put it another way, they are a form of shorthand, akin to mental space savers. Concepts take whole chunks of reality—in this case, all the enormous number of tables past, present, and future—and condense them into one unit. The result, for us, is a whole new scale of consciousness immensely more powerful than anything possible to animals. Because of this condensing ability, for instance, we can apply the knowledge we have

---

* See Ayn Rand, *Introduction to Objectivist Epistemology*, Expanded Second Edition (Plume, 1990).

learned from just a few cases to all the members of that field, and thereby get to know universal principles, scientific laws, something impossible to animals. Animals may perceive the same original concretes that we do. But they cannot unite them into a whole; they cannot deal with that scale of information; they cannot *conceive* it. Consequently, they are reduced to passive observation.

While it is true that concepts give us magnificent advantages, they also create a problem. Or, to put it another way, they impose a responsibility. Animals may not get too far cognitively, but as far as they go, they are always clear. On the perceptual level, you are automatically tied to entities out there in reality. If you look out there at a table, you see what you see. It is sharp and delimited (leaving aside cases in which there is fog); there is no effort required on your part as an adult. You, or the dog, or the cat, or whatever, look and see that it is sharp and clear. Concepts, however, as a shorthand, are a complex creation. They are neither automatically clear, nor necessarily formed correctly, nor even necessarily tied to reality.

Most people learn concepts from other people, and often do so without basing those concepts on any actual facts. The result, in such people's minds, is what we call "floating abstractions"—abstract terms with no connection to reality. For instance, suppose you ask the typical student in class today what he thinks of freedom, and he says he is all in favor of it. Then you ask him what he means by the term "freedom," and he says, "Well, freedom is doing whatever you want." You say, "Does that mean you can punch somebody else in the mouth?" And he will say, "No, you have to say 'as long as you do not make other people unhappy.'" So then you say, "In other words, then, if you get an A in this course, that is going to make your neighbor unhappy, so you have deprived him of freedom." "Well," he will say, "I did not mean that. It means not making other people unhappy in improper ways." And you say, "What is an improper way?" "Oh, well, I do not know; we have to go by majority rule."

This is just a condensed example. But does this type of individual know what "freedom" means? He actually does not. He is thus ripe for legislation restricting it and annihilating it in the name of majority rule, and therefore "freedom." Now, in his mind, and in the minds of most people in this category, "freedom" is not an empty noise devoid of any meaning, like "triddle." It has a tenuous connection to something. He may have a mental image of a body racing down a beach without fetters; he may have an emotion, or one or two examples, or a sense of a positive connotation. But he does not have a concept actually subsuming a number of instances integrated by some essential. With such a floating abstraction, of course, he can neither think clearly nor communicate.

To say what you mean, and to know its implications—in other words, to mean what you say—has to be *achieved*. Or, to put it another way, it takes work to acquire clarity in your own mind in the use of concepts. Just the same way that a lens in seeing has to be focused, so does it in thinking. But whereas in seeing, clarity is given to you automatically, in thinking and communicating, it is not; it has to be achieved and maintained by you. Clarity means an unbreached tie to reality; to your listener, therefore, clarity means that he sees, at each point, what in reality you are talking about. Clarity has to be achieved by definite, specific techniques. That is inherent in a conceptual consciousness.

You may think that all that is required is to define all your terms. To be sure, definition is important, but it is not the only technique or method required. Even if you had a perfect definition of every term you used, you could not pepper your readers or listeners with a whole string of such definitions. That would stun them. At most, in any given presentation, you can offer only a few central definitions. In fact, there are a whole variety of methods, techniques, and skills required to keep that lens focused, so that at each point, you know exactly what you are thinking and your audience knows exactly what you are saying. These include answering such questions as: Where do you start in any presentation so that the base in reality is clear? What do you cover? What do you omit? On the perceptual level, there is no equivalent of that. You can see something in your path, and turn and see something else, and turn back, and it does not interfere with the clarity; each step is clear. On the conceptual level, though, what you include or omit is essential to the clarity of what is there. Other issues include: What confusions should you pause on and answer? When should you ignore something, even though it occurs to you? In what order should you proceed in a presentation? What options are there? What kinds of things are not optional? Should you give examples? When? How many? Why? The answers to these questions, and many more, are the types of things that have to be learned, by the very nature of a conceptual consciousness.

In summary, on the conceptual level we are not plunging in from scratch. We are speaking in an advanced shorthand; we are counting on a whole structure of knowledge that has to be tied to reality, and we have to know how to do that.

Knowledge as Contextual

A second aspect of a conceptual consciousness, one that is essential to clarity in both proper thought and communication, is that human knowledge is contextual. We do not acquire knowledge in a vacuum. Our knowledge is based on previous knowledge. Of course, we have to begin by sensory observation. Thereafter, though, we build a whole structure. At any given point, there is a certain sum that represents what we know on a given topic, and that is what permits us to go on to learn more. That sum, we say, is the *context* for the new point. The context means the cognitive sum that conditions everything that is still to come. It determines how we understand the new point, estimate it, interpret it, and apply it.

The point here is that in all thought and communication, there is a context that conditions what is occurring. Knowledge, to look at it another way, is relational. It is not a mosaic of independent, disconnected pieces, but a sum of interconnected elements, each bearing on and relevant to the others. Contrary to the claims of religion, knowledge is not a series of revelations, each a kind of separate, disconnected thunderbolt that you have to accept apart from its relation to any other revelation, or to anything else you know. Human beings have no way of dealing with ideas except by relating one item of knowledge to the rest, connecting it to the context. In a vacuum, we can do nothing.

You can see the role of context in human thought, knowledge, and communication very simply. Suppose you come late to a lecture. You arrive in the middle of the lecture and sit down, and the first sentence that you hear the lecturer say is, "All human beings have a right to life." Your neighbor then turns to you and says, "Wonderful! Do you agree with him?" Obviously, you believe that men have rights; but as you will see immediately, you do not know what has conditioned this statement; you do not know what the context is. Depending on the context, this statement can have enormously different implications and significance. For instance, if it is made by a follower of Thomas Jefferson, that is one thing, and in that sense, of course, Objectivism would certainly endorse it. But suppose it is made by an advocate of socialized medicine who has just made a speech claiming that if you do not have medical care, your life is threatened and rights become meaningless. In that context, the statement "All human beings have a right to life" takes on a completely different significance. Suppose it is made by an anti-abortionist who has given an implicit definition of "life" as applying to the fetus or the embryo, or by a pacifist who has implicitly defined war as an assault on life, or by an opponent of capital punishment. There are many, many different contexts in which, by the time a person gets to this particular statement, "All human beings have a right to life" takes on an entirely different significance or implication. The context profoundly conditions how a given statement will be interpreted. You, then, have to know what the framework of a given statement is, where it appears, what affects how you are going to interpret it, analyze it, apply it—in short, what the context is.

To look ahead for a moment to how this would apply to communication, you are going to have to know your audience's context. What do your listeners or readers know? What are they coming to your talk or paper with? What ideas will govern their interpretation of what you say? What errors do they bring that might confuse them? What obvious points do they already know that you will simply bore them with if you repeat? All of that and more is part of the context that they are bringing to your presentation, and that will certainly have effects on what you should include. It will also affect the organization of your material, because the essence of a good structure is that each point you present paves the way for the next. In other words, each point creates the necessary context, so that what comes next will be clear and understandable.

The Crow Epistemology

The third basic principle of effective communication is a metaphysical principle. Metaphysics is the branch of philosophy that studies the nature of the universe as a whole. The principle of metaphysics that I want to stress here is the one first defined by Aristotle: the Law of Identity. A is A. Everything is something; it is what it is; it is definite, it has a nature, it is something specific. To put it another way, everything that exists is *limited*. There is no such thing as an infinite quantity or an infinite number of attributes, because "infinite" means a quantity without any specific identity. According to Objectivism, this law applies as much to space and time as to every other aspect of the universe. A is A; everything is limited.

Let us apply this to epistemology. Consciousness, too, is limited. It, too, obeys the principle that A is A. This is not an insult to consciousness; it is inherent in the fact that consciousness exists. Everything that exists is something specific, and so is consciousness. It can deal with and hold only so much. Informally, we call this point the "crow epistemology," a term I will use throughout this course. Let me explain briefly why it is given this name.

An experiment with crows was conducted, as described in *Introduction to Objectivist Epistemology*.* In this experiment, if one man came to a place in the woods where some crows were gathered, the crows would

---

* Chapter 7, pp. 62–63.

hide, and they would not come out until the man left. If three men came, they would hide, and if two left, they still would not come out, because they knew that one was still there. But if five men came and then four left, the crows would come out. To put it in human terms, the crows figured: "Many came, many left, so it is safe to come out." The crows could distinguish and hold only up to about three units. They could, in effect, grasp "one, two, three," but beyond that, they could not hold a further number of units in mind. So their arithmetic, so to speak, would be "one, two, three, lots."

The point here is that some kind of limitation, in principle, is true of every kind of consciousness, not merely that of crows. Human beings are better off than crows; for instance, we can retain an awareness at one time, let us say, of six objects (that is, perceptually, without counting or concepts). But there is a limit for us, too. After a certain figure—when it reaches dozens, let alone hundreds—you simply cannot distinguish or deal with such a number of units at one time, not perceptually. Your mental screen, so to speak, is limited in what it can hold in any one frame. Any consciousness is finite. It has a specific scope of material that it can deal with, and only that much in any given frame. A is A. There is only a limited number of units, therefore, that a consciousness can hold in awareness at any one time. Beyond that number, the content simply becomes a blur; the mind cannot encompass it or take it in. It is against this background that Ayn Rand explains one of the crucial functions of concepts, which is that they enormously broaden the scope of the material that we can deal with, precisely by condensing a vast number of perceptions into one new whole. They reduce all the vast number of percepts of a given type into one new unit, the concept, which subsumes all of them.

Grasping this point of the crow epistemology—that consciousness is limited in what it can deal with in any given frame—is essential to all communication. You must always remember that your audience can retain and deal with only so many units. Therefore, it is up to you to economize the units, reducing the number wherever possible. Otherwise, you overload your readers or listeners by giving them too many points. As a result, their ability to grasp breaks down, and communication comes to an end. When this takes place, it is exhausting as well as demoralizing to the audience members; they characteristically give up, flatly and defiantly, for the rest of that encounter, and you have your work cut out ever to get them back again.

The principle of the crow epistemology has applications on every level of communication, from a single sentence to a book as a whole. The point, on whatever level you look at it, is that the members of your audience have to hold on to the parts you give them. If you give them too many before you add up those parts into a unit, then they have to give up, of necessity, because they cannot deal with the overload.

Observe your own mental process, for instance, if I utter a sentence like this: "The man who, having hit his friend (the doctor who graduated from Columbia with the highest grades of his class that year) during an argument which was very bitter and committed many fallacies over which of them was more intelligent"—and I am still going on here, while you are still holding "The man who." At a certain point, you cannot do it anymore. You will find that, if you really try to follow me, you get a little tense, and it starts to mount very rapidly. At a certain point, the mechanism snaps, and you say the mental equivalent of "What the hell," and tune out. That is the crow epistemology asserting itself. It would not make any difference if the wording were the clearest you could imagine, the context perfect, the audience passionate—the mind cannot retain it, and therefore communication is over.

If you think no one does such a thing in real life, consider a sentence chosen at random from the world-champion violator of the crow epistemology: "To gain assurance that [category and judgment] do actually accord, we must observe that in all disjunctive judgments the sphere (that is, the multiplicity which is contained in any one judgment) is represented as a whole divided into parts (the subordinate concepts), and that since no one of them can be contained under any other, they are thought as coordinated with, not subordinated to, each other, and so as determining each other, not in one direction only, as in a series, but reciprocally, as in an aggregate—if one member of the division is posited, all the rest are excluded, and conversely." That is from page 117 of the Kemp Smith translation of Immanuel Kant's *Critique of Pure Reason.**

This point applies not only to individual sentences, but to your piece or presentation as a whole. I once heard a very interesting paper that violated this point inadvertently. The speaker wanted to discuss the importance of thinking in principles. Hoping to intrigue the audience, he started with three long examples, which he did not explain at first. The audience had one, and then he said, "Now hold that," and then he gave them a second, and then a third. Then he thought, "Now I am going to explain the theory"—which itself was fairly complex—"and then I will show how it applies to these examples." The audience was waiting, and you could see the tension. And when he got to the second point of the theory, they lost the examples and tuned out. He did go on, finally, and he gave a perfectly good explanation of the three examples, but it absolutely could have been in Greek to that audience, because they had tuned out. It was just too much to hold.

You have to remember that as soon as you start to speak, you are setting up a certain tension in your listener. They have to hold what you are saying, then connect it to the next point, and so on. You, in turn, have to keep tying it all up for them, reducing the number of units. You see that there is a certain problem here. Suppose you are giving a paper, and you want to start with examples to create the right context so that your audience will understand what you are saying. You then have the problem of how to set the context in such a way as not to overload your listeners. You have to know how to set that context, what kind of examples to use, in what order, and at what pace, being sure to avoid certain misinterpretations, all without causing your audience to overstrain. You see, therefore, that you have to strike a balance between being clear and being economical.

---

* *Critique of Pure Reason*, trans. Norman Kemp Smith, revised 2d ed. (Palgrave Macmillan, 2003), p. 117.

We will see the issue of the crow epistemology recurring throug͟ this course. In fact, it is true in every field, even beyond that of commu͟ nication. Consciousness is something, and that necessitates certain methods of dealing with it. If you violate these methods, you are assaulting human consciousness as such, and you therefore make communication impossible. If you want a visual example, remember the McLuhan method in television: very fast jumps from frame to frame and from shot to shot, too quick to take in, to grasp, or to connect. The result is nil. It does not add up to anything; it is outside human epistemology. The net effect is simply visual irritation. This is an example of what is more broadly true of every form of consciousness and every form of communication. You have to direct your communication to the requirements of human consciousness.

These three points—that knowledge is conceptual, that it is contextual, and that A is A and consciousness is limited—are the briefest I can make the philosophic base of this course. Hereafter I want to apply it; I want to work out various principles of communication, and then go into details.

CHAPTER 3

FOUR ESSENTIAL PRINCIPLES

AT THIS POINT I want to turn to several broad principles or methods of effective communication, which are based on the foregoing philosophic points. I want to look at these methods in a general way, with the details to follow later. For the most part these are elementary, widely known points, but I want you to see why they are necessary on the basis of the kinds of philosophic issues we have indicated: knowledge as conceptual, knowledge as contextual, and the crow epistemology.

The crow issue also applies to the way you use this course. You, too, can deal with only a limited amount. If you try to learn everything and then hold it all in mind as you write each sentence or deliver each sentence to someone else, there will be too many points to deal with, and your mind will break down. Therefore, what I suggest is that you take in what you can and, when you go to actually address someone or write something or argue, focus only on the content. Do not, in that moment, try to hold the content of what you are doing plus six proper methods of doing it, or you will simply paralyze yourself.

Finally, always keep in mind that there are a great many options in applying these methods. I am considering broad principles, not concrete rules, and there are many different ways of using them. It is roughly analogous to ethics. If I were lecturing you on ethics, I would say, "You should have a productive occupation"; but that leaves open a wide range of possibilities—it excludes being a bank robber and a dictator and a few other things, but it includes many legitimate options. The same is true of the principles we are going to be discussing. To put it another way, it is not true that the absolutely perfect version of your article or presentation already preexists in some Platonic dimension, with every single example, formulation, and so on all worked out flawlessly, and you are trying to reach that one single, preexisting, concretely perfect ideal. There is no such thing as a Platonic superrealm, including no such thing as the perfect article in another dimension. You could take the same theme to the same audience and deliver it in a great many different ways, each perfectly legitimate. They would differ in their form, in their emphasis, in many different attributes; they would keep the same essentials, if they were all good. You have to keep in mind, therefore, that there are a great many options in the field of presentation. Always remember that we are speaking of broad principles within that framework.

Motivate the Audience

The first principle is that whether you are speaking or writing, you must give the audience a reason to care, to be interested in what you are saying. By the sheer act of addressing them, you are asking work from them; you are asking them to commit time, effort, attention, focus, and thought. Any philosophic or ideological subject is difficult and complex, even in its easiest aspects. You therefore have to tell the members of your audience why they should do all of this work, because they will not do it causelessly. Sometimes, if you are a teacher, you get students who are being forced to take your class as a requirement; they may be unmotivated, but they will drag themselves to class and listen. Even so, that is not nearly as good. You will not communicate nearly as much, or as well, as when they care, are eager, and want to learn. You cannot force a mind. Even if your listeners try to follow you out of a sense of duty, at the first obscurity or difficulty, they will mentally wander off. You need an active mind if you are to communicate, and an active mind means a *motivated* mind.

The broader point here is the role of values in human life. According to Objectivism, all rational actions involve the pursuit of values, as against simply selfless duty. This is true for intellectual actions also. Or, if you want to look at it another way, the relevant Objectivist point here is egoism—the virtue of selfishness. A mind must be inherently selfish in the realm of cognition if it is to enter that realm at all. A person has to use his own judgment, and it must be for his own sake, his own curiosity, his own interest, his own knowledge. You cannot think, nor ask people to think, selflessly. You must therefore show your audience, in some terms, why your talk or point advances their values. You have to attach your subject to what they care about, so that they see that it will benefit them to follow you.

All of this is particularly true today, given people's skepticism about the realm of ideas. People are profoundly disillusioned with ideas, which they associate with boredom, useless talk, and time wasting. I advise you, therefore, to expect your audience members to be skeptical of the very field of ideas, and not to condemn them for it. You have to understand it; you have to understand its roots in today's ideas, and then you have to show your audience that you are better.

The fact that *you* are interested in the subject is not enough. You understand its importance, let us say. But the point here is the one made earlier: You must, first and foremost, take the audience's context into account—in this case, their evaluative context. For instance, with college students I take the attitude: "This subject, you believe, is a waste of time—and you are entirely justified. Given what you know, you have every right to think you have been railroaded into a nightmare of junk. I hereby give you the right to regard me as guilty until proved innocent, and any part of this subject as worthless until proved a value." I lay that on as thick as I can at the beginning, simply to try to pierce the screen of their disillusionment and skepticism about ideas.

There are different forms of motivating an audience, which vary according to the topic, the audience, and the length of time that you have. But somewhere near the outset, in some form, you must indicate, "So what?" You can think of it this way: You have a double assignment as soon as you open your mouth, namely "what" and "so what"—what are you trying to communicate, and what difference does it make to the audience? In short, you are responsible for providing both the content and the reason your listeners or readers should want to absorb it. I, personally, favor open statement. That is, I come right in without much subtlety and say, "So-and-so is the reason you should listen. Now you are motivated, so let us start." That has the virtue of clarity, even if it is not exactly elegant. I did this at the beginning of this course. I made a few brief remarks—the world is falling apart, clear thought and communication are crucial, and so on—and then launched into the subject. Brief as it was, that was definitely superior to my coming in and saying, "Good evening. Effective communication is based on three philosophic issues. Number one"—and simply lopping off the whole base of the subject. If you start properly, you activate your audience's value context, telling them, "This is the value I am going to serve; this is the purpose. If you agree with this purpose, that is the standard by which all the rest of it is going to be conducted; that is going to determine what I include, and that is your test as to whether or not what I am doing is relevant."

Even in a very short article, you have to indicate the motivational element in some way. Suppose, for instance, that you are writing a paper on axioms—a very technical philosophical subject, but let us say you are writing it for a general audience. You have to say *something* to motivate your readers. You cannot go into a big production in a short paper, because if you go into five pages of motivation, you do not have time to present your topic. But you have to say something like, "All knowledge rests on axioms. If they are not reliable, everything collapses and that is the end." (You would say it a little more elegantly than that.) Then you have attached your subject to something your audience presumably cares about, and you can go on from there.

You have to tie your subject to the values of the people you are addressing—their *actual* values, as distinct from their professed values (if there is a difference). Many people profess to be interested in "culture," for example, but an interest in "culture" in the abstract sense will not sustain anyone for very many minutes, because there is no actual reason anyone should care about something as undefined as that. If you want to communicate with people, you have to find a way to tie what you are saying to something they actually do value. Objectivism is very valuable in this connection, because it holds that ideas are practical, that they do affect and shape our lives. This is an enormous asset in your attempts to motivate an audience. You do not have to talk about a noumenal dimension à la Kant, or a supernatural world of Forms à la Plato. You can present ideas as necessary for living on earth, something that is an actual interest of the great majority of people.

Sometimes you will encounter an utterly skeptical audience, one that you know will not believe your general position. At such times, heroic measures become necessary. I knew an executive who had to give a compulsory course to a group of office workers who profoundly, bitterly disapproved of having to attend. There were actually good reasons that the course would benefit them, but since they had been compelled to attend, they came in very hostile. This executive decided to devote the first meeting entirely to the office workers telling her why this course was a waste of time and why they were bitter about having to be subjected to it. She told them, "If you can give me a good argument as to why this course is worthless, I promise not to give it." She let them give every argument they could think of for a whole hour. Since she had a good case, she refuted each objection; her audience became attentive, and the course went over very well. In an extreme case, it is worth it to cut your material in half, if that is what you have to do to break through your audience's initial skepticism. If people just stare stonily at you, communication is impossible, even if you give the most eloquent presentation in the world.

Remember, too, that an initial motivation is not enough. Occasional reminders are very helpful, depending on your audience and the length of the topic. But you have to keep tabs on this issue. Think of it this way: When you get up in front of a group of people, you make a contract with them; you promise them, "I am going to deliver value X." Every once in a while, you have to say, "See, I remember; I am keeping my promise." It is very easy to lose an audience, particularly today. A yawn is always on the periphery; the glaze of boredom is always waiting to set in. Therefore, you have to do anything you can to keep the value context activated. This requires that you define your audience carefully in advance: Are you speaking to one person, and if so, an adult or a child? If you are speaking to a group, is it a professional group, a group that is generally educated, mankind as a whole, or what? Are you assuming a professional interest or not? What can you expect this particular audience to know about the subject?

Point one, then, is that you have to catch your audience economically and convincingly, and then hold them. That is the precondition of everything else.

Delimit the Subject

You cannot cover *every* aspect of any intellectual topic. Selectivity is necessary on any project, whether you are writing a telegram or an encyclopedia. All knowledge is interconnected, which means that if you tried to tell the total about any one point, you would have to tell the total about everything. In other words, you would have to communicate omniscience. Even if you wanted to tell me everything about this table, that would include the last details of physics and forces and molecules and so on. This point is particularly obvious in intellectual and philosophical issues. Suppose you wanted to give a talk on the virtue of honesty, and you decided you were going to give the full presentation—that is to say, every single point that could be possibly made, or relevant to, explaining honesty. What would you have to include? Of course, you would say, "Dishonesty is departing from reality." But what is reality? You would have to go into that. You could say, "Reality is what you perceive with your senses." But are the senses valid? And so on. You might also say, "In telling a lie, your mind abdicates control." Then the question would arise: Do you have control? Does man have free will? And so on. What about so-called white lies, lies told to benefit other people? Well, is altruism good or bad? What about those who say, "Mankind is too stupid to know the truth, so you have to lie"—are people necessarily stupid? What *is* human nature? And so on.

That is just a taste. Ten volumes would not cover everything you could ask with some plausibility about telling the truth. Knowledge is a total. Whenever you present a point, you are extracting one element, one topic or theme, from that total. Thus there is always a vast amount that you have necessarily left unsaid and uncovered. This is true even in a long book. In college, writing school papers of ten or fifteen pages, I used to think, "Oh, how great it will be when you finally get out and can write a book and not constantly have to select one out of fifteen crucial points— you can say everything." But in writing my book *The Ominous Parallels,** I found that I had to be just as selective as I was then, if not more so; and that if I tried to put in all those points that I never could get into the school papers, it was so much that I, let alone an audience, could no longer retain the theme of the book. By the crow epistemology, it was too many units, too much material, to hold. In other words, I learned that you have to give up the idea that you will say every last word on a given topic. Some people, too, have the idea of the impregnable presentation, by which they mean that every conceivable objection is taken care of in advance. That is impossible. What you can do, as long as you do it well, is to choose the essentials, assuming a certain context. But you cannot do everything.

Some of you will now feel vulnerable, because you will think, "If I leave something out, the audience is going to descend on me and tear me to pieces." The only effective answer to that is: Do not write for the kind of audience that is going to do that. You have to assume a rational audience. With the irrational, you cannot communicate, convince, or argue.

---

* *The Ominous Parallels: The End of Freedom in America* (Plume, 1983).

Here I mean the *irrational*, not the ignorant or the mistaken. An audience is necessarily ignorant of what you are presenting, so that is not a point against them. They may also hold mistaken views, which you may have to correct. But by an "irrational audience" in this context, I mean, in effect, a hostile group that is out to distort what you say, tear your statements apart without any basis, change context on you, switch terms, throw authorities around, spew emotional venom, and so forth—in other words, exactly what people are projecting when they worry that their papers are not impregnable. With that kind of audience, you cannot do anything. Whatever answer you give will simply be met with further distortions and further objections.

A rational audience is concerned only with the objective requirements of the subject. It understands that you have to delimit; it does not expect the impossible, only the essentials. What you have to do, therefore, is go over your topic in advance and decide what are the essential points required, in reason, to cover this subject. You can list possible elaborations that are desirable if you have the time. But you have to decide in advance what are, in your judgment, the necessary essentials. And then you guiltlessly set aside all the rest of the material. You have to say, and say aloud if you have doubts, "I simply cannot cover so-and-so. By my understanding it is not necessary, and I will not cover it, period."

We will go into more detail later as to how to decide what to include and what to omit. But very briefly, it depends, in essence, on three factors: the subject, the audience, and the length of time you have available. First, in any subject, certain points are obviously indispensable by the very nature and the logic of the topic. Certain points are the essence of your message, and those, therefore, have to go in with whatever is required to make them clear. This is the bare minimum that you should decide on in advance; whatever else may be left out, this has to stay in, because it is the heart of your message. For instance, if I were giving the Objectivist concept of "egoism," the bare minimum would be, "You have to live for your own sake, neither sacrificing yourself for others or others for yourself, and following the judgment of your own mind, that is, going by reason." I would have to tie it to reason and the impropriety of sacrifice either way. That would be the absolute minimum; otherwise, I would not even get into existence what I was talking about. If I were a guest on a radio show, that might be all I could say; I could literally just utter that, without further elaboration. In an article, a lecture, or a book, on the other hand, I can progressively elaborate, go into the philosophic base and political effects and possible confusions, and all the rest of it. In each framework, though, I have to know what is the bare minimum, and then be sure to get that much in.

Second, with regard to the audience, you have to know what its knowledge and motivation are. That will, in turn, affect what you have to include. The audience is relevant. Obviously, the more your listeners or readers know, the more you can leave out, because they already know it—and, on the other hand, the more complex the material you can cover, because they will not be baffled or lost when they hear you. Conversely, if they are beginners, uninitiated, or children, the less you can cover and the more simplified you have to be.

Finally, there is the length of time or space that you have available. Whenever you write or prepare to talk to someone, you must have some specific outlet in mind, which will carry with it some idea of length. Are you writing a paragraph, a few pages, or a volume? Is this a ten-minute statement, or a two-hour lecture? This will enormously affect, not the essential core of your subject, but the extent to which you can elaborate upon it. As we will see later, what you would cover in five minutes is extremely different from what you would cover, on the same subject and to the same audience, in thirty seconds.

In general, therefore, I would suggest that when you are preparing a presentation, you make a list of points that you think are plausible given a certain audience and time frame; then decide in advance, insofar as you can, "This is what I have to cover, and this is what I can definitely omit." You may also have an intermediate group of points about which you say, "I will see how this develops; maybe I can work some of these in, maybe not." But you have to make a basic decision on delimiting the subject from the start.

Organize the Presentation Logically

To have a logical structure, your presentation must be a series of points or steps, each resting on or coming from the preceding, each paving the way for the next. You have to pick some appropriate starting point, material that will be understandable on its own terms to your audience, to set the basic context. Then you build on that start. Guided by the theme you are trying to communicate, you ask yourself at each step what would come next: "Is there something coming later that I want to prepare the way for, something that depends on something earlier, which I have to get in here?" Above all, you have to ask yourself, "What does my audience need to know to understand and accept the points that are coming later?" You have to organize your material so that you create the necessary context, preparing the way for each new point as you go. We will see examples in which a given point at one place in a progression is clear, illuminating, and convincing, because it has been prepared by the preceding context; whereas the exact same sentences that were so eloquent at one point will be arbitrary, confusing, and unconvincing when put in a different position.

You know that when you list in brief form the main points that you are going to cover and their order, that is called the outline of your work. Here I am simply saying that you have to be able to defend your outline logically. You have to know why you chose that particular order. It is not enough to say, "Point one is the one that occurred to me first." Is it a good starting point, or does it depend on something else?

On this, as on all the other points, there are many options. There is no such thing as one mandatory order. But there must be a reason for your order. For instance, as a very simple example, I can say, "I love you; let us get married." That is a structure—it is the cause, then the effect. Or I could say, "Let us get married; I love you." That is the effect, then the cause; it is also a logical structure, and in some contexts it might be preferable simply for its shock value. But I could not say, "Turnips taste good; let us get married," because the sheer juxtaposition makes it sound as if the marriage has something to do with turnips, and the statement becomes baffling. There are thus options within limits. You might, for instance, give a general principle first, and then give examples; or you could give examples and then give the principle. Or you can give a shocking conclusion first and then explain it, or vice versa. Or, if you are giving history or a narrative of events in time, you can use chronology. Or maybe you are simply doing a survey of art, and you cannot think of any reason why you should cover music before painting or vice versa; you can then say, "Let us look at art in no particular order," and that is then your order. But there has to be some defensible framework, "defensible" in the sense that you observe the logical connections of your subject matter and the context of your audience.

Note that it is a good thing to have surprises, shock value, or mystery. Do not equate the point that you have to have a logical structure with the need for a deductive or geometrical presentation. It is not necessary to say, "Point one, from which I deduce point two, and then point three," in the manner of Euclid. You can start out with something that the audience does not grasp at all, and then explain it. But the point is that if it is a mystery, it has to be a good mystery. One requirement of this is that the audience has to understand what they are supposed to know and what they have not yet had explained to them; then they can follow what you are doing. A bad mystery—the kind in which there is a litter of points, clues, or events, with no indication of what is happening or why you are being told this—does not belong in any form of presentation.

Ideally, not only should you have a good structure, but your audience should also know it, at least in principle. They should know why you are at any given point and where you are going. There is a saying that the standard lecturer is supposed to have three parts to his presentation. In part one, he tells the audience what he is going to do; in part two, he does it; and in part three, he says that he did it, as summary and review. Such a structure is not literally necessary, but the idea behind it is very valuable: namely that you should keep your order clear to the audience so that at each point, they know where they are. Here, for instance, I have tried to follow that by saying, "First we are going to cover philosophy, three points; then we are going to cover its application to communication, so-and-so many points." Numbering is helpful in letting your audience know your order. It is by no means necessary but, especially if yours is an oral presentation, numbering helps people pin it down. Moreover, every audience sighs with relief when you get to the end of a number, because they think, "Oh, good, that point is over; now we can go on to the next one."

Balance Abstractions and Concretes

"Abstraction" here means any broad general principle or theory. "Concrete" means the particulars that come under it—examples, illustrations, instances of it. The point is that abstractions have to be accompanied by concretes in the cases where this is required, as explained below.

A concept is a condensation of concretes. It is a shorthand, and you must always remember that. It is not automatically tied to the actual particulars in reality that it represents. Therefore, in your presentation, it is urgent that you keep any key idea or principle that you are focusing on, that your presentation is centered on, tied to reality, meaning to the perceptual level. In other words, you have to bring it down to earth. Otherwise, you will have a floating abstraction, and even if it is tied to reality in your own mind, in the audience's mind it will not be.

The crucial method of tying abstractions to reality is to concretize by giving examples. For example—now I am concretizing the advice to concretize—take the abstract argument for cause and effect. Suppose I just come into a group of people and say, "Every entity has a nature and has to act in accordance with its nature; that is the Law of Identity applied to action. Therefore, everything acts as it has to. Therefore, there is cause and effect." That is more or less clear, yet it is so abstract that people will not know, in concrete terms, what I am talking about. But if you give even one simple, boring, academic example, such as a piece of chalk, and you say, "This is an entity, and you see I have it here in my hand, and it is something—it has a certain density in relation to the air—and when I let it go, under those conditions its nature permits only one action, and that is what it has to do; therefore it will fall, like this, and you see, it will always do that under these circumstances"—then cause and effect takes on a reality that it did not have for the audience in its abstract formulation.

This actual example, causality, played a role in my own development. I first learned cause and effect in a discussion with Ayn Rand many years ago, before *Atlas Shrugged* came out. Causality was very abstract in my mind, and she suggested that I go for a walk and try to find examples of cause and effect on the streets of New York. I was a little dubious about whether I would find them. But I saw trucks turning, and people moving, and feathers floating, and planes flying, and so on, and I noted each one down and worked over how in each case it was an entity of a certain nature acting accordingly. I remember coming back with a real sense of astonishment and telling her, "Causality is all over the place!" And since that walk, it has had a solidity in my mind that it never had before.

The point is that every abstract paper should have some such element of concretization in it somewhere. You should train yourself so that as soon as you utter a broad abstraction, that sets up a certain pressure in you, as though it is an IOU, and you now have to pay off that IOU by concretizing and illustrating so that the audience gets the meaning in reality. A magnificent example of this is Ayn Rand's novels. Not that she wrote them for pedagogical purposes, but the events are the concretes, and then Galt's speech or Roark's speech at the end is the abstract summary, which has a luminous clarity in conjunction with the concretes.

One caution: Do not get carried away. In your zeal to concretize, do not simply inundate people with examples. The reason is the crow. The other side of the floating abstraction is being concrete-bound: that is, giving a whole series of instances with no unifying abstraction to tie them together. That is a violation of the requirements of the human epistemology, and as such is unretainable. If I, for instance, walked in and just gave you twelve examples from that causality walk, there would be an enormous pressure on your mind. I would have to do something to tie them together, to summarize and integrate them. A real-life example of this error would be the type of history book that puts everyone to sleep with things like "the fourteen causes of World War II." It lists page after page of examples and concretes, from Hitler's childhood to Japanese exports, with nothing to tie it all together and no way in the world for the reader to retain it. This is what gives people the idea that the study of history is simply memorization with no intelligibility. Whereas, of course, if you know the Objectivist view of history, you will know what kind of abstraction would unite all of those examples—in this case, the moral collapse of the West. For details, you can read *The Ominous Parallels*.

In short, you have to find a balance. You have to discover when it is necessary to come down to concrete examples, to bring the discussion back down to your base in reality, and when to tie your concretes together with an abstraction because your audience can hold only so much. This shuttling back and forth between concretes and abstraction is a crucial requirement of intellectual presentation.

To summarize, the four basic principles of communication that we are concerned with are motivation, delimitation, structure, and concretization. *Motivation* means the way in which you convince the audience to care about the subject. *Delimitation* means your recognition that A is A, that the crow epistemology is true, and, therefore, that the audience can retain only so much. *Structure* means having a logical sequence of presentation. Finally, *concretization* refers to the balance of abstractions and concretes; you must go back and forth between giving examples of an abstract point and then tying them up abstractly.

Analyzing "Philosophy: Who Needs It" (Appendix A)

Let us now apply the principles of communication concretely, so that you have a clear example. Our example is the first part of "Philosophy: Who Needs It."*

* Part one, the first half of the speech reproduced in full in the Appendices, was published in *The Ayn Rand Letter*, vol. 3, no. 7 (December 31, 1973), pp. 277–80.

Motivation

Here, you have to project the problem from the beginning. This is a speech for undergraduates at West Point. Their attitude toward philosophy is the standard attitude of people who know nothing about philosophy except for what they hear—namely, the impression that philosophy is a series of floating abstractions with no relation to them, mankind, life, or anything. Therefore, in giving a speech like this, you already face a certain wall of skepticism or disinterest built up in advance. Given an audience of people who have this preliminary skepticism, you have to do something to motivate them. You have to give them the conviction that this has something to do with their values and interests.

The first thing about this talk that works toward motivating the audience is the title, because it states, very economically, precisely the motivational problem. "Who needs philosophy?" is just the question on the listeners' minds (although they would be asking it in a kind of cynical way). If the author, right at the beginning, takes cognizance of the fact that that type of question is on the audience's mind, and flaunts it, saying, "Fine, you think nobody needs it? I am prepared to meet that challenge head-on"—that is already intriguing. Of course, no four words are going to establish motivation, but such a title does make people think, "Maybe there is some reason to listen—at least the author knows what's on my mind."

The next element in the talk that is specifically designed to enlist the interest of the audience is the short story at the beginning. It is wonderful to start with a short story, because everybody likes one. Naturally, you cannot make an absolute out of this, but just as an example here, it provides a certain intrigue right at the beginning. It helps to break down the cynicism or skepticism of the audience, because something interesting is being said, something no one would expect in a discussion of philosophy. This is what you can call a "grabber." It serves to get the audience interested right off the bat; it breaks the ice and holds the audience fast. It has been said that the beginning is one of the most crucial elements of a piece, because it is going to be determined very close to the beginning whether you have an audience or not. If your beginning is poor, boring, or too abstract, people will simply tune out and stop listening (or reading). But if you can do something to grab their attention, then you have a little breathing space, and you do not have to be quite so exciting while you lay out your basic context.

Notice that Rand not only uses an intriguing little short story, but specifically uses, as her example, an astronaut. Theoretically, she could have used any profession, such as a fiction writer or a professor. But in this context, it is helpful to her to use an astronaut as an example, because the speech is addressed to West Point cadets. Military hardware and space exploration are so-called hardheaded, tough subjects, subjects that students would usually think are far removed from philosophy. An astronaut, though, is in their league, so to speak. Therefore, to use this example straightaway is to start with the implication, "This has something to do with you; this applies to you; this is relevant to your concerns." I was actually there when this talk was delivered, and it certainly worked that way; the audience was interested and settled down right away. The question on their minds was obviously, "What could a real-life subject like an astronaut have to do with philosophy?" There was thus a good motivating element right at the beginning.

Notice, too, that Rand uses "you" throughout this piece. That is by no means mandatory. But in a speech of this kind, where her particular stress is, "This applies to *you*," it is more effective and more motivating to say "It applies to *you*" than "It applies to man" or "It applies to all rational beings," because in such cases the audience would have to go one step further—"I am a rational being, and therefore it applies to me." Rand wants to hammer home the idea, "Philosophy—who needs it? *You* do." Therefore, she uses the second person very frequently. That also is a motivating element.

There are many other motivating elements in this beyond the opening. Notice, for instance, that throughout the talk Rand consistently keeps in mind what possible skeptical question might occur to a rational audience at a given point. Frequently, she puts that question explicitly into words. In effect, at those points where she expects that this audience might legitimately think, "What has this got to do with me?" she says, "Now, you may think, what has this got to do with you? The answer is . . ." For instance, just at the point at which an audience would be thinking, "All this about the astronaut is very interesting, but what has it got to do with me?" she says, "This is fantasy, you say; you would not act like that and no astronaut ever would." Right away, she states the thought in their minds, which then opens the line of communication for her to go on and elaborate what it has to do with them. Shortly after that, right after she states the three questions ("Where am I? How do I know it? What should I do?"), the audience will think, "Oh, well, I know the answer to those questions." In other words, there is a certain skeptical element in their minds stopping them from being motivated. So she immediately says, "By the time they are old enough to understand these questions, men believe that they know the answers." And the audience listening will think, "I *do* think I know the answers, but she obviously thinks I do not, because she is taking account of that fact"—so again, they are still with her. At each point, by anticipating what we could call the audience's skepticism, or at least the question that would occur to them that might make them tune out, Rand stresses, "This is relevant; *you* need it, you specifically. I know the thought on your mind, and here is the answer to it." Her listeners are being carried along, because she is anticipating the type of question that would undercut their motivation.

This technique is not mandatory; there are many different options. But if you can anticipate a legitimate question on an audience's part at the very moment when that question occurs to the audience, that is marvelous, and every audience loves it. They feel, "I am in sync with the speaker; he knows what is on my mind and is actually talking to me." That keeps them interested in what you are saying. You should, of course, try to anticipate *rational* questions on the part of the audience. If you have an invincibly ignorant audience of people who would not be motivated even if you told them that their sexual performance would be improved by your talk, you cannot do anything. Given a rational audience, though, everything you can do to motivate them is crucial, and one method is to anticipate the points where they are going to have a problem and tell them that.

Notice also that Rand is not content simply to give her listeners a good, strong motivation at the beginning and then go into the subject and forget about it. Throughout this first part of the speech, as a kind of leitmotif, she keeps very briefly reminding her audience of the practical role of philosophy. For instance, after she has stated the questions of metaphysics, she says right away, even before defining the subject: "The nature of your actions—and of your ambition—will be different, according to which set of answers you come to accept." At this point, she is discussing what metaphysics is, so she cannot go into a detailed discussion of why those questions are crucial, but by the way they are selected, it is enough to keep the issue alive for her listeners, and she states it just to remind them, "I know what I am talking about; I am after the same point, and this is, you see, relevant to your life." After stating the basic questions of epistemology, too, she says, "The extent of your self-confidence—and of your success—will be different, according to which answers you accept." Similarly, when she comes to ethics, she says, "I do not have to point out the different consequences; you can see them everywhere." Then, of course, comes a summing-up of her proof of why you need philosophy. That is an example of a motivational element running throughout just the first part of this talk.

Delimitation

The West Point talk had to be strictly delimited. It had to be reduced to two questions, with a third question rigorously omitted. The two questions that the author is definitely going to answer are, "What is philosophy?" and "Who needs it?" The question that she is definitely *not* going to answer (as she states explicitly later in the talk, saying, "It would be a disaster if you tried") is, "What is the proper philosophy?" Of course, Rand suggests such a philosophy by her wording. But she does not say, for example, that selfishness is right, that logic is valid, or that Kant is evil. As soon as she did that, it would open up a whole raft of questions that would be impossible for her to cover in this presentation. The whole talk is consumed by what philosophy is and why you need it. As to what is true, that is another talk, and she has to adhere to that principle throughout.

Notice, too, that she is as brief as she can be. For instance, when she gets to politics, she is much briefer than on metaphysics and epistemology. Now, you could give a lengthy explanation of what politics and aesthetics are. But that is not central for her theme, because her theme is "Philosophy—who needs it." The real thing she wants to sell the audience on is metaphysics and epistemology, so those get much fuller treatment. For politics, though, she needs only the briefest mention that it is a branch of philosophy, and aesthetics is actually thrown away in a single sentence. It is not going to be the focus, so she does not say, "By the way, aesthetics deals with psycho-epistemological concretization," and so on; that would lose the audience completely. She simply decides, "That is out, and I am not going to try to do it."

This issue of delimitation is true not just of the overall points chosen for inclusion in this talk, but also of all of the specific formulations in it. Rand is very careful not to raise issues that she cannot explain. Every point is carefully formulated, given its purpose. If you change some of the wording, you will needlessly fall into a morass, because you will open up a question that you have no means of dealing with. To show you how to avoid raising questions that you cannot answer, I am going to reword a couple of things to show you what would be nondelimitation and would open up a whole kettle of chaos.

For instance, suppose Rand had on her mind at the beginning of the talk the idea, "As part of the way to sell philosophy, I want to show that philosophy is necessary for human happiness, so I will get that in early."

So let us suppose that where she says, "This is fantasy, you say, but this is the way most men live their lives here on earth," she then added just one sentence: "That is why they are so unhappy." The immediate thing that would arise in a listener's mind is: "Is it true that people are so unhappy?" People have all kinds of different views on that question, and without anything to prepare you for the idea that people are so unhappy, it is not at all plausible that they are. Or, for those who do agree people are very unhappy, the most common explanation is, "Because everything is falling apart, and prices are so high, and we do not have the good movies we used to," or what have you—in other words, the state of the world has caused the unhappiness. That is understandable; if the audience already knew that philosophy was a necessity of human happiness, they would not need this talk. Therefore, if you uttered that sentence at that point, without any context, it would raise the need to go into a whole dissertation on happiness, what it depends on, what its causes are, and how it is related to philosophy—and you could not possibly do that to this audience at this point, because they do not yet know what philosophy is. The formulation would not be self-contained; it would not be understandable on its own terms, and you would have shot down your own talk.

Notice that Rand was able to get in a glancing reference to happiness a couple of paragraphs later. It shows the difference between a prepared (not yet proven, but prepared) statement and a completely unprepared statement. She says that men believe they know the answers to these three questions ("Where am I? How do I know it? What should I do?"), but "the only trouble seems to be that they are not very active, not very confident, not very happy." She does not there come out with, "Philosophy is a precondition of human happiness," because if she put it in that form, she would then have to discuss it. She makes this understandable on its own terms. We have already had the three questions and the example of the astronaut's disorientation and fear, so we know that philosophy has some kind of relation to human emotions. We have now also translated the questions to people as they actually are. Finally, we have given the example of people being not too sure of what they should do, but doing what every-

body else does. Rand then says, "But that makes them not very active"—
and her listeners can see, in logic, that if you do not know what you should
do, you will not be that active. Then, of course, right after that comes "not
very confident." If you are not that active because you do not know what
you should do, then it becomes, "I do not know what I *am* doing, really,"
and you are suddenly a little bit more aware that you are shaky, you are
confused, something is upsetting your balance and functioning. In that
context, "not very happy" has become more or less obvious.

Notice, too, that Rand does not say, "This is a proof that philosophy is
a precondition of happiness." She suggests, within a framework that she
has prepared, that philosophy is relevant to your level of activity, your confidence, and your happiness. She does not go beyond what she can establish. She says men are "not *very* happy." In fact, of course, she would say
that without philosophy you would be miserable; but she does not say that
here, because it would be unprepared. "You will not be very happy" is an
objective formulation in this context. And by the end of the talk, on that
basis, she can then tell the audience, "You will be miserable without it."

Here is one more example of a formulation needing preparation. In
the section illustrating the questions of metaphysics, suppose that all remained as written until the sentence, "Are you in a universe which is
ruled by law, or are you in an incomprehensible chaos?" Suppose now that
at that point Rand were to add, "like the universe of the Christian religion?" That, while true and relevant, would be impossible in this case. To
see why, consider another form of the same error. Suppose she were to say
in the next sentence, "Are the things you see around you real, or is there
a God?" That, in fact, is completely defensible. But although such examples would certainly bring metaphysics to life, she would lose metaphysics
altogether, because the immediate question in her audience's mind would
be, "This is an assault on religion; how can she possibly defend that?" It
would raise all kinds of legitimate questions in the listeners' minds: "How
can she say religion is against a universe ruled by law? What about natural law as dictated by God? And if religion is the opposite of natural law,
what about a great scientist like Newton, who thinks that space and time

are the sense organs of God? What about the Founding Fathers and deism? And how can you say it is either reality or God? God is the author of reality, so there can be both." It would be enormously confusing.

There is no way in this talk to go into an attack on religion. It is not possible. That would be a whole talk in itself. Therefore, in a talk such as this one, what you have to do is say to yourself that you are going to illustrate metaphysics, and even use religion, but in such a way that you do not raise topics you cannot cover. You might say, for instance, "Are there laws, or are there miracles? Does knowledge come by reason, or by supernatural revelation?" The elements "miracles" and "supernatural revelation" connote religion. Ayn Rand's attitude as a speaker is: If the shoe fits, wear it. If the listener's idea of religion is that it is miracles and revelation, then so be it; now he will see what that does to human life. If it is not, that is a separate problem; she is not here arguing religion.

Structure

There are, broadly speaking, four main divisions to the first part of "Philosophy: Who Needs It." This may be helpful to you in planning out your own pieces. Remember that before you have written a piece, you do not know what is in it. You know your idea, but you have not yet worded it, organized it, and so on; you just have a mass of material whirling around in your mind. What you want to do is reach an outline that will indicate where you will start, where you will go from there, and where you will end up. Let us break this down in the West Point talk in order to see the structure of a real case.

The first subdivision of this speech is what you could call the motivation or the orientation. It is, in effect, the introduction. Its purpose is to get the audience into the subject and establish the minimum context necessary. The whole talk up to "There is only one science that can answer them—philosophy" is orientation. This includes the introduction, the astronaut, the real-life versions of it, and what we are dealing with. Part two is then the question of what philosophy is, including its branches. Of course, there is also an order within it—metaphysics, epistemology, ethics, politics, aesthetics. The third part is what I would call the concretization of the fact that philosophy is inescapable. The last part is the explanation or abstract statement, of which part three offered the examples—what it is about the human mind that makes you need philosophy, why you cannot get away from philosophy.

There are various forms in which you can do an outline. Some people prefer a highly detailed outline, some a much briefer one. But there is such a phenomenon as an "outline on a matchbox"—a tiny, tiny outline condensing just the main points in your mind as a guide. Doing it very briefly helps you easily retain what your main divisions are. If I were doing this, the bare minimum that would be my working outline would be:

1. *Intro*—that would tell me to get the thing started;
2. *Philo.*—that would be my shorthand for "What is philosophy" (and if I wanted to be sure to remember, I would put "*Br.*" after it, meaning "cover the branches");
3. *Inescapable (concretes)*—in other words, that you cannot get away from philosophy, and I am giving only the examples;
4. *Inescapable (theory).*

Of course, within each of these headings, you can have as many subdivisions as you want, depending upon how much you can retain and how clear it is in your mind. For instance, under the second heading, "What is philosophy," I would not have to outline, "metaphysics, epistemology," and so on, because I have given that speech for so many years that if I were just pressed the right way, it would come out by itself. But under "Intro," I might not be sure what I was going to start with. So I would have to decide, "Am I going to start with the astronaut, for instance, or am I going to make some introductory remarks first? Am I going to say, 'Good evening, glad to see you, first keep in mind such-and-such,' or am I going to start right away with the story?" Those are the kinds of decisions you have to make. You thus might want to indicate the structure of the introduction and then, under your various later headings, what points you are making and in what order. Break it down. Do not break it down in too great detail, though, or you will be writing your piece before you have outlined it, whereas the purpose of your outline is to tell you what you are going to cover in what order.

What is the virtue of this particular structure? Remember that there is no such thing as one perfect, Platonic structure for any given topic. There are many different ways that you could do it. But taking this structure as it is, you will see some very obvious virtues in it, virtues that will become apparent if you try a different order.

For instance, suppose I started with the definition of "philosophy," omitting the orienting introductory material. As we have already seen, that would be boring, unclear, and too abstract. When it comes after some preparatory words, though, even as abstract as it is, people can take it. Or suppose we switched points three and four; suppose, after we presented up to the end of "what is aesthetics," we then went from there right over to, "You might not be interested, but here is why you should be"—in other words, give the audience a really good reasoning, only without the examples in advance. That would be much too abstract and unconvincing. It is much more effective to say, "You do not think that this is relevant to you? Well, you hold this, do you not, and this, and this?" At a certain point the listener begins to wonder, "Why in the world do I hold all these ideas, since my view is that I do not need philosophy?" At that point, he is ripe to hear what the reasoning is.

Or suppose we started the talk with the examples. That is a more plausible organization. In other words, suppose I came in and said, "Good evening, ladies and gentlemen. You may say, 'Philosophy has nothing to do with real life,' but I want you to check that claim. Have you ever thought or said the following?"—followed by a whole group of examples, such as, "Do not be so sure; nobody can be certain." That is a fairly common way for good professors to start a course in philosophy, because they know that the class comes in terrifically skeptical, and they want to do whatever they can to enlist the class's interest. Although that is possible, if you start that way, the crow epistemology sets in. There is only so much people can retain, and when they hear six or eight examples, they immediately begin to wonder, "What have these things all got to do with each other? What is the connection?"

When the examples are given at a later point in your structure—after you have explained what the subject is, established what its divisions are, and given some idea of its relevance—then each example that you list adds more fuel. It is more convincing; the listener thinks, "Oh, there is another example of this subject." Given out of the blue, though, examples may be intriguing, but they leave an audience disoriented and wondering what all these concretes have got to do with one another. There are ways of getting around that, but it is definitely a problem. In addition, if you start with your examples, the question on people's minds becomes, "So what? I hold these or I do not hold them—what is the difference? What does that have to do with my actual life?" Whereas in the context of the astronaut story and the discussion of the branches and the issues of philosophy, they already have enough to see that it has *something* to do with their life. Starting with the examples, in short, would not be nearly as effective.

The above is simply an indication of the virtue of the structure overall. Within each passage as well, Rand has a definite structure of subpoints, and within each paragraph a definite order. Again, I do not want to inhibit or frighten you into thinking that there is one absolutely right structure—every paragraph could be written in many different ways. I simply want to give you an example or two to demonstrate that there is a need for a certain progression in all writing, in the overall point structure and then within each development, even within each paragraph. If you write it a certain way, certain sentences prepare the way for what is to come and make it intelligible; if you do not give the necessary preparation, the same content falls flat.

For instance, consider the discussion of the subquestions that come under metaphysics. These are simply examples, concretes designed to illustrate what metaphysics is. But notice that they are in a certain order, and that if you changed that order within certain limits, the thing would simply fall, even though the questions and the earlier context remained the same. As an example, suppose I kept the paper as it is up to the sentence, "Philosophy would not tell you whether you are in New York or Zanzibar, but here is what it would tell you." Then suppose that the first question I gave as an example was, "Are things what they are, or not?" The listener's immediate answer would be, "Who needs to know that? Obviously, things are what they are, so philosophy is a useless subject." You would have, in effect, shot down your own motivation. You built it up, and then in the presentation of it, it went back to being a useless abstraction even though it was supposed to be a concretizing example. A beginning audience is able to take a question like, "Are things what they are?" only if the groundwork for that question has been laid by the earlier examples. You start with something that the audience grasps: "Is this a stable universe ruled by laws, or is it an unknowable chaos of miracles in which your mind is impotent?" If you put it in those terms, even freshmen know that there is an actual issue there.

Take one other case where changing the order would ruin it. Suppose the question we started with was, "Are the things you see around you the object or the subject of man's consciousness?" The immediate response would be: "What does *that* mean?" You would have to add, "By the way, I mean by 'object' that which exists independent of consciousness," and then you would be giving the audience a technical definition at a point where they do not see why they need it—so suddenly the whole thing stops, and they are given a boring theory. Contrast this to the way Ayn Rand does it. She asks, "Do the things exist independent of the observer or are they created?" after giving the basic questions of metaphysics. Then, "Are they the object or the subject of man's consciousness?" is self-intelligible, because it has been defined by the preceding sentence.

Concretization

The West Point talk is particularly excellent at balancing abstractions and concretes. It is a very difficult assignment to take a beginning audience and tell them what philosophy is, with all its branches, subdivisions, and interrelations. The subject is formidable and abstract, and the people listening wonder what it has got to do with them. The only way that you can make it clear and interesting is to concretize. But if you concretize too much, then the crow epistemology sets in, and your listeners cannot retain what you are saying. You have to give certain concretes so that they know specifically what you are talking about; then you tie it up, and then, when they understand it in abstract terms, go back and give some more concretes.

In the case of "Philosophy: Who Needs It," the talk is what you could call inductive in its approach, rather than deductive. By "inductive" here I mean that it starts with examples and then draws the wider abstraction, rather than starting with theoretical definitions and then illustrating them, which would be a deductive presentation. The first three questions that the astronaut asks are the first concretes relevant to the theme—"Where am I? How can I discover it? What should I do?" Those are simple, concrete questions, asked by a specific (fictional) person. They are clearly understandable. Yet those are the very issues of the whole later discussion. The first question is the example that is later going to be built up into metaphysics; the second, epistemology; the third, ethics. In telling the story, Rand introduces examples of the three branches of philosophy in a self-contained, clearly understandable way before she goes near talking about what the abstract branches are. She also does it in a very intriguing way, for purposes of what is coming later. The astronaut does a bad thing in each of these areas—he is afraid to look, he does not trust his instruments, and he sits there paralyzed while these creatures are coming—and the whole thing is presented in a plausible way. It is not highly likely that an astronaut would do this, but it is not inconceivable.

Thus, in concrete form at the outset, it is suggested that there are certain types of questions that this person had to answer, and if he gave the wrong kind of answers, which is possible, a listener could see that that would be very bad.

That is all that is communicated at the beginning. There are no abstractions yet, just some questions in a particular case in which you can see that the answers would definitely make a difference. Of course, it is quickly going to go—and Rand herself says so—to the fact that these questions apply to all men. That is another concrete, in the sense that she has not yet stated what broad issues those questions involve; she is simply taking the very questions that the astronaut asked and putting them a little more broadly, and then giving the kind of concrete answers that people would give—"I am in New York City. How do I know it? It's obvious," and so on. She is thus repeating the first three concretes on a little broader scale. Notice, by the way, one other thing that she has illustrated without yet discussing, and that is the order of those questions. What comes first is, "Where am I?" Then comes, "How do I know," and finally, "What do I do?" She has not yet said that there is a certain structure here, but it is obvious in the framework of that concrete story; you do not know what you are going to do until you know where you are, and certain questions therefore depend on others. Before she comes to abstractions, she has given concrete examples indicating the nature of the subject, its interrelations, and its significance, without saying any of it, except in the form of a concrete example.

Rand then turns to the abstract: "Philosophy studies the fundamental nature of existence, of man, and of man's relationship to existence," followed by the contrast to the special sciences. Try to imagine the difference if you came to an audience and started with, "Good evening, ladies and gentlemen. Our subject is 'Philosophy: Who Needs It.' Let me give you a definition to begin with. Philosophy studies the fundamental nature of existence, of man, and of man's relationship to existence." Two things immediately take place in the audience's mind: "What is he talking about?" and "Who cares?" "What is he talking about?" because what do you, the speaker, mean by "the fundamental nature of existence"? That is an enormous abstraction. "The fundamental nature of existence" could mean whether it is made of matter and energy and subatomic particles, or who knows what. By itself, that is an extremely broad phrase. The same is true of "man's relationship to existence." For most people, the only answer to that question is, "He is in it." They have no further idea of what you would take as man's relationship to existence; the whole question simply does not have any concrete significance in their mind.

If you started that way, then, your listeners would simply look at you in a kind of glazed way, without any specific idea of what you meant. Rand, in contrast, starts with the astronaut. The point still needs a lot of elaboration, but there is a concrete to anchor it. It is clear why the astronaut had to say, "Where am I?" If that is the stand-in for "the nature of existence," it is also clear that there is something there that you have to know. She still has to go on and illustrate it, but she has prepared the ground. By the same token, she has given her listeners the "So what?" because if you simply came in and said "the fundamental nature of existence," they would say, "Who cares?" but after the astronaut example, they have enough to see that this type of question makes a difference. On the base of the first concretes, then, Rand can go on to give the very abstract formulation.

Notice that with regard to the branches of philosophy, each branch is presented with concrete questions and then an abstract summary. The whole thing is always shuttling back and forth between concretes and abstractions, because the abstractions are so broad that they convey nothing without examples. You cannot just give a whole bunch of examples, though, because then they do not add up to anything, and you have to tie it up or you will lose your listeners because of the crow epistemology. The whole essence of excellent writing in this regard is the shuttling back and forth. In this section on the first three branches of philosophy, you see how Rand does it.

For instance, notice that on metaphysics, there is a paragraph that gives a number of specific questions, which are then added up into "the study of existence as such, or being *qua* being." Again, if you said just that, no one would know what it meant. Even if they had some idea of "the fundamental nature of existence" from the astronaut, what is "being *qua* being," or what could "the study of existence as such" possibly consist of? But if you give examples of the type of issue that come under it, such as, "Are there natural laws? Are there miracles? Are things real?" and so on, then you provide some content. Then, when you say, "This is the study of existence as such," they get an idea that there is a field there, and see what specifically it would deal with. The same is true of epistemology: Rand lists a group of specific questions of a kind that a beginning audience could understand, and then gives the definition.

Notice, however, that the procedure changes when she gets to ethics. In metaphysics and epistemology she gives the examples first and then the abstract summary; in ethics she plunges right in with the definition, and then gives examples. This is because you can take for granted that people know, in a general way, what ethics is. They know that it has to do with good and evil, right and wrong, and how you should live. They also, of course, have some idea that ethics has something to do with life. Therefore, the term "ethics" will not strike people as a horrendous, vague abstraction that has nothing to do with anything, so you can give the definition first and then go into a few examples to concretize it. In metaphysics and epistemology, by contrast, the subject matter is so abstract that you have to concretize it first.

In the discussion of ethics, Rand's concretizations are not so much concerned with illustrating what ethics deals with, because that is generally known. Her examples illustrate something else. Notice that she gives examples that come from metaphysics and epistemology and then tries to show how they lead to different views in ethics in concrete cases. So her main focus in this paragraph is to concretize that ethical questions have to be based on metaphysics and epistemology. She knows that people know what ethics is. Her focus is always to show "Philosophy—who needs it"; that is her theme. Since people will have an idea that they need ethics, what they need to be sold on is that they need metaphysics and epistemology. Therefore, her concretization is focused not on what ethics is, but on what kind of metaphysical and epistemological questions you have to an-swer in order to get to the kind of important ethical questions that you know influence you.

As one more example of concretization, suppose I were to redo the passage like this: "You might claim, as most people do, that you have never been influenced by philosophy. However, this is false. You must have been influenced, because after all, you live in reality, and no one who lives in reality can be indifferent to it." That would be a true, theoretically accurate statement. But it would not have anything like the impact of Rand's version, because it is too abstract. A person could follow it, and since there has been some preliminary concretization, he could get it, more or less, but we are making a very important different point now. We are now switching from "Philosophy—what is it" to "Philosophy—you need it." That is so crucial to the theme of the discussion that Rand is not going to make that point until her listeners have ample evidence in their own case. Therefore, after concretizing the branches, the next main thing is to go to, "You do not think you hold this? Look, here is an example, and here is another, and here is another." Now the listener says, "I see what all these examples are, and I see that I do hold this. I wonder why." He is thus set up for you to say, "The reason you hold them is because you cannot escape it," after which you have the final summary.

There are more examples, but you should get from this an idea of what we call shuttling between concretes and abstractions. Different pa-pers, different articles, will require different forms of it. If you do not have as abstract a theme as this talk does, you do not have to concretize so heavily. With a completely raw audience, you may have to go more slowly, give more examples, give them metaphysics one week and the next branch the following week, or whatever. But in some form commensurate with your audience and your subject, you have to go back and forth, and this speech is an excellent archetype to keep in mind.

CHAPTER 4

KEEPING MATERIAL
SELF-CONTAINED

KEEPING YOUR MATERIAL self-contained is a crucial aspect of the principle of delimitation. You can include only so much, and the self-containment principle is a specification of this—a way of applying the broader principle that you must delimit your point. The self-containment principle is this: Include only that which you have room to explain or clarify, given your time and audience. This applies to the basic points you include, and to any given statement or example within it. Stated as a kind of formal rule, it would read: *Do not include issues, statements, or examples that directly raise legitimate questions you are unable to deal with.* Notice I say *directly* raise, because indirectly, every article raises every question; all knowledge is interconnected. Raising issues directly means asking questions like, "Is the universe chaotic, or is there a God?" by which you are directly raising the issue of God. Remember, too, that I stress *legitimate* questions. As far as illegitimate questions are concerned, you need not worry about them; there is no such thing as the unanswerable, impregnable piece. You have to assume a rational audience, but one that does not know your particular material; if it already knows it, there is no need for you. Within that framework, you have to decide what your readers or listeners would need to have explained to them, and if a certain issue would be unclear and require for them to grasp it more elaboration than you have time for, you must excise it ruthlessly.

Naturally, it takes a lot of experience and sheer practice to know when something needs explanation to a certain audience and when it does not. One of the best ways is simply to talk to people and take note of when they become baffled. If you see that certain points characteristically baffle them, eventually you will realize that those points have to be explained. The best thing that ever happened to me, in this regard, was when I was teaching many years ago. I gave what I thought was a perfectly clear presentation, and as I read the first set of exams, I went into a shock from which I did not recover for a long time. I realized then that things that you think are clear, are not clear. This was most borne in on me when one student, in a paper on free will and determinism, said that free will was guaranteed by the American Constitution. From that time on, when introducing free will and determinism, I have always said, "This is not politics. If free will is true, it is true in a dictatorship; if determinism is true, it is true in the United States." That has turned out to be a helpful clarification, one that I learned only from experience.

You build up from experience a certain knowledge. But you can also use yourself as a standard in this situation. If you are unsure what to include, it is sometimes helpful to ask yourself what you needed to learn when you first discovered this material. Remember that everything that you are going to present to the audience, you had to learn at some point. Ask yourself, "What was unclear to me in those days? What would I have liked to have been told when I first heard this point? What would have made it easier for me to grasp?" If you can re-create that, you will find it a helpful thing to use in deciding when a point is self-contained and when it needs further elaboration.

One caution here: You cannot use only your personal autobiography, particularly if you are a college student, because all of us who have gone through college, and particularly graduate school, have in many ways had our minds warped—I include myself in this—by outlandish teaching and all kinds of vicious ideas that get thrown at you so fast you do not even know how to begin untangling them. By "warped," I do not mean permanently, but I mean to the point at which you are thoroughly confused and it takes a long time to delouse yourself, intellectually speaking. You may, as a result of schooling, have become so confused that what you would need in order to become clear is much more than a normal audience would ever dream of needing. Therefore, take into account your audience. When you apply this autobiographical standard, be sure you are not reflecting the added confusion that is your heritage from going to a modern American university. But if you set that aside, asking yourself what you, as a rational being, would need to know is a helpful test. Whatever is a legitimate question by that standard, you have to be prepared to answer. Otherwise you must omit the point, or recast the piece so that it does not come up.

A few qualifications are in order. There may be some things that you have to comment on in your piece without being able to cover them fully. In that case, you can make what is known as a glancing reference; you can indicate in passing, "I know I am raising such and such issue, but I cannot cover it here." Let us say you are giving a talk on emotions to a group of psychologists, and you know that they are all advocates of determinism, but you have not got the space or time to go into free will. You can say, at some point, "I am addressing you on the premise that man has free will. If you want to argue about that, do it later. But I cannot argue about it or discuss it today." Then you have put your cards on the table. Your audience has to know, "Is this a point he is going to cover, or is this something he is assuming but not going to cover, and we are not expected to follow or to agree with it?"

Some things, I should point out, do not need *any* explanation to a given audience. For instance, if you are giving a talk to a general audience today, there are many things that are not philosophic primaries that you can blithely say without elaboration, because they are regarded as common sense and obvious. For instance, "The world does not owe you a living." That is not a philosophic primary; in fact, that comes out of ethics, and if you wanted to give a proof of it, you could go on for hours just to give the bare bones. But that is not necessary. It is not necessary even to give an indication to an audience today, because you can take that much for granted as common sense. If someone then in a question period or afterward wants to discuss it, you can do so. Or, if you are addressing an American audience, you can say, "I agree with the Founding Fathers that man has certain inalienable rights."

To a certain extent, this kind of issue is contextual. When I first started arguing against the draft, you had to give a whole song and dance before people would even dream that such a viewpoint was possible. Eventually, though, many audiences would nod their heads right away; they agreed the draft was wrong—probably for the wrong reasons, but nevertheless, less of a discussion was necessary. So you do have to take into account what the audience already understands. Leaving aside this type of point, though, when your material raises legitimate questions, you must cover them. This is essential to making your material clear and self-contained. Otherwise, you may say the truth and nothing but the truth, and yet your whole presentation will collapse; it will baffle or alienate the audience because of the form of your presentation. The broader topic here is the context of the audience's knowledge. Note that I am not saying that you should avoid controversy or be noncommittal. You can take passionate stands, make absolute commitments, say the most outrageously shocking things in the world. That is not the point. The point is, say what you can explain or clarify within an understandable framework.

Let us now illustrate the issue of self-contained presentation by means of two complete opposites on this point. Recall that when you present ideas, you have to delimit your formulations, the specific points that you include and the way you word them, so as not to raise questions that you are unable to deal with or answer, here meaning questions that *directly* and *legitimately* rise out of the material that you cover. If you *do* raise such questions and then do not deal with them, you simply baffle, confuse, or antagonize your audience.

This sounds easy enough, but there is a certain problem in actually knowing how to delimit your material. The problem arises from the fact that all knowledge is interconnected. On the one hand, in your desire to give a strong case for your material, you feel obliged to put in more and more, to cover all the foundations of your argument, all the objections it might face, all the kinds of examples that would make it so convincing. On the other hand, when you get to a certain point, you pass the limit of what can be self-contained in that presentation. The problem thus becomes what to put in so as to give the best possible foundation within the limits of the space available to you, and what to leave out so as not to spill over into the un-self-contained. It becomes a balancing or a juggling act. For this, experience is very helpful. You simply find, time after time, that you either put in so much that you baffle your listeners, or put in so little that they are utterly unconvinced, and after a while you begin to get the hang of it. But it is also helpful, particularly at the beginning, to analyze the presentations of other people who have either mastered or flagrantly violated this principle. That is what we will turn to now.

Let us turn first to Ayn Rand's article "The Wreckage of the Consensus," specifically to the part that begins, "The institution that enables our leaders to indulge in such recklessly irresponsible ventures is the military draft."* This latter half of the article is an excellent example of making self-contained something that could very easily sprawl all over the place and ruin itself. The context, as set out in the previous section of the article, sketches the general anti-ideological state of the mixed economy— the unprincipled deals, the compromises, the gang warfare—and then applies it to the Vietnam War as one example, and then to the draft as another example. I am not concerned to point out Rand's outline, but specifically the issue of self-contained writing—what she chooses to say, and how she is able to make it self-intelligible, as against the next presentation that we will look at.

Rand starts out right away by giving the argument against the draft, saying that the draft is a violation of individual rights. Note that from the beginning, she pitches her philosophical proof on what you could call a

---

* *Capitalism: The Unknown Ideal*, pp. 226ff.

political level. In the field of politics, the issue of individual rights is the basic philosophic issue, in terms of defending a free economy and a free country. This is, therefore, a political issue. Rand does not begin with the basic standard of morality, from which she deduces rights. Nor does she offer, in this article, any proof as to why man has rights. There are a few indications from which you could glean what type of argument she would offer, but she does not say, "I believe in rights for the following reasons: Man is a rational being, and so on and so on and so on," because then she would raise many issues more complex than the draft. She pitches it right away on rights. She could not have done this, say, in the seventeenth century. At that time, the idea of individual rights would be a revelation, and if you just plunged in like that, people would not know what you were talking about. But thanks to the Founding Fathers and John Locke and the whole tradition of the Enlightenment, people in this country recognize the idea of rights, and it is therefore self-contained and intelligible, given a paragraph or so of elaboration.

To make it crudely obvious what Rand does not do, she does not say, "I am against the draft because of the Law of Identity." Nor does she begin by saying, "I am against the draft because I am an advocate of reason." And yet, if you asked her and kept asking why, eventually she would reach the point of saying that the basis of her opposition to the draft is the fact that A is A, reality is real, and reason is man's means of knowledge. If she started there, though, she would have to go through a whole philosophical dissertation, and the paper would be long over before she ever got to the draft.

Rand continues, "The most immoral contradiction is that of the so-called conservatives," and goes into a brief paragraph criticizing the conservative and liberal views. Again, she could easily attack the liberals and conservatives from the point of view of their philosophic foundations, as she has done in other papers—the skepticism of the liberals, or their Marxist viewpoint, or the conservatives' ties to religion. But if she did so, she would lose the discussion of the draft in a whole bunch of other equally or more controversial issues. In the present context, she attacks the liberals and the conservatives on the level of their view of rights, on which she has already indicated her own view. In other words, she attacks them only within the framework of the base she has already laid down.

At this point you might ask, Why does she even raise the issue of liberals and conservatives? Is this not, in itself, a distraction? Why does she not just present her own view? The answer is that she accomplishes something philosophical here, by way of making her own view clearer. Remember that rights are a long, complex subject. If you wanted to start from scratch, you would have to say what rights are. There are many different theories of rights, and the sheer fact that you say, "I am for *individual* rights," although a beginning, does not, by itself, make your view clear. One way of making your view clear would be to go into a long dissertation with theoretical definitions, but that is impossible if your main focus is the evil of the draft, which is just one application of rights. Briefly, another way of making your own view clear is contrast. Set yourself off from a view that is not yours, as in the sheer act of saying, "Now remember, when I say 'rights,' I mean *rights*; I am not the type that says 'I am all for property, but I am against life,' and I am not the type that calls welfare handouts rights." This amounts to saying, "When I say 'rights,' I mean rights in the original American sense, which is a sanction to action based on the value of life." Rand does not go into that whole theory. But by quickly warding off the two sides, she makes her view more convincing and more defined. She says what it consists of, in a way that is still self-contained and shows that the opposition to it is contradictory—glaringly so, because they talk about rights while denying the right to life.

In the next paragraph, she goes into a discussion of the notion that rights impose obligations. That is a widespread viewpoint, commonly invoked by advocates of the draft. Rand therefore gets it out of the way right at the beginning, so that it does not impede the reader's understanding. Observe how she refutes this argument. The theory that rights impose obligations is actually a version of altruism—the idea being that man owes his life to others, and that they give him certain permissions to be free as long as he serves them. If Rand were to say at this point, "This bromide—that rights impose obligations—comes from the theory of altruism," and move on, that would sink the discussion, because that claim is much more controversial and complex than the issue of the draft. Instead, she covers this on the level that she has already discussed, namely, only rights. She is counting here on the fact that people know, or can at least quickly grasp, the difference between a right and a gift or permission. Accordingly, she says simply that the idea that rights impose obligations would mean that we do not have rights at all, but gifts, and that would mean therefore a complete rejection of the idea of man's rights. Of course, if she wanted at this point to write a different article, she could go straight into a discussion of why you cannot have freedom without an ethics of egoism, but then she would not be addressing the draft. Here, she has indicated enough of a base to answer this argument without having to go into questions that she would have no way of covering, and that the audience does not need.

There is an old joke about a little boy who asks his mother where he comes from, and—thinking this is the moment she has been waiting for—she gives him the whole story, from egg to womb to birth. At the end, he says, "Oh, Bill came from Chicago, and I was just wondering where I came from." This is analogous to the situation with your audience. A lot of people think, at the beginning of the writing process, "I have got rights and, supposedly, obligations—that is altruism; now I have to tell the whole story of where altruism comes from, why it is evil, and so on." But in fact, you do not. You need merely say the equivalent of "Chicago" in that joke—that is, put your point in terms the reader can understand, and do not make a big production where none is necessary. (Do not, however, draw from this the conclusion that you should always avoid major philosophic issues. That would be a grave mistake. The concern here is only how to deal with such issues in contexts in which you cannot discuss them at length.)

Rand then turns to the question of the need for a volunteer military. If she omitted any reference to that, the reader would be left thinking, "If there were no draft, who would defend the country then?" You cannot take the cavalier attitude of saying, in effect, "I have proved that the draft is immoral, so my job is done. If the reader is left wondering how the country will be able to survive, that is tough. I have shown the moral basis, and I am not concerned with vulgar details such as the survival of the nation." If you make a moral point that you know is going to raise questions of practicality, it is up to you at least to indicate that it would work out practically. If you have no space, you can cover, very briefly, enough simply to show that you know this issue exists. If you had, for instance, no space at all, you could say, "As far as practicality is concerned, all history testifies to the practicality of volunteers," period, without saying any more. You would not have proved it, but you would have indicated that you are aware of that issue, and if people were then interested in pursuing your viewpoint, there would be a further answer.

In this article, Rand goes into some detail on this issue. She discusses why a man would volunteer to fight, and she even answers the question, "But what if people do not?" She gives the two reasons they would not, and concludes that neither of those is relevant in a free country. She ends up by showing that the volunteer military is not only moral, but practical, in the sense that it prevents the government from pursuing an adventurist foreign policy that the citizens do not see the value of; she also goes on to make the other practical point that modern warfare is technological and requires a trained military. In general, it is always valuable to include an indication of both the moral and the practical when these issues come up. If you include only the moral, you leave the implication that you are a mere theoretician, with your head in the clouds and no concern for reality. If you include only the practical, even supposing you have shown that it has worked, the immediate question in your reader's mind is: "Why has it worked? Why must it work? Is there any theoretical basis to its success, or is it just that up to now a volunteer army has worked, whereas in the future it may not?" But if you combine the theory and the practice, the reason it has to and the proof that it has, then that is very powerful.

At this point, then, Rand has established that the draft is not practically necessary, and that it is a basic violation of the principles of America. It then becomes relevant to point out the motive of people who advocate this type of institution. It would be completely wrong, of course, to begin the section on the draft with that question. That would sound like starting off with an ad hominem argument, that is, not discussing the validity of the draft but simply attacking its proponents. And the reader's immediate answer would be, "Well, their motive is to save the country from an aggressor." First, therefore, you have to show that the draft is obviously not a practical means of defending the country, and that it is immoral as well. Then you can say, "Now, on that basis, why would anybody advocate it?" In other words, you have to prepare a question in the reader's mind; he must see that there is something here that has to be explained.

Notice that Rand does not answer yet, because she wants to build up to what the advocates' motive is. So she simply lays down that that is the question she is concerned with, and then she starts to give some background. She states the historical context—the conscription of labor in World War II—and makes people think there is something more at stake in the draft, obviously, than what we are being told, because here is something similar to it in the past, and look what direction that measure is moving toward. Then she discusses the alleged financial motive and the actual real cost, which is small in comparison to today's government expenditures, implying that the motive cannot be a financial one. The question thus becomes more and more insistent in the reader's mind: "What could the motive be, then? It is nothing that any of these people say. There must be something fundamental being concealed here, because all the things they say are senseless on the face of it, and yet they are advocating this monstrous measure. Why?" You gather more and more momentum the more you unravel what they say.

Rand covers one point further before she goes into what could be the motive—the results of the draft on the youth of the country. This is the touch needed to show how truly horrifying this institution is. This qualifies as concretization; she is showing you what the draft would mean in the lives of the actual people whose rights are being violated. She shows

briefly how the draft would affect specifically the *minds* of these boys—
they are as yet unformed; they are put in a world of the unknowable; they
do not know when they are to be called or for what; they are given a sense
of impotence; they feel bitter—and then she points to the signs of that
bitterness that anybody can see: the "Now!" generation, the young people
losing their minds on drugs, and so on. One could write an entire dissertation on "the draft is destructive to the minds of the draftees," and go
on to the requirements of the mind, including why force is the antithesis
of mind. But that is a separate topic in itself. What Rand does is simply to
concretize: What would force, in this case and context, do to the victims?
By simply touching on a few things, she is able to evoke this unknowable
and terrifying world they would find themselves in, and it becomes clear
that they would give up and there would be all these negative consequences. She goes on to say, "This is what a volunteer army could spare
us, this kind of torture to the youth, as opposed to the junk that a rela-
tively small amount of money is spent on now."

What, then, is the real motive of those who advocate the draft? Now
we have a true horror. We have exposed as false all the main alleged jus-
tifications of the draft. We have shown that it is immoral, impractical,
and indefensible. We have also, in effect, intimated that there must be
something truly monstrous behind this kind of advocacy. Now Rand is
able to say what the real motive is, and it comes out of the horse's mouth,
which at this time was General [Lewis Blaine] Hershey and Secretary of
Defense Robert McNamara. You see the quotes from them leading up
directly to the idea that what they want is not to advance the welfare of
the country, not even to help the people in the slums, but destruction for
its own sake, sacrifice as an end in itself. It is at that point that she can say,
"What they are after is to turn the youth into sacrificial animals." By the
time she says it, it is clear from the whole preceding context. Therefore,
she can say, "The real issue is whether you are a sacrificial animal, whether
your life belongs to the state or not." Notice that she has come back to her
starting point. She started with the idea that man has rights, that his life
does not belong to the state, and now she has shown that the monstrous

motive of the people advocating the draft is precisely to turn men into wards of the state, to make them sacrificial animals that the state can dispose of as it chooses. And she has done this in a way that makes it nakedly clear that that could be their only motive, because everything else has been covered.

That is just enough to give you an idea of the types of issues that Rand covered, indicated, and avoided in this article, and why the article is self-contained as long as you know the idea of individual rights.

For contrast, let us now turn to the following short essay on the draft. I wrote this as an exercise, deliberately violating the principle that writing should be self-contained. I just took whatever came to mind first and batted it out without worrying about whether it would be intelligible or not. Then, whenever I dug a hole for myself in one paragraph, I tried to get out of it in the next one by digging even deeper.

> The military draft is an evil institution, which should be rejected by every civilized government. The draft is a gross violation of the rights of the draftees.
>
> The conservatives today favor the draft, but they can be ignored, because they argue on the basis of religion, which is irrational and unproven. The liberals are against the draft, but only because they disapprove of the present war. The war, however, is not really that important. The issue is one of principle.
>
> Since man's life is the basic standard of moral value, by which all actions must be judged, any action that harms or threatens human life is wrong. And the draft, incontestably, threatens and often harms the lives of the young men drafted: It sends them off into foreign wars, against their own choice, where they can easily be killed or wounded.
>
> It may be said that the draftees will help to save an entire country from the enemy and, therefore, that the net effect of the draft is to preserve man's life. This is the altruistic idea that service to others is good—which I firmly reject. Altruism

holds that man should suffer (e.g., Kant). Selfishness is the only proper approach to morality.

Selfishness does not mean trampling on others or doing whatever one feels like. It means acting in such a way as to preserve one's own life, without sacrificing for others or accepting their sacrifices. And to fight in a war one does not believe in is definitely a sacrifice.

I don't mean to suggest that one should act on whatever one happens to believe, regardless of the reasons for it. One should always act on objective conclusions, which one can prove by logic. Even if a young man is mistaken about the advisability of a given war, however, it is still objectively wrong to force him into it against his own beliefs; when you force a man into the army, you are really forcing his mind, and thus destroying it in the long run. Even if the young man has been irrational about rejecting the war, it is still his mind's conclusion, and as such it must be respected by others.

It may be said that if a young man is wrong about a given war, then the government, in forcing him to act on the proper viewpoint, is forcing the truth on him, and thus is really helping his mind. How can the government be so certain of what is true? Does it know more than the citizens? How can it set itself up as the absolute judge? Is there no room in a free country for disagreement?

History proves that the draft is impractical. In a free country, men always volunteer (if they approve of the war), and they perform more efficiently than conscripted troops. This is especially true in the modern age, with our different weapons. The real issue, therefore, is motivating men to enlist voluntarily, which means: paying them enough, i.e., the real issue today is money. We need merely cut out some useless welfare programs and give the tax money instead to the military.

Of course, a government should not have the power to tax,

any more than it should have the power to draft. But you cannot undo all the controls at once. And the right to life is more important than the right to property, since it is the source of all rights.

Those who grasp the above will have no difficulty in seeing the draft as merely one more example of the evil of the statists, whose only concern is to augment their power over the country. If one understands what the draft champions are proposing, and what it would do to this country's youth, the statists' evil becomes inescapable.

The first point in this paper at which I raise an issue that I have no business raising is the gratuitous attack on religion. It is unnecessary, and the people reading it would not see any reason for it. Moreover, they would not even see why a conservative has to be religious. A lot of people might think a conservative is simply somebody who supports his country and advocates the draft on patriotic grounds. The connection to religion has not been explained. Therefore, it is as though I am simply going out of my way, first, to make my opponent philosophical when I have not given any reason why he must be philosophical, and then second, to take a swipe at his philosophy. It is simply unconvincing. There are many contexts where you can attack religion directly, but in an article of this scope, it is irrelevant.

Next, I say that the liberals disapprove of the present war, and then I say, "The war, however, is not really that important. The issue is one of principle." That is a perfect example of a sloppy formulation. Taken as is, that statement can legitimately be interpreted to mean that ideas are more important than lives. In other words, thousands of people are dying, but that is not so important; what really counts is that a philosophic principle is at stake. If you put a formulation in such a way as that, your reader can very easily think, "What is the matter with this guy? What is the purpose of principles if they are not relevant to human lives?" The actual, unstated intention of this formulation, which is not objectively clear, is that you cannot resolve an issue like this by focusing on only one concrete. In fact, if I were to develop that idea, I would say, "If you are concrete-bound, your stand against the war will not save you from another war in the future, one that will also take thousands of lives needlessly and irrationally. Consequently, if you are concerned with life, you have to be concerned with principles." It would actually be very undesirable to go into this whole excursus here, though, because then I would be going into a dissertation on the role of principles in human life before I even discussed the draft. It would simply sidetrack the reader, and it would not be clear.

At this point in the paper, we go into the basic argument offered against the draft—which is in conspicuous contrast to Ayn Rand's argument. "Man's life is the basic standard of moral value. Any action that harms or threatens life is wrong. The draft threatens life, and therefore it is wrong." The concept at which I pitch the base of this argument is not "rights," but "the value of human life, man's life as the standard." According to Objectivism, this is indeed the foundation of ethics, and man's life is the standard of good and evil. That determines every such question as what is right, what is wrong, how man should live and how he should not. If you know that, though, you also know that a very lengthy discussion is necessary to explain what you are talking about: Why is this the basic standard? Does it mean, then, that suicide is always wrong? Isn't God supposed to be the standard, or society? If you are going to raise the question of the basic standard of ethics, you cannot just throw it out carelessly, because it is much more controversial than the draft. Moreover, a further question in the reader's mind will immediately arise, because there is no definition here as to what "man's life" means according to this theory. Does it mean life at any price? Does it mean all men as a group, collectively, as the standard? Nothing is here said to explain this; it is simply "man's life" tossed in without any elaboration. I then go on to say, "Anything that threatens human life is wrong," which could legitimately be taken to mean literally *anything* that threatens human life, from fighting in a war to crossing a busy street. So does "man's life" as the standard mean that you must never risk anything?

The way I have written this passage, I am relying on a gigantic context, one that says that man's life requires certain basic principles, and that anything that threatens those principles is wrong, but I have not said what the principles are. The result is that I go from the basic proposition of ethics to a last consequence in politics, with everything in between omitted. As a result, it is completely indefensible and unclear. In my [1976] lecture course on the philosophy of Objectivism, I took some three whole lectures to get from life as the standard to the evil of the draft.* In between, I had to say, "Life is the standard, and that requires reason; and that requires egoism; and that means a whole set of virtues—independence, integrity, productiveness, and so on; and socially, that means a policy of trading value for value and respecting the freedom of others; it means the evil of the initiation of force, and it means individual rights, and the function of the government should therefore be . . ."—and only on that whole foundation did we then get to the draft. At that point, if I say, "The draft threatens human life," you see the whole structure and grasp that the draft threatens every requirement of human life. But in this passage I have not said any of the requirements, and it therefore sounds like anything other than lying in bed is anti-life. It is ridiculous, and it collapses the whole case.

Since I have not said what "man's life" means, I have left it perfectly open for a person to say, "Well, the draft will help to save the whole country, and there are a lot of men in a country; so, on balance, the draft is *for* man's life." Considering that I tossed in "man's life" without any elaboration, that is a perfectly legitimate confusion. Therefore, given that I was writing in this irresponsible way, I had to counter that. When Ayn Rand got to the issue of sacrifice in her article, it was only after giving a number of examples, so she could touch on it very briefly and clearly. Here, though, I simply, without any preparation, take altruism baldly and say, "What you just said is service to others, and I reject it."

---

* In Dr. Peikoff's book *Objectivism: The Philosophy of Ayn Rand* (Dutton, 1991), the section "Man's Life as the Standard of Moral Value" begins on p. 213, while the draft is not mentioned until p. 366.

At this point, an uninitiated person can legitimately say, "What is wrong with service to others? In an economy, for instance, we exchange goods and services—your dentist gives you a service, i.e., he serves others." That is obviously an equivocation. But there is nothing here to explain what altruism actually does mean, so the person can honestly say, "What is wrong with doing something for other people?" In Rand's article, by the time you get to altruism, you know what altruists have in mind; you know that it means destruction of the able and the healthy for its own sake. Here, though, there is absolutely no explanation. I then make it worse by saying, without explanation, "Altruism holds that man should suffer (e.g., Kant)." The straightest way of taking that would be, "Altruism holds that man should suffer (for example, Kant should)." This could very well be read as, "Kant is an example; he should suffer," or, "Kant's philosophy advocates suffering," or who knows what; there is no grammar; it is just "(e.g., Kant)." It amounts to telling the reader, "Whatever the word 'Kant' connotes in your mind, that is my thought." (I put this kind of sloppy formulation in deliberately every once in a while, because you have to read things as they are written, without knowing what is in the writer's mind.)

Then I finish up this paragraph by saying I am for selfishness. I have to, because I have to say what else I am for, if not for altruism. That, of course, raises the whole question of selfishness, which people think means cutting other people's throats and running around like a maniac and doing whatever arbitrary thing you feel like. So I have to clarify it in some way, and in the next paragraph I toss off, "Selfishness does not mean trampling on others (and so on). It means preserving life without sacrificing or accepting sacrifices." That is certainly true, but it is wrong to treat the issue this way, without preparation or elaboration. I have not given any examples of what "sacrifice" would consist of. Anybody is free, therefore, to take it to mean anything. An audience might think, "How can you live this way? Take the case of the draft that you were discussing—if you go and serve in the army, you are sacrificing for your country, and if you do not, other people are sacrificing for you, so either way somebody is sacrificing. Somebody has to fight in the war. Therefore, this ethics is impractical." A proper explanation would indicate that it is not a sacrifice to fight in a legitimate war. But I have given neither definition nor elaboration; I have just tossed in "no sacrifice," and the result is "no time to explain" and completely unconvincing.

After going into this whole dissertation, I say, by way of tying it back to the draft, "It would be a sacrifice to fight in a war you do not believe in." That immediately suggests to the reader that doing something you do not believe in is a sacrifice, so you should always just do whatever you believe, regardless of how you arrived at that belief. To avoid that implication, I then toss in a paragraph saying, "You should be objective; you should prove everything by logic." Now, you know you are in bad shape if you are already into objectivity and logic. Everything I write is digging me in deeper and deeper, taking me further and further away from the draft. Suppose you tell an unprepared audience in this context, "You should always act on conclusions that you can prove by logic." The immediate reaction will be, "The author says that you should act on logical ideas. So if a man is wrong about a given war—and the government should know—then he should not act on his views, and it is perfectly okay for the government to draft him."

To cover that, I go right away to the next point, which is, "Even if a man is mistaken, it is still wrong to force him. Because when you force a man into the army, you are really forcing his mind, and therefore you are destroying it in the long run." That, of course, is true, and we saw in Ayn Rand's article in what context and in what form she was able to indicate that. Here, though, I say absolutely nothing to make it understandable, and it again leads to an obvious question. I have not given any indication here how the draft destroys the mind, or in what way; I have simply said, "It destroys the mind." That is completely arbitrary. Any decent, commonsense person will take it to mean that the draft drives its victims crazy, like brainwashing or something, and he will reply, "That's a small minority. A lot of draftees came back sane." The point is completely unconvincing. Rand covered this very briefly, but she had a context and just enough points so that by the time you got there, you could see how, in the long run, it ruins these people. But without context, it just sounds silly.

Notice, too, another bad formulation: "Even if a man has been irrational in coming to a viewpoint, it is still *his mind's* conclusion, and as such it must be respected by others." Such a statement throws you into the depths of subjectivism: "You should respect his conclusion, regardless of how irrational it is," implies that his conclusion is true for him. Here, I really mean to say, "A man has a *political* right to come to this conclusion; you should respect that right, even though his actual viewpoint, let us say, is completely wrong." But no such distinction is made. I just say, "It must be respected." The formulation is so sloppy that it is not even clear whether the "it" is his conclusion or his mind.

The next paragraph makes my argument worse still. I make up something that a neutral listener could say—"If a man is wrong about the war and the government is forcing the truth on him, is that not helping him?" The only way to answer this would be to discuss what the mind is, why it requires freedom, and why you cannot force truth on people. But that is a big subject, one you could not cover in a paper of this length. So, in desperation, I suddenly turn on the audience and start asking rhetorical questions. In itself, that is fine, but observe the questions that I ask: "How does the government know what is true? Does it know more than the citizens? How can it set itself up as the absolute judge? Is there no room for disagreement in a free country?" This writer obviously feels that he has to get rid of the idea that the government can force the truth on you, but the issues involved are simply too much for him, so he goes on the offensive. Only, by the way those questions come up, their net effect is skepticism, in the sense that nobody can know anything. If you ask, "How can the government be the *absolute* judge?" the clear implication is, "Who can say what is absolute truth? There are no absolutes; it is all a matter of opinion. How can the government be so certain? We cannot be certain." So the phrasing does not state, but it implies, skepticism and subjectivism. Mixed in with that at the same time is another viewpoint— not a bad epistemological view, but a legitimate political view: "In a free country there can be disagreement." Thus, two entirely different questions are conflated: "Is truth objective?" is an epistemological question about the status of human knowledge, while, "Should man have a right to reach conclusions by his own judgment, or be subject to governmental coercion?" is a political question. But this paragraph simply mashes the two together, thereby leaving the implication, "If you advocate freedom, you have to be a skeptic; on the other hand, if there is absolute truth, we can give the government the power to force it on us." It is a devastatingly harmful implication, simply by the nature of the questions.

In the next paragraph, I am supposed to be now turning to practicality, having allegedly given the theoretical base (which is, in fact, a catastrophe). But the token discussion of practicality is unconvincing, because I do not offer any illustrations. The brilliant thing that I say is, "Men always volunteer if they approve of the war." The question that immediately arises is, "Would they approve of *any* war, or would they all take the attitude, 'To hell with the war, let us just mind our own business and be overrun'?" In Rand's article, she says they would approve, except under conditions A and B. But I have just passed that by, so my case is completely unconvincing.

Notice also the sentence, "This is especially true in the modern age, with our different weapons." That is a small but eloquent example of poor communication. It is entirely ambiguous: What do I mean by "different weapons"? Different from what? Do we have bows and arrows now? And what has that got to do with anything? In point of fact, I actually have in mind technological advancement, nuclear weapons, and so on. But this is a typically modern sloppiness, in which no one bothers to say what they mean and what they are talking about. In the process of writing, the first thing that may occur to you is, "There is something different about our weapons today from those of the past, and that is relevant to the draft." Then you properly take a pause to think, "What is it that is different? Well, today's weapons are much more complex; there is much more technology and so on; what is the right word to express that?" And you have to grope until you can say, "Ah, this is exactly the point I mean, and now it is clear." But instead, people today are taught to be "natural"—that is, to blurt out whatever comes to mind. The first thing that would logically come is, "Things are different today," and so they would say, "This applies especially today with our different weapons," which does not state the point and simply leaves the point vague and unconvincing. A great deal of modern writing is exactly that. It is, in effect, a subjective hint at meaning, not an actual objective statement.

The next statement in that paragraph says, "The real issue today is money." As a formulation, that makes it appear as though the whole issue of the draft is only a financial question, with nothing ideological about it, nothing philosophically or morally important. That, of course, is what the advocates of the draft would like everyone to believe. This passage thus throws away the whole case by a sloppy statement. True, in writing this I do not mean that the real issue is money; I mean that the practical way to resolve the problem is to pay the volunteers more money so that they will enlist. But instead of saying that, I just blurt out, "The real issue is money"—a formulation that, taken straight, implies simply that money is all that counts.

The next paragraph simply makes things worse, because, having given a poor case against the draft, I then go on to say, "On top of that, the government should not have the power to tax." That idea is even more controversial than the draft and would take a much longer article, but I simply drag it in, too. I then say, "We do not have to worry about taxes now, because the right to life is more important than the right to property, since it is the source of all rights." That is a disastrous formulation: "The right to life is more important than the right to property." The clear implication is that sometimes we have to choose between the two, in which case the right to property is not so important; after all, the right to life is its basis. If that is true, the advocate of the draft can perfectly well come back and say, "The right to life is the source of freedom, too, so if it is more important than property, then it is more important than freedom. Thus, if we can get rid of property when we need to, we can get rid of freedom also. After all, it is in the name of saving the country from aggressors and preserving the lives of the citizens."

A formulation like "The right to life is more important than the right to property" is a self-inflicted, mortal wound. With it, you destroy your case, your argument, your logic, your conviction—you would effectively have to burn the whole article and start over. In a rough draft, such a formulation is acceptable, as long as you then strike it out and state clearly what you really mean. In this case, though, you should not cover that issue at all, because there is no space to do it justice.

At the end of this paper, I conclude: "If you grasp all of this, you see why the advocates of the draft are so evil—all they want is power, and they are destroying the country's youth." That is a completely unprepared, absolutely arbitrary statement; I do not give any idea as to why I would say it, and therefore it just falls completely flat. In Ayn Rand's essay, by contrast, by the time you get to that point, the basis for it has been completely prepared.

Let those two essays on the draft, then, serve in your mind as the good and the bad examples of the principle of keeping your writing self-contained.

CHAPTER 5

RATIONALISM

WE NOW TURN to what you can call the *quality of argument*, your approach to argument as such. In that context, I want to discuss the topic of rationalism. This is the most widespread and harmful error of today's intellectuals. It is virtually inescapable by college students, certainly by graduate students in the humanities. It also has the effect of enormously alienating nonintellectuals or nonprofessionals in the field. Rationalism is the arch-disease of today's intellectuals. If you have not got it yourself, I congratulate you. But even if you have not, you still need to understand it. Otherwise, you will find today's intellectual world unintelligible, including your professors and their publications, and you will simply end up, in effect, deciding that people are hopeless, and withdrawing. If you understand this error, however, you can inoculate yourself against it and explain the countless forms of it that you see around you.

In philosophy, the term "rationalism" is used to designate a broad school contrasted with "empiricism." These are two technical terms, standing for two schools of philosophy that have been at war with each other from ancient Greece to the present day. Rationalists, roughly, are those philosophers who stress the role of reason or logic in the acquisition of knowledge, while disparaging or denying the senses. They include thinkers like Plato, Augustine, and Descartes. Empiricists, on the other hand, include people like John Locke, David Hume, and the modern pragmatists, all of whom stress the role of experience, or sensory evidence, while denying or minimizing logic. As pure philosophy, both of these schools lead to disaster, and Objectivism rejects both camps. Objectivist epistemology entirely repudiates the idea of reason versus observation, because it says knowledge is acquired by the use of reason *applied to* observation. Knowledge is thus the integration of logic and experience, not an either-or situation.

In this book, I want to focus on rationalism in a somewhat different sense from the technical definition that I have just given, and that is rationalism as a profoundly mistaken *method of thought*. In this sense, it is used not only by technical rationalists, but also by most of the people who call themselves empiricists, as well as by many others who have never heard of either school. The essence of rationalism, as I am using the term, is: deduction without reference to reality. In other words, this method consists of ignoring reality, ignoring observational evidence, seizing in a vacuum on some idea, some premise or theory that sounds plausible to the writer, and then proceeding to deduce from it a set of consequences. The result is like a floating construct. It is completely arbitrary, even though it may appear imposing. There may be a whole chain of "If this, then this; if this, then this; therefore, therefore, QED," and so on, with all the apparatus of deduction—but it all rests on nothing, like a castle in the air. Very often it culminates in a conclusion that is blatantly the opposite of observed facts, but the person says, "What can I do? I have proved my conclusion, so much the worse for the facts." In other words, the rationalist starts with an arbitrary preconception, unthinkingly taken as self-evident, the practical equivalent of Plato's innate ideas. Then there is a chain of deductions, which usually follow quite rigorously, leading to a conclusion that completely defies reality. It is thinking without looking at reality; thinking as a kind of game of manipulating words without reference to what is out there, to existence; thinking in which the primary concern is the relation of one idea to another idea, not the relation of ideas to reality.

Ayn Rand once invented this eloquent example: A rationalist would come out with some argument such as, "Man has only two eyes; therefore, he should be able to see only two things, one with each eye." The rationalist does not ask why; it sounds neat and symmetrical—two things, two eyes, it all fits. At this point, two schools of philosophy would arise. One would say, "We have to accept the conclusion. Men do see only two things; everything else, they do not actually see—it is all an illusion." To that, the opposing school would reply, "Men *do* see countless things, not just two, but that is because of all the hidden eyes that they have." If you then say to such a rationalist, "Look, it is not true; if you look at reality, you will see that men do, in fact, have only two eyes, and they do see many things," he will find that irrelevant. Reality does not have any status in his thinking. He has decided that his conclusion about eyes is good, and his idea supersedes all facts.

What rationalism amounts to is obliviousness to reality on the part of a thinker. It is the placement of ideas above reality. Remember that the first crucial point of communication is that it is conceptual, and that you must always bear in mind that a concept is shorthand for concretes. Rationalism represents a total failure on this particular point. A rationalist's concepts are cut loose from reality altogether, and he creates his own world of concepts. It has a definite structure (rationalists are very big on logic); there is a beginning, a middle, and an end; you always know where he is and where he is going; and there is always, "Therefore, therefore, QED," just as in geometry, which rationalists love as a subject matter. But it all floats, cut off from reality. The conceptual shorthand, which is supposed to be our way of holding a mass of concretes in a reduced number of units, becomes a world of its own, just like Plato's world of Forms. As a result, if you ask the rationalist about his imposing structure, pointing to his starting point and asking, "But why that?" he generally looks at you, baffled, and says, "What do you mean, 'why'? That is where I start." His whole structure, in other words, collapses very easily.

You can be a rationalist positively, using this method allegedly to prove something of your own—or you can be a rationalist negatively, using this method to refute an opponent. The latter leads to what we can call *rationalist polemics*. In this case, you are trying to refute an opponent, but not by pointing out facts of reality that he overlooks; you forget about facts. Instead, you show him that his ideas contain an internal contradiction. In other words, in this type of polemics, you accept the basic premise of your opponent. You say to him, "I will concede your fundamental point, but I am going to show you that somewhere along the line, you contradict your own beginning." This is a very inadvisable method of arguing. There is obviously nothing wrong with showing a man that he has contradicted himself; that can be a valuable thing to do. But if you engage in this type of approach as a characteristic method of arguing, you tend, after a while, to become oblivious to reality. You train your mental eye to focus exclusively on your opponent, to see how you can trap him while accepting his premises. You train yourself to focus not on the relation of what he says to reality, but on a world of ideas apart from reality. This is very harmful to your intellectual development, to your ability to argue or present ideas. It trains you to widen a breach between your mind and reality. It also characteristically fails even as polemics, because once you accept your opponent's basic premises, he sets the terms thereafter, and you are at his mercy.

This method of rationalism is characteristically used by theologians, to take another example. They have decided in advance of thinking—by means of revelation, they say—what conclusion their reasoning is supposed to lead them to. Then they simply ignore facts. They are oblivious to reality, but they want to "prove" their conclusion because they claim to accept reason, or at least many of them do. Therefore, they cook up an argument that will lead them to the conclusion they know in advance they want to establish. They juggle ideas around until they get them into the pattern in which the ideas allegedly justify the conclusion that was sent by revelation. This is reasoning as rationalization. It is not following reality, or following the facts where they lead, but going through a pretense, making up arbitrary premises and connections in order to come out at a prearranged spot. Unfortunately, this is something done more widely than merely by theologians. It is invalid, and I urge you not to do it.

Obviously, if people engaging in rationalism said openly what they were doing, there would be no problem in detecting it. Usually, however, rationalists do not exist in a really pure form. What you get in a typical real-life case is an individual who ignores reality, but not so consistently that you are dazzled by his ignoring it. He smuggles in facts and observations as necessary, because it is very hard, even in today's schools, to be completely out of touch with reality. The result is the usual paper, which is half floating free of reality, half tied to some facts. Typically, though, since the facts are smuggled in, they are not introduced in the proper order, or with the right context, and consequently they are unconvincing and fall to pieces the moment you so much as breathe on them. Therefore, you have an allegedly convincing, deductive, impregnable structure that just dissolves into nothing as soon as you ask a few "whys."

I want to illustrate this by reference to a paper on certainty that was submitted by a graduate student in philosophy a number of years ago (Appendix B). This paper is a very good example of rationalist polemics. Some of it, if you are a beginner in philosophy, may seem technical, but do not worry if any particular point or paragraph eludes you; it is not that important that you grasp every point of it.

Let us begin by observing that this paper on certainty is detached from reality in two crucial respects. It is from a graduate seminar course in philosophy, and the professor has asked the question, "Can you be certain? Is knowledge with certainty possible?" The student is arguing yes. Observe his method: He says right away that he will attempt to demonstrate his viewpoint "by pointing out that any other position involves one in a contradiction." So it is perfectly well stated from the beginning that this is going to be internal polemics: "I am going to take the opposing viewpoint and deduce from it contradictions." In what ways, therefore, is the paper by its very nature detached from reality? In the first place, there is no consideration in this paper of any argument in favor of skepticism, the belief that there is no certainty. There is no discussion of any reason anybody would be a skeptic, of what considerations, arguments, facts, or observations might lead to the conclusion that certainty is impossible. Reality is simply irrelevant. The author just begins, "My opponent has a viewpoint. Where it came from, I do not know; it is not up to me to ask. He has an idea, 'There is no certainty,' and I use that as my starting point."

Observe the difference if you were to start by referring to reality. Suppose you said to the skeptic, "Why would anybody think that you cannot be certain?" He might say, just to take one of the many arguments that skeptics actually offer: "People hallucinate; they see things that are not really there—so how do you know, at any given time, that you are not hallucinating? Maybe you are always hallucinating, and therefore you never can be sure of anything." That is not a good argument, but it is an argument that attempts to start with some actual observation—there is such a thing as hallucination, after all—and then to build a structure on it. If you began like that, then immediately you would have a line of response that would tie you back to reality, because—assuming you knew some philosophy—you would then say to the skeptic: "If you are talking about hallucination, we have distinguished hallucinations from times that we are not hallucinating; otherwise, how would we ever get the concept? As for how you know when you are not hallucinating, it is very simple—the difference between a pink elephant and a real elephant is that when you climb up on the back of a real one, it hurts when you fall to the ground, and you can ride the real one, and the pink one is only visual but you cannot integrate the other sense data, and so on"—and you can show the person that he is making a conclusion unwarranted by the facts. You remain in touch with reality, because you made the skeptic give an argument that started from somewhere. Not in this paper. This is rationalism, and there are no restrictions and no question where the theory came from. There is merely: "He said it, and I am going to deny it."

The second way in which this paper is, by its very nature, oblivious to reality is that it offers no positive argument in favor of certainty. At no point does the author give a definition or a characterization of certainty, even though that is the central topic. It is certainly controversial, but there is no reference anywhere to what it is. The author is not concerned. His implicit premise is, "Whatever it means, I am going to refute its opposite anyway. Whatever you say against it, I am going to show that you are led to a contradiction, so what do I care what it means? I am not out to show that we *can* be certain by pointing to any kind of facts of reality. I am out to show that your statement that we *cannot* be is wrong. That is all. Therefore, it is up to you to worry about what it means." Notice the difference if the student had begun simply by observing that we have minds, we are capable of perceiving reality, and sometimes the evidence is conclusive and sometimes it is less than conclusive, in which case we make a distinction between the certain and the probable; and, obviously, probable evidence presupposes certain evidence, because "probable" means less than certain, so first we have to grasp the certain; and each of the items of the probable has to be certain itself, so that the sum of it can be said to be probable; and so on. In such case, he would be able very easily to say, "By the nature of consciousness, we start out in contact with reality; we are aware of reality; that is certain," and there would be no problem. This paper does not do that. It does not try to establish certainty positively, or even ask the other side to refute it negatively. It just starts, with the author ready to deduce contradictions.

This is unconvincing even on its own terms, because suppose the author does deduce contradictions from the original statement. The immediate question is left, and nowhere answered: Why does this thesis lead to contradictions? The student who wrote this cannot say. He does not know what in reality raises the topic. Therefore, all he can say, at best, is: "I can jiggle your formulation around in such a way as to come out with a contradiction"—but why, and what it all means, is not explained.

How, in fact, does the author go about establishing the contradictions? At each crucial point, he makes a passing reference to some certainty or other, some absolute, some framework that is serving as his foundation. Naturally, he does not say, "I am here taking this for granted as certain," because he is not supposed to be taking anything for granted; he is supposed to be just refuting. Consequently, instead of forthrightly stating his viewpoint and his base, he smuggles it in. When he feels that he is sinking, he brings in something else as further ammunition. But it is not convincing, and, having conceded to the skeptic in advance the right to make the original statement that you cannot be certain, he will never convince anybody by that method.

Here are just a few points to illustrate the futility of this method. At the very beginning, the student says, "I want to point out that any position other than 'certainty is possible' involves one in a contradiction." Any skeptic worth his salt would immediately say, "So what? Everybody's viewpoint on everything is contradictory; that is my whole reason for being a skeptic. No one can ever attain consistency. So what does that prove?" Or the skeptic will say, "Just because it is a contradiction, how do you know it is wrong? We do not know anything—that is my whole viewpoint." This student is trying to say that if you cannot know anything, then so-and-so follows. But think of that idea: If you cannot know anything, what follows from that? Nothing. If you cannot know anything, close up shop and go back to the cradle. You cannot say, "Let us assume we know nothing; now here are all the things that follow from total ignorance." You would not get into that position if you said at the outset, "You are denying the existence of human consciousness, because certainty is inherent in consciousness as such." The author, though, has left out reality. He is not saying what certainty is, or what the facts are, and therefore he is doomed from the outset.

To take another example, consider the infinite regress argument as elaborated in the second paragraph. It amounts to this: A skeptic says, "You cannot be certain," and then his opponent says, "Are you certain of that?" and the skeptic says, "No, I am not certain of that," and then his opponent says, "Are you certain of that?" and then he says, "No, I am uncertain that I am uncertain that I am uncertain," and so on. That is something like party polemics. But by itself, without anything further, that is not a valid argument. Observe what would happen if you had a knowledgeable skeptic. A knowledgeable skeptic would immediately come back and say, "I can do exactly the same thing with 'certain.' I can force you into an infinite regress, because you say, 'I am certain of so-and-so'—well, are you certain of that?" And you say, "Yes, I am certain that I can be certain." "Are you certain of that?" You say, "Well, I am certain that I can be certain that I can be certain." As many times as you can ask him is he certain of uncertainty, he can ask you whether you are certain of certainty. So you, too, are in an infinite regress. Immediately, of course, you feel in your mind that there is some funny difference here. But this paper does not say what the difference is—namely, that both sides are claiming knowledge, and knowledge implies certainty. The advocate of certainty is happy to say, "Yes, I imply a whole infinite chain of certainties," but the skeptic cannot be happy, because he is denying certainty and therefore systematically contradicting himself. What is it, though, that we have to establish to make that distinction? *Why* does knowledge require certainty; *why* does every claim commit you to certainty? The fact of infinite regress does not establish that. What does? The fact that certainty is inherent in being conscious as such, and skepticism is the invalidation of consciousness. Since that is so, any skeptic who opens his mouth is forced into a fatal infinite regress, because he is trying to say something while saying that he is incapable of it—but only because of the essential fact here, to which the author of this paper is oblivious.

In the third paragraph, the author goes on to the next step. He says that this version of skepticism is itself not an intellectual position, that nothing is being said, and therefore, nothing is being asserted that you could consider or refute. That is the neatest trick of the week. Not only has he just refuted the skeptic's position; he went on at great length to do so; but if nothing has been said, how could he be doing this? If *nothing* has been said, that would be as though the advocate of skepticism were saying, "Ish de triddle da gloop de tweedle." There, nothing really is being said, so you cannot refute it. Here, though, the argument is, "You said nothing, and here is what it leads to." Of course, what the author means is, "You are not saying anything with certainty." But the skeptic comes back and says, "Of course I am not saying anything with certainty. My whole point is that I cannot; you cannot; there is no such thing as certainty. Why should there be?" There is nothing in all of this that answers that point. The author concedes the opponent's premise. He is allegedly going to show what follows from it, but nothing follows from it, and in conceding it, he has wiped himself out.

Observe also that in the same paragraph he says, "The truth of this derives from the Law of Excluded Middle, which states that anything either exists or does not exist." Notice that we are leaving open the question of whether you can be certain of anything; we do not know that yet. Right at this point, though, the author brings in a basic law of logic. He has not said, "My foundation is that certain axioms are absolutes, and logic is one of them," because then the question is, "Can you be certain?" and he is omitting that. But if you cannot be certain, how do you suddenly bring in the Law of Excluded Middle, as if no one could possibly contest that? If the skeptic is going to contest all consciousness, he is certainly going to be prepared to contest the certainty of logic.

I am passing over many other points, but I want you to see how what seems to be at least partly plausible just simply disintegrates. Take a look, for another example, at the fourth paragraph, in which the author is trying to imagine that the original position has been amended to take account of his allegedly destructive criticism. The skeptic's amended view is now, "You cannot be certain of anything except one thing, and that is uncertainty." And now the author is going to say, "Let us accept what the skeptic says as the given; I will not bother with the fact that it is a contradiction. Now I am going to show all the other things he says that he would also have to be certain of." Let us see if any of this stands up. Imagine what a skeptic, standing over the author's shoulder, would reply to each of these arguments. The author says that the skeptic must be certain that something exists about which he is uncertain. The author thinks that he has established existence, so he is happy. But what would the skeptic say on the basis of what has been stated here? He would say, "Yes, something exists about which I am uncertain, namely uncertainty." You might say, "What are you uncertain of? How can you have uncertainty without recognition of reality?" But that is the positive base that has been left out. If you just go by the formulation, "Something must exist about which the skeptic is uncertain," the skeptic would say, "Yes, uncertainty exists, and that is what I am certain of." To the next phrase, "He who is uncertain exists," the skeptic would say, "Indeed, and all I am is a state of uncertainty." Or the author says that the skeptic, "who is certain of uncertainty, is capable of being certain of (at least part of) that which exists." To which the skeptic might reply, "Yes, the part I am uncertain of is certainty." Or the author says that the skeptic must be certain that you can communicate to others; the skeptic would say, "I do not know if there are others; maybe there are, maybe there are not."

As another example of rationalist polemics, look at the next paragraph. The author is starting a new tack now. He is still not satisfied that he has really wiped out the skeptic, so he is going to try to show that all of the arguments for skepticism must have something in common. He does not *give* the arguments for skepticism, because he is here concerned not with facts, but with deduction. So he is going to show what the skeptic argument would have to be if the skeptic were to offer it, which he has not. This is very typical of rationalist polemics. The author figures, "How could my opponent defend this case, even if it is not, in fact, what he says?" Then he refutes this complex argument that he has made up. Almost invariably, his opponent then hears it all and says, "But that is not the argument I would have offered." And the rationalist is very disappointed, because he has analyzed the whole thing, only it is not the argument.

There are a number of standard arguments used to justify skepticism, such as the existence of illusions, hallucination, or error. But the author of this paper has made up his own: "The skeptic would have to show that the very concept of certainty is itself contradictory." Why? He says, "That is the only thing you could know could not exist—a contradiction. So if you know that certainty does not exist, you have to know that it is a contradiction." How does the author establish that that is the only way you could demonstrate the impossibility of certainty? He says nothing about that. He has in his mind, "We know that 'A is A' is an absolute; and if something violates 'A is A,' it could not possibly exist"—neither of which points, of course, he has made in this paper. He is prepared to stop there; if there is any other way of something not existing, he cannot think of it. To a rationalist, this sounds good enough. He thinks that gives him a nice firm basis to go on, and then he is going to show that skepticism cannot hold this position. But the whole thing is completely arbitrary. All the skeptic has to say is, "Where do you get this idea that the only way to prove that something does not exist is by means of a contradiction?" There is no argument offered in this paper for that idea, which is certainly much more controversial than the question of skepticism.

The same thing is true in the next paragraph. The author is now trying to show that the skeptic's position is meaningless because contradictions are meaningless. Observe that he has left open the question, "Can you be certain of anything?"—in other words, "Is man conscious?" He is prepared to leave that debate open. But he does know for certain that in polemics, he can use the idea, "Anything contradictory is meaningless." He has a theory and a definition of meaning, but he does not know whether man is conscious. How does he know that his theory of meaning is true? There are all kinds of questions here that the author is simply oblivious to. If it is true that everything that does not refer to reality is meaningless, what about the term "Santa Claus"? It does not refer to reality, but is it meaningless? What about the term "God"? It does not refer to reality if you are an atheist, but is it meaningless? If it is, there is an awful lot of discussion that is completely meaningless.

This author simply decided as follows: "I have got a good argument here: If something is contradictory, it does not refer to reality, and if it does not refer to reality, it is meaningless; therefore, if it is contradictory, then it is meaningless. The skeptic would have to show that certainty is contradictory, but then certainty would be meaningless—and then his argument is wiped out, because his very position is meaningless. That is what I am going to do." He is in his own rationalist world; he has got his perfect little deduction, which ends up wiping out the opponent's position, and he is simply oblivious to such an obvious objection as, "How do you know what is meaningless, and what about these words that do not refer to reality and are yet meaningful?"

That much should be ample simply to give you an illustration of rationalist polemics. This paper is well structured and clear, and it did receive a grade of A, but it is thoroughly rationalistic. Even if you do not remember the particular examples, or if you find any particular point abstruse, you should try to just hold in mind such parts as you can get, because it is such a terrific example of this problem that I could not resist using it.

To conclude, let me tell you that the author of this paper was me. This was one of the first papers I submitted in graduate school, and I did not do it as a literary exercise. I thought this was perfectly good at the time that I submitted it. I was quite convinced; I thought I really had refuted the skeptics. This was my first year in graduate school, and this was entirely how I had been trained. It took many years to overcome this kind of rationalism, but I think I have shown you that across time you can do it.

CHAPTER 6

OBJECTIVITY

I WANT TO turn briefly now to a broader theoretical issue: the concept of *objectivity* as such. The issue of objectivity in communication includes many of the points that we have already discussed, but it is a broader way of looking at them. It includes the issue of keeping your material self-contained, rationalism and what is wrong with that, and many other sins and problems. I did not start with this, because certain concretes and background had to be established to make the issue clear. Now, though, we can discuss it abstractly.

What, then, is objectivity in communication, whether we speak of writing or oral presentation? The term "objective" is used in the branch of philosophy known as metaphysics, which studies the nature of the universe, and it also has a separate meaning in epistemology, which is the theory of knowledge. So let us look at each of those, and then see what it would mean as applied to communication.

In metaphysics, "objective" means "independent of consciousness." A fact is said to be objective if it is what it is, independent of anybody's consciousness. In other words, the object, the thing out there, sets the terms, as opposed to the subject, the mind, the consciousness. So if we look at a table, we can all of us look at it, wish desperately that it go out of existence, pray that it go out of existence, plead, pretend, do whatever we want within the mind, within the subject, but the object is immutable—it is independent of what goes on in consciousness, and in that sense it is objective. And of course, according to Objectivism all facts are objective. A is A, and things are what they are, regardless of who thinks or feels what. This is one of the sources of the very name of the philosophy. The opposite of "objective" would be "subjective," which would mean "dependent on consciousness." A subjective fact would be one controlled by consciousness, one that goes in or out of existence depending on the whims of the consciousness in charge. The ostrich, for instance, is supposed to be a subjectivist in this sense—he does not look, and he assumes that if he does not see a thing, then it goes out of existence. Obviously, Objectivism denies that facts are subjective.

In epistemology, the term "objective" applies not to facts but to minds, to mental processes or mental contents. To be objective, as the term is used in epistemology, designates a certain way of using the mind. In essence, that method is adherence to the object: in other words, to the object of cognition, which is the thing out there you are trying to know. To be objective means to adhere to reality in using one's mind and coming to conclusions; in other words, to be guided at each step of one's mental processes by facts. The opposite would be to be guided by the arbitrary content of the consciousness of the subject, such as feelings, desires, and so on. Thus to be objective, in this sense, is to accept as the base of all your mental activity the fact that A is A, that facts are what they are, and that your mind is the faculty of looking out and grasping facts, not of creating them. Therefore, in reaching conclusions, in thinking, in conducting your mind, you have to adhere only to the facts and get your guidance from them. If you start making things up out of whole cloth by the arbitrary promptings of the subject, you will simply be wrong. Here, the classic example is the famous line from the old Jack Webb *Dragnet* show from many years ago: "Just give us the facts, ma'am." Epistemologically, that is the essence of objectivity: focus outward on the object, the out-there, the factual.

We can summarize by saying that in metaphysics, objectivity means that the object comes first, that it is what it is, independent of the subject; and in epistemology, it means that the object must set the terms of your mental functioning, that you have to conform your thought to what is out there.

These are the purely philosophic uses of the term. How would it apply to communication? What would an objective presentation be? You cannot apply the term in a simpleminded way, because you might say, "Well, if 'objective' means independent of consciousness, then an objective presentation would be one that is independent of consciousness." Obviously, that would be impossible, because we are talking about a conceptual presentation that depends on you, the presenter, and has no meaning aside from the consciousness of somebody or other who is going to grasp it, hold it, interpret it, and so on. What, then, does "objectivity" mean applied to communication? Objective communication is communication in which you have been objective in presenting the material—that is, in the epistemological sense, your mind has functioned objectively—and the result is that the meaning and the validity of your paper are now independent of your consciousness, clear without the need for any intervention by you. Epistemologically, objective communication means that in presenting your material, you have followed facts, you have been objective, in such a way that the result stands independent of you. Its meaning and its validity are now clear without anything further from you, and in that sense it is now an entity apart from you. If your presentation has been objective, you do not have to rush in each time a person reads a sentence and say, "No, I meant so-and-so," or, "Oh, I forgot to put in this," or, "If this is not clear, look at it this way." If your presentation requires that, then it is obviously still dependent on you; it is like a baby that is half-born and half still trailing the cord. When you have an objective presentation, by contrast, you have so thoroughly adhered to reality in organizing it, delimiting it, taking your audience's context into account, concretizing, and so on, that the presentation now stands on its own. It is therefore as though your presentation is now like an external fact, an object apart from you. In that sense, it is objective.

To summarize, in an objective presentation, you are using your mind objectively, and the result is that the product becomes like an object apart from you. A subjective presentation, on the other hand, would be one in which you have departed from reality; you have been arbitrary, you have in some way or other been subjective in your presentation, and the result is that your product needs continual clarification, elaboration, examples, and answers to objections, without which it would legitimately be misinterpreted and unconvincing, and would not stand on its own. "Subjective," in this sense, means that the piece is dependent on the writer or speaker to add in more than is already there. His message is not there, real, on paper. For example, statements like, "War is not all that important; what counts is the principle," or, "The right to life is more important than the right to property," or, "Money is the real issue," are all nonobjective formulations. In all cases, they do not stand independent of you; you have to rush in and say, "No, no, I did not mean such-and-such," and it is legitimate for the person to interpret you as meaning that. Your goal, in other words, has to be to present ideas in such a way that they stand clearly as facts by themselves.

Of course, this depends on the audience's context. Assuming a certain context, though, the presentation must stand by itself. This means you have to learn to see your writing as you would a legal document—not a legal document interpreted by a shyster, because then anything goes, but by a rational lawyer (assuming such could be found). You have to read your writing with the same seriousness that you would read a legal contract. You would not sign a contract that said, "In case of disagreement, something drastic will happen to your property, but we will worry about it when the time comes." You would be very eager to know what exactly is going to happen, who decides what is drastic, whether there are any limits, and so on. The same has to be true for all writing, particularly ideological writing on which the fate of the world depends. You have to mean what you say and aim to be precise in your statement and its implications, just as you would in a legal document.

To do that, you must read what you have written after you have finished writing and editing it. Look at it as an outsider. Set aside everything that you know inside your mind, and look only at what you actually have on paper. Look at it as a neutral audience, not a mind-reader, would see it, and ask yourself: "What misinterpretations or confusions would be possible to this kind of neutral audience?" Again, you have to assume a rational audience, because—I stress this—if you are going to allow irrational misinterpretations, there is no way to do this. There is no way whatever to satisfy the irrational; anything you say can be distorted or misinterpreted by hecklers. Assuming, then, an audience that is not irrational, look at your presentation cold and ask, "How might this legitimately be misinterpreted, and what can I do to avoid that possible misreading?"

This is a skill. It takes time to acquire. You have to learn to throw the switch. First you write, and you are concerned with getting what you have "in here," in your mind, out on paper. Then you look at it coldly for its objectivity, and you do so strictly as an outsider; you cut yourself off from everything you have inside your mind that you did not put on paper, and you ask, "What have I actually said?" If you want, it may be helpful to look at it as somebody else's paper and say to yourself, "What has he actually said?" Look at your paper as though it had not been written by you, and then read it from that perspective, adding in nothing. You will sometimes be very surprised. You will see whether the thing is an object, or you are still counting on the subject to ward off misconceptions.

As a personal example, I once prepared an excerpt from my book *The Ominous Parallels* for *The Objectivist Forum.** The excerpt is a presentation of American history that ends on Richard Nixon. As actually written in the book, this excerpt indicates that the country got fed up with the New Left and people turned to the political right. I decided to cut the excerpt off at the point in the book where I wrote, "There was no one there but Richard Nixon." Obviously, I wanted to convey the idea that if this is what the country was offered, then it was a hopeless fiasco. In the book, that was perfectly okay, because this came after several hundred

---

* "The 'Spirit of the Sixties,'" *The Objectivist Forum*, vol. 1, issue 2 (April 1980): 1–6.

pages, and my view of conservatives, and Nixon, was so clear that there was no question about what I meant. But when I read the excerpt over just by itself, without any of the other hundreds of pages, it was obvious that that sentence is susceptible to an entirely different interpretation, one I would never have dreamed of originally—namely, as a bitter, post-Watergate crack: "There was no one there but Richard Nixon—he stood alone, the sole figure on the Right who could have saved the country." Nowhere in the article do I state my actual view, and that last sentence comes across like a bitter complaint that the great hope of the future was destroyed by the leftists. This sentence, then, is nonobjective. I know my intention, but in that context it did not come across. It took a minor re-wording to eliminate the problem. I simply rewrote it as, "The people turned to the political right. There was no one there. All they found was Richard Nixon." That keeps the same idea, only by changing it to, "There was no one there," I make it clear that I reject the conservatives entirely. It is almost exactly the same wording, but put this way, it closes out in advance the possibility that someone would think I am sympathetic to Nixon. That is a small example of what typically comes up in writing all the time. You know exactly what you intend, but if you do not read it objectively, you will be astounded at what people could legitimately interpret it to mean.

There is no way, in my knowledge, to write except to commit this error thousands of times, and gradually discover from experience how to repair it. Do not, then, feel that it is a disaster if you make inadvertent subjective formulations. Little by little, you will develop your ability to write objectively.

The following are some different categories of nonobjective formulations. I have more or less arbitrarily chosen three different but overlapping categories. These can serve as a rough guide to break down this broad discussion of objectivity.

1. *Arbitrary statements:* The most obvious form of nonobjectivity is the arbitrary, undefended statement. This is really the issue of not being self-contained. In other words, when you say something unprepared and

unexplained, it is not clear why you say it, and therefore the statement is not objective. Since it does not stand on its own, the audience needs you to add in some reason why you are saying this. Obviously, you cannot prove everything, so you have to delimit your piece in some way. The important thing is, if a point is significant to your talk or your paper, yet it is not self-contained, you have to defend it in some terms; you cannot make just a simple arbitrary assertion. Otherwise, it is not objective, because the audience does not see why you are saying it.

2. *Poor formulation:* This pertains not to the lack of defense, but to the actual wording of a statement. A poor formulation is one that can legitimately be taken in different ways. It may be vague and undefined, so that you have to grope for what it might mean. It may be ambiguous. It may have two or more different meanings at the same time. It may have misleading implications and therefore commit you, by implication, to something that you would never dream of accepting, such as the statement in the paper on the draft, "The war is not that important," which implied, in its context, that ideas are more important than mass slaughter. Any of those problems would make a sentence nonobjective—not in the sense that you are not arguing for them, but in the sense that they are simply not clear. They are susceptible to different meanings, and therefore, for the person actually to grasp what you are saying, you have to rush in and say, "Oh, I did not mean that; I meant this."

Here is an example of poor formulation:

> In a proper capitalist system, as a matter of law, no individual and no government can exert a deleterious influence on the achievement of any other person's rightful values or goals.

Suppose I say, for instance, that my rightful goal is to attract students and make money. Under capitalism, nobody can put a gun to my students' heads, nobody can steal my money, so that is a perfectly true statement. Yet there are other ways that someone could take away my students—he could, for instance, have a more interesting lecture. If we take this statement literally, the person giving a lecture in the next room is exerting a definite "deleterious influence" on the achievement of my rightful goal, and consequently, we have to have anticompetition laws to protect my rightful goals.

What permits that kind of interpretation is the word "deleterious," which is so vague that it encompasses any kind of negative influence. In a capitalist legal system, you can have every kind of negative influence that you want over other people except one, and that is the initiation of physical force (or fraud, which is an indirect version of force). That is all the law prohibits. Therefore, no government, as a matter of law, can affect your achievement of your values by the initiation of force. But as this statement is worded, it leaves that point wide-open; we have no idea what the writer is talking about, and the result is that he leaves himself open to every kind of misinterpretation, and every kind of bad law.

Notice also a minor error. "In a proper capitalist system" needs a comma after "proper." Otherwise it implies that there are two kinds of system, a proper capitalist system and an improper capitalist system. And there is no such thing. With a comma ("In a proper, capitalist system"), it means "in a system both proper and capitalist," which is just what the person means to say. Whenever you use an adjective, it implies the existence of the nonadjective; a "proper capitalism" implies an "improper capitalism," an "old woman" implies a "non-old woman." So always remember that you have to punctuate appropriately. But punctuation is beyond our purview here.

3. *Poor placement:* A third category of nonobjectivity pertains not to the formulation, but to its context. The formulation might be okay—it might be true, plausible, understandable—but its *placement* is misleading. In other words, it is in a context that makes it imply something that the author does not mean. So the statement is clear and true, but where it is, is wrong. Therefore, it does not stand alone. The author has to rush in and say, "Well, just because I put this together with that other statement, do not draw such and such a conclusion."

Here is a good example of a problem with placement:

According to Hume, we value whatever is pleasant and call evil that which is painful. But there is nothing to guarantee that the values selected in this manner will be based on the standard of life. Thinking, for example, is a painful process for many people, yet thought is man's primary tool of survival. On the other hand, a man may avoid thinking and perhaps live pleasurably off the effort of those who do think, by either begging or stealing; but by the code whose standard is life, nonthinking is evil because it destroys man's life. Therefore a man whose values are acquired by Hume's method could hold irrational values, and, in fact, it would be very unusual to find a man holding a rational, consistent set of values which he had acquired by seeking pleasure and avoiding pain.

This is a very good example of nonobjective placement. The statements are true, clear, and understandable—but their placement carries a definite implication, one the author does not intend. In effect, it amounts to something on the order of, "You should seek pain and avoid pleasure."

Here is the situation. Hume takes a certain kind of hedonist view: that the only way to define good and evil is by pleasure and pain—a view that the author of this passage, as an Objectivist, wants to refute. The author wants to show, in effect, that simply going by what gives you pleasure and pain will not necessarily lead you to a rational conclusion. So he thinks, "Well, a simple way of showing it will be to say that thinking is painful for many people, and yet it is necessary for life, so if we go by pleasure and pain, a lot of people would choose not to think, and that would obviously be irrational; therefore, Hume is wrong."

That argument, as far as it goes, is correct. It is true that thinking is often painful to many people, and to everybody (in some form) if it is thinking about really difficult material. But the implication in this context, by the sheer placement of it, is: "To hell with pleasure. I hold life as the standard of value, and the fact, therefore, that something is painful does not matter to me at all. Maybe something *will* be terribly painful by the standard of life; even so, you should do it."

You could not defend such a proposition as, "Something leads unavoidably and necessarily to protracted pain; nevertheless, it is good for man." If you know the Objectivist ethics, you know that life and happiness or pleasure come down to one fundamental issue, namely the achievement of values, and that what fosters life also fosters happiness and pleasure. You also know that it is not true that life points in one direction and pleasure in the opposite and you have to choose between them; and you know that if such a choice *were* necessary, then you would have the horrible clash of the moral versus the practical, and all the disasters of the history of philosophy. Finally, you also know that it is true that thinking is painful for some people. But those people for whom thinking is characteristically painful will generally find *everything* more or less painful. They will be out of control, anxious, and self-doubtful, so they will be more or less miserable no matter what they do, and the most they can hope for is momentary relief from the pain of the moment until it strikes them again tomorrow. They are, as such, hardly an example of human nature.

This is a simple example of poor placement leading to nonobjectivity. It is certainly true and clear to say, "Thinking is painful for many people." But if you said it in this context, trying to refute pleasure as the standard of ethics, the implication is, "The ethics I advocate is oblivious to pleasure. I do not care one way or the other whether you suffer or not; I only care about what life requires." This author, in short, had an easy polemic against Hume at the price of implying a whole theory that he himself does not subscribe to.

The same is true of the statement that people can live pleasurably off the effort of others, in other words that nonthinking may be pleasurable. It may be pleasurable to some people, in the sense of momentary relief, but again, it is not true, in the sense that it is not applicable to human nature. If it were true in this connection, why should you think at all? If it were true that you could avoid thinking and live pleasurably off the effort of those who do think, why not do so? It is no use to say that reality is against it, because then you are saying that reality points one way and pleasure points the other, which means that man is intrinsically at war with reality. Once you accept that view, then you are completely lost philosophically, because you are saying that man has to defy reality or suffer.

By the attempt to get a polemic of this kind against Hume, the author of this excerpt makes true statements in a context that commits him to something that he would never want. The last sentence of the paragraph also indicates that the author was not clear on his view when he wrote this, because he says it would be "very unusual" to find a man coming to a rational, consistent set of values by following Hume's method. That implies that it is unusual, but possible. In fact, if we define our terms, Hume's method means being a rampant emotionalist—if something makes you feel good, accept it, and if not, not. If you understand why ethics is necessary to begin with, you understand that such a method makes it impossible to have a rational code of values. You know that man is not automatically set to choose the right code, that he has to figure it out in principle, that he may have out-of-context emotions, and so on. So if you know why reason is man's means of knowledge, then you know that it is more than "very unusual" to reach Objectivism by following your emotions as your standard—it is impossible.

Objectivity in communication, to sum up, revolves around three things: your formulation, the reasons you give for it, and the context—in other words, what you say, why you say it, and where you say it.

The following excerpts test these three issues, sometimes more than one of them—plus a fourth one, namely rationalism. These excerpts will be vague and imprecise; or they will contain something arbitrary and undefended; or their placement, the context of some part of them, will be misleading; or they will be rationalistic.

The following excerpt is supposed to be a definition of "justice."

> "Justice" means having the right idea about men, and acting
> on it at all times. By the "right" idea, I mean one based on the

facts of reality. Most times, the appropriate action is a trade, i.e., giving others the equivalent of what they give you.

First of all, this is vague. The author says justice means "having the right idea," but what does that mean? He goes on to say "based on the facts," but that, too, is vague. It would be perfectly compatible with this formulation to say, "As I see the facts, all men are really vicious; they are out to lie and cheat, they want the government to help them, and so on; so the right idea, one based on the facts of reality, would be that everybody is rotten. 'Justice' means having the right idea about men and acting on it at all times; so then 'justice' means recognizing that everybody is vicious, and acting on it." The author goes on to say, "Most times, the appropriate action is a trade, in other words, giving others the equivalent of what they give you." So someone could say, " 'What they give you' is usually something rotten that they do to you; therefore, I will do it to them before they do it to me." A person could thus read this paragraph and say, "Now I know what 'justice' is according to Objectivism—it is going up to a stranger on the street and punching him in the mouth."

That is not an exaggeration; this formulation leaves open an interpretation of that kind. It is extremely vague; it does not give you any guideline as to what is a "right idea," and what is an "equivalent." Consequently, it is simply wide-open. It tells you in effect, "Somehow have an appropriate idea about other people, and do something commensurate."

If you wanted to tie this down and make it more specific, you would have to say: "Justice is a virtue; it pertains to estimating men's characters. You have to estimate them according to a certain standard of value, according to the actual facts and not your arbitrary desires, and you have to act accordingly. By 'trade,' I mean give value for value by mutual consent," and so on. In other words, you say something to make it more specific than, "Have the right idea and do something about it," which is so vague that it is open to any interpretation.

This excerpt, from a paper on why the pursuit of happiness cannot be arbitrary, is an example with a subtle problem.

Just as everything else in the universe has a specific identity, so does man. No man, to be sure, is the same as any other; there are innumerable stylistic, optional, particular differences among individuals. But the unalterable fact is that man must *use* the single most important tool of his survival—his mind. He must at once seek, and want to seek, nothing but the goals consonant with the life of a rational being.

Everything that the author says in this paragraph is true. There are no bad formulations. Assume also that in the rest of the paper he defends this point, so the problem is not that it is arbitrary. The error is the placement of the second sentence. If that sentence were moved to a later paragraph, there would be no problem, because then you would say, "Everything in the universe has a specific identity, and so does man. His identity is that he survives by the use of his mind. He must therefore seek and want nothing but rational goals." Then you would have laid down clearly what the common principle among men is, and that this is the requirement of survival and happiness. Then later, after you had elaborated on that, you could say, "Of course, there are many differences among people. But all those differences are lesser. They are within the fundamental framework that we all have reason and have to use it."

The way the excerpt is actually written, however, we are told that there are innumerable differences among men *before* we are told that we survive by the mind. Therefore, the question arises right away: "Maybe all the optional differences apply even to the point about using the mind. Where is the solid, universal fact?" If we read this in its placement in the context as written, it comes out like this (if a bit exaggerated): "Everything is something specific. Of course, every man is different, very different, from every other. But still we have to use what we have in common, although, to be sure, we can use it very differently because none of us is really the same." If you get that implication in, you are on the path to subjectivism, which will infect all the later formulations. Whereas if you simply took that issue of the differences between people, and waited until you had firmly established what is the same and what is the objective basis, then the subjectivist interpretation would not arise. Otherwise, the placement here colors everything that is to come.

The next excerpt comes from a college assignment on the topic "Will America's obsession with repentance prevent Senator [Edward] Kennedy from gaining the Democratic presidential nomination in 1980?" It has a very good opening but then makes an error.

> It is a good thing that Americans are "obsessed with repentance." "Repentance," in this context, means concern about morality. If anyone ever gave pause to a moral man's mind, Edward Kennedy would certainly be at the top of the list. And he is growing closer to the bottom of America's presidential candidate list for the same reason.
>
> There are two essential things a voter must judge about a candidate: his ideas and his character (has he got integrity, honesty, rational judgment, etc.). By his political ideas alone, Kennedy is evil. But the campaign has focused more, so far, on his character, which, as people are beginning to see, is as bad as the ideas that molded it.
>
> Kennedy is a man who thinks he can get away with anything. And he has. He is caught cheating in college. He is caught trying to outrun the police in a speed chase. He is well-known for his adulterous affairs. He panics and is responsible for the death of a young woman and lies about it repeatedly. How does Kennedy get away with such blatant immorality? He has the Kennedy family power and image to rescue him. It has operated for him in the past. Today, in a losing struggle for the esteem of Americans, Kennedy is panicking again. He embarrasses himself by declaring (in answer to Vice President Mondale's accusation) that neither he nor any of his brothers can be accused of disloyalty. A statement like that from this man means that he is sinking and will say anything to save his

image, even if it means robbing the graves of his dead brothers
for the prestige he will never earn.

This student is obviously having no truck with the professor, whose
viewpoint you can get simply from seeing that he describes Americans
concerned about Chappaquiddick* as "obsessed with repentance." This
student is laying down his context from the outset. "You imply," he says
in effect, "that this is a bad thing; from my viewpoint, it is a good thing."
That is forthright, nonappeasing, and self-contained. It is self-contained
because it says right in the second sentence, " 'Repentance' means concern with morality." If the professor wants to contest that, he in effect is
put in the untenable position of saying he is an amoralist. Therefore, this
excerpt has a good, forthright opening.

But the student got carried away. He was doing fine, he laid down his
terms, but—and this is very typical of a rough draft—on the rush of feeling a fury at this kind of thing, he went to the next statement, which is:
"If anyone ever gave pause to a moral man's mind, Edward Kennedy
would certainly be at the top of the list." In other words, if you made a
list of immoral people, the type who would make a moral man recoil, at
the top would be Edward Kennedy. That is another way of saying that
Edward Kennedy is the worst man in history, or the worst man alive
today. Obviously, the *least* you could say about that is that you cannot
regard it as self-evident. Actually, of course, it is an overstatement. Edward Kennedy would be high up on such a list, but there are some numbers of people who have done many worse things. So the effect there is
one of an undefended statement. That is unfortunate, because it makes
the opening look merely emotional, as if the author cannot really defend
his viewpoint.

The next paragraph is also well organized. The author says there are

---

* "Chappaquiddick" refers to the 1969 incident in which Edward Kennedy drove his car
off a bridge in Massachusetts. Kennedy managed to escape, but his passenger, Mary Jo
Kopechne, drowned. Kennedy later pleaded guilty to a charge of leaving the scene of an
accident after causing injury.

going to be two issues involved, and he is going to focus only on the second. But one thing in that paragraph is also nonobjective: The statement that Kennedy's ideas are evil is unsupported. We are not told which ideas are evil, or why they are evil. That they are wrong is one thing, and even that would require some vindication. Normally, though, a person who does not have a specific philosophy, and does not look at things from the perspective of a certain code of morality, would say, "What is evil about political ideas? Kennedy wants, let us say, national health insurance, and he wants wage and price controls, and he wants peace in the world, so that we should not have trouble with Afghanistan and Russia and so on, so he really is thinking of the little people and inflation and trying to make things easier. What is evil about all that?"

If your subject is going to be Kennedy's character, as indicated by the assignment, then how should you handle his political ideas, as distinct from his character? You cannot just baldly say, "This is evil." You have to make a choice. Either say something like, "His political ideas are bad enough, but that is not my subject"—which is then clear—or find some brief way to indicate the reason that Kennedy's ideas are evil without making a big production of it. Thus you could say, "Kennedy's political ideas are consistently on the side of extending government power over the individual, violating his rights and restricting his liberties." A liberal who hears that will not be opposed to Kennedy for such ideas, but the liberal will at least grasp that there is such a thing as a viewpoint that does not favor the continual expansion of government, and that there are people who believe in freedom, rights, and so on. He may not be convinced, but he will get the idea of what this author objects to. A more honest person might just brush the statement aside, thinking, "Well, that is too bad, but you have to do something and save the poor," but he may feel a little qualm. That would be one possibility. You could even say, "I regard as evil the systematic attempt to destroy the middle class in favor of those who do not work for a living." That is a little more extreme, but it gives an idea of what you are talking about.

As the point is stated in the original excerpt, though, it is nonobjective, because the person reading it has no way of knowing what the author means by "evil," and why he regards Kennedy as evil. You would not be able to convince anyone in the amount of space given, but you should be able to give an indication of why you say it. Otherwise, misinterpretations are unavoidable. For instance, since religion has such a monopoly on the terms "good" and "evil," your reader may be led to think you are a fervent anti-abortionist who thinks Kennedy is evil because he is pro-choice. The statement, therefore, is nonobjective.

There is one more example of nonobjectivity here. In the last part of the last paragraph, the author notes that Kennedy declared that neither he nor any of his brothers could be accused of disloyalty,* and says that this means Kennedy "will say anything to save his image, even if it means robbing the graves of his dead brothers." There is one element of nonobjectivity in that, which is again typical of a rough draft. The student had a definite idea there, but he did not make something clear, and the result is that that passage is actually baffling if you do not know the intention of the author; in other words, this is a case in which you have to ask the author what he means. The writer's actual intention was to bring in how Kennedy always invokes his brothers; in effect, if you said to him on the campaign trail, "Would you like a Coke?" he would say, "My brothers always wanted a Coca-Cola, when one was president, back in the glorious age of the sixties," and so on. But the way it is presented here, there is no stress, nothing to emphasize that the author is talking about Kennedy's constant invocation of his brothers. Therefore, the connection is simply not clear; the sentence seems to say that Kennedy protests that he is loyal, and that makes him a parasite.

That is the kind of thing you catch by reading over your rough draft. You know what is in your mind, but you look coldly at what you have written and you ask, Does this point follow? Then you see that you have not stressed enough that the issue is that Kennedy constantly brings up

---

* In response to Vice President Walter Mondale's comment, in late 1979, that Kennedy was disloyal for criticizing the recently deposed Shah of Iran, a former U.S. ally.

his brothers. Therefore you just reword it so that the connection becomes clear: "Kennedy embarrasses himself not only by declaring, in answer to Vice President Mondale's accusation, that he is not disloyal, but by needlessly invoking his brothers to say they were not either." In other words, you say what Kennedy did, and then you say something like, "If he does that, he is robbing the graves of his brothers." (Remember that in the rough draft, you just have to blurt things out as they come to you. If you try to edit your work in the process of writing it, you will paralyze yourself, because you are trying to perfect what is not there yet. First you just have to let it come, just pour it out, and then you look over it objectively, check for clarity, and make the adjustments that you need.)

This next excerpt is from a polemic against altruism.

> If you chose to be an altruist, you would have to devote your time, your effort, your life to serving others. But if you did, when would you have the time to sustain your own life so that you could go on serving others? For if you wanted to be moral according to altruism, you could not take a single action that would benefit yourself. To do so would be immoral. Your mind, therefore, would have to stagnate. You would not be able to earn money to buy food. To do so would benefit no one but yourself. You would starve.

The problem with this is that it is too extreme. If you say to an altruist, "According to altruism, you cannot take a single action to benefit yourself," you are saying, in effect, "If you are an altruist, you cannot eat, because after all, that benefits you, and you are supposed to live only for others." A commonsense person on the street, if you gave that argument, might say that you are supposed to place the good of others before yourself, but that does not mean you cannot do *anything* for yourself. A typical altruist will say, "Eat, so long as you can show that that is necessary to keep up your strength so that you can serve others. I do not say you should *never* eat. I do not say *never* use your mind. I just say, when you do it, justify it by the service that will ultimately redound to others." In other words, this is a case of polemics in which the author interprets altruism, without any context, as simply excluding any action of which the actor is the beneficiary, even indirectly, provisionally, or temporarily. That is not objective. The altruist, without any preparation, will reply, "That is not my viewpoint."

It certainly is possible to establish that altruism would lead to the conclusions listed in this passage—that is, that you could not earn money, you would starve, stagnate, etc. But that would not follow from only one sentence saying what altruism is. To sustain the main point here, you would have to set a whole context. You would have to define "altruism" and show why, by its nature, it means a philosophy of sacrifice; that its concern is not with the welfare of the recipient, regardless of what it says, but with the sacrifice of the donor; that those who are to be sacrificed are the able, and those to whom they are to be sacrificed are the incompetent, *because* they are incompetent; that no one benefits from this, that everybody loses, that it is sacrifice for its own sake, that it is destruction as an end in itself. Once you lay that down, then you can say, "Therefore, altruism means stagnation," and so on. But the whole necessary context is here omitted, and the result is that it seems as though the conclusion is deduced from the statement that you should live for others, whereas from that statement alone, it does not follow. So I would say that this is a conclusion that is too extreme, because the context for it is not there. It is a true conclusion, but the placement destroys it.

The next passage, which is excerpted from a longer paper, is nicely written, colorful, and clear. There is definitely a good future for someone who can write in a lively, straightforward way like this. There is, however, a definite problem in this content.

One stock charge made against lecturing is that it is "spoon-feeding" the student, that the student never has a chance to think for himself.

I am sure that the "spoon-feeder" type of lecturer is definitely bad, for his lectures amount to muttering a few facts about the subject matter of the course and, most often, spouting many evaluations. This "spoon-feeder" takes the liberty and the power (of being in front of a class) to inject his personal opinions whenever he gets the chance. His commonest comments are something like this: "Of course, today, we know that Aristotelian logic is out-of-date and completely indefensible," or "Obviously, Milton was the greatest poet ever to have lived." The "spoon-feeder," I am sure, never even conceives the possibility that someone believes Aristotelian logic to be sound and very relevant to today, or Milton's poetry to be poor. He may think of this possibility and consequently allow a few students to disagree with him. Many times the "spoon-feeder" glosses over the student's disagreement by saying that everything is a matter of opinion. At best, the "spoon-feeder" may give some careful consideration to the student's opinions.

The point, however, is that the teacher dare inject any of his own opinions in the classroom at all. And this is the major fault of the few teachers who do lecture. Colleges are supposed to be citadels of the intellect with the pursuit of truth as their major goal and academic freedom as the means to that goal. This means that each student comes to college in order to pursue knowledge and truth; and each student must decide for himself what constitutes truth in any particular field. Consequently, any teacher who frequently injects his own opinions in the classroom is denying the student his academic freedom to pursue the truth as he sees it. In other words, the greatest sin any teacher could commit in the classroom is to inject his own opinions in his lectures. The evaluations must come from the students; the facts, from the teacher.

This passage falls on one crucial flaw: There is no definition of "spoon-feeder." This is even given away typographically, by the fact that the term is used throughout in quotes. In other words, the speaker is half endorsing it and half disowning it, without ever telling you what it is. This, therefore, permits him to have his cake and eat it, too, in a number of different ways.

What is a "spoon-feeder"? If you had to define that concept in connection with lecturing in college, the metaphor is one of feeding a baby: He does not have to pick up his food by himself; you stick the spoon in his mouth for him. A "spoon-feeder," then, would mean a teacher who makes the material too easy, who predigests it, breaks it up into little tiny bits, and treats his students as though they are infants. Now, I may say that given the problems of oral presentation, and of today's students, it is virtually impossible to find such a thing. Therefore, if there is such a thing as a spoon-feeder, I have never encountered it—never—in all my years of listening to a class. I have heard many lectures that were too hard, but none that were too easy. Therefore, I have great skepticism. But let us say that theoretically, there is such a thing as breaking material up into too tiny steps and going into such detail that you do not give the class credit for anything. That is one concept.

The author of this presentation also includes in his definition of "spoon-feeding" the lecturer's own evaluations, thereby creating a package deal.* The unstated assumption is that if the lecturer gives his own evaluations, he makes it too easy for the students, and therefore it is really spoon-feeding. The thought in this author's mind is, in effect, "Anything against making the student think is bad. There are two ways of preventing him from thinking: One is to give him too much help, and the other is to give him your opinion." And he combines the two into one term without definition. Counting on the fact that the reader will obviously disapprove of lecturers making lectures too easy, the author goes on to

---

* "'Package-dealing' is the fallacy of failing to discriminate crucial differences. It consists of treating together, as parts of a single conceptual whole or 'package,' elements which differ essentially in nature, truth-status, importance or value." Leonard Peikoff, editor's note to Ayn Rand's "The Metaphysical Versus the Man-Made," *Philosophy: Who Needs It*, p. 30.

attack lecturers giving their opinions, without raising or answering the question of whether giving one's own evaluation does, in fact, make it too easy for the student and prevent him from thinking. But the answer to that question is that it entirely depends on how the lecturer gives his evaluation. It is exactly the same issue as that of how he presents his material. A lecturer can give his evaluation, in principle, in such a way that the student has even *more* to think about, because he goes home and has not only the material, but also a provocative evaluation from the lecturer to ponder. Far from evaluations making it easier, then, they can give the student even more stimulation and be the exact opposite of spoon-feeding. But, of course, the author of this excerpt does not think of that, because he uses this central concept without giving it a definition and can oscillate back and forth from one point to the other.

The author's solution to spoon-feeding is given in the third and last paragraph. There, he is led into a problem. Because he wants to prevent this teacher from giving his own opinion, he is led to a very misleading conclusion. A statement like, "Each student must decide for himself what constitutes truth in any particular field. . . . [He has to be free] to pursue the truth *as he sees it*," can be taken in two entirely different ways. One is that truth can be anything the student thinks it is, so each student has to "decide for himself" what constitutes truth. Therefore, if you feel that two and two is nine and a half, we have academic freedom, and if you do not, that is fine as well. Of course, the author certainly does not believe that. But he was thrown into wanting to stress that the student has to think on his own, and he did not make clear the distinction between politics and epistemology. You have the right to think, meaning no one can force an opinion down your throat, but that does not mean that you are logical no matter what you think, nor that whatever you think is right, no matter what it is. You have to preserve freedom without implying subjectivism, as this paragraph does. The whole problem arises because of the confusion about "spoon-feeding." The moral here is thus: If there is a key term, do not assume that you know what it means. If it is one that is really central to your presentation, have in your own mind a firm definition.

The following excerpts are just brief examples to highlight precision of formulation.

> An "axiom" is an explicit statement of fact so fundamental as to be self-evidently true. (Self-evidence is one of the distinctive features of an axiom.) The primary philosophic axioms are: "Existence exists," "Existence is identity," and "Consciousness is identification."

We are in the hardest type of writing here, namely writing on epistemology. I put this in just to give you an example of the type of considerations involved in writing on epistemology, in which you have to pick every word with care.

"An axiom is an explicit statement of fact so fundamental as to be self-evidently true." This statement clearly implies that if something is fundamental, it has to be self-evident. But are all fundamentals self-evident? Fundamental is that which is at the foundation or base. Some things that are at the base may be self-evident. Other things, at least according to Aristotle, are at the base of nature; they are the fundamental laws of nature, but we arrive at them only after centuries, so they are certainly not self-evident to us. "Fundamental," in short, is a term that can be used in many different contexts. You cannot just assume automatically that whenever a thing is fundamental, it is self-evident. But this formulation implies it. A further problem is the implication that self-evidence is distinctive to an axiom. Not everything self-evident is axiomatic. The color of a tablecloth is self-evident, but philosophy's axioms do not begin, "This tablecloth is yellow." All perceptual data are self-evident, but that does not make them all axioms in the sense of philosophic axioms.

This statement contains, then, two wrong implications, despite a basically correct intention. It is very, very tricky to word a definition of "axiom" so that you restrict yourself to what you mean without giving false implications. To give an exact definition, you would have to say something like, "An 'axiom' is an abstract statement of facts available self-evidently to perception," and you would have to also include, "in such a way that it serves as a primary or starting point for all subsequent human knowledge." The main ideas that you would have to get in are that an axiom is basic data, or self-evident facts, but an abstract statement of them; and that it is used as a primary, as the beginning on which all subsequent knowledge is built. That was the intention of this author, but it did not come out correctly.

By way of a review of Objectivism, take a look at the three things that the author names as the primary axioms. "Existence exists," "Existence is identity," "Consciousness is identification." Those are certainly three statements that Objectivism subscribes to. But they are not the right statements of the three axioms in a beginning context. "Existence is identity" is already the relationship between existence and identity; it establishes the relationship between two axioms, rather than serving as a simple statement of one. It is a later elaboration that presupposes the knowledge of what the Law of Identity states. For a beginning audience, you would start by stating the Law of Identity in the simplest form possible—something like, "Everything is something," or, "A thing is what it is," or, "A is A." "Consciousness is identification," too, already presupposes something—namely, that there is a faculty of consciousness. This statement tells you the function of consciousness, what its cognitive goal is; but the more basic statement, as Galt formulates it, is, "One exists possessing consciousness." The axiom is really, "There is such a faculty," and what it does is a later elaboration. Finally, "Existence exists" is okay as a formulation. But Galt's exact formulation was, "Existence exists—and the act of grasping that statement implies two corollary axioms: that something exists which one perceives and that one exists possessing consciousness, consciousness being the faculty of perceiving that which exists."* Therefore, if we are going to do the two, existence and consciousness, it would be more straightforward to say, "Something exists; consciousness exists; A is A." That would be the simplest way to state the

---

* *Atlas Shrugged*, p. 933; "This Is John Galt Speaking," *For the New Intellectual*, p. 152.

three. You see how much is involved in a very brief formulation, but of course, on a very, very difficult topic.

There is no big philosophic issue with this next excerpt, just a simple inadvertency.

> Most species of animal are adapted to their environment. Their tools of survival have a limited range; beyond that range they cannot function. Man is different. Because he can adapt his environment to himself, he is not limited to a specific natural habitat; there is no natural condition in which he could not, in principle, survive. There is, however, one social condition incompatible with the human form of existence, a condition that vitiates man's means of survival. That condition is coercion.

This is well written, but susceptible to a misinterpretation that the writer would never imagine, but would immediately see once it was pointed out. He deliberately wants a dramatic opening. He wants to say, in effect, "Nature can do anything to you and you can get along, but people can wreck you." That is a way of motivating an audience, because it is a striking opening. The question is, "What is this power that people have that nature does not?" Only, the wording makes it seem that man is an exception to the Law of Identity. The author says that most species have limited tools and cannot function outside a limited range, but man is different; "he is not limited to a specific natural habitat; there is no natural condition in which he could not, in principle, survive." The "in principle" tries to save it, but what obvious condition would come to mind here? Earthquakes, plagues, tidal waves—all the things that the religious philosophers struggled with in the so-called problem of evil. That is not the norm. In writing, you have to be committed to the last implication, and if you say flatly, "Animals are limited to some extent, but man can survive anywhere," then you are committed to *anywhere*, and if the reader says, "In the middle of a volcano?" you have to say, "Yes," and if you want to exclude volcanoes, you have to say, "leaving out volcanoes." I put that in simply to show you a case of overstatement. Obviously the person did not intend it, but it is too much.

The next excerpt is from a discussion of women's books.

> Any attack on the other sex—as a collective—is an attack on one's own sex. Attacks on females as a sex are more devastating to the male than may seem likely at first glance. It is too little realized that women have been used as decoys behind which the attack on the male has continued unabated and unidentified for years.
>
> In almost any novel you pick up, you will be informed at least once and usually more often, through narrative, description, or dialogue, that "all females are treacherous" or "illogical" or "untrustworthy" or a "necessary evil." But if this is so, what does it say about the men who love women? It says that they are corrupt and self-destructive by nature.
>
> You have heard it repeated in movies, novels, and from coworkers that the presence of a woman in an office filled with men is trouble; that the simple fact that a woman is around means that men will behave in an unseemly manner; that it is the presence of a woman that is the cause of such behavior. In other words: Women are responsible for men's actions. But if this is so, what does it say about a man's view of himself? It says that he is a crawling, helpless robot at the beck and call of another human being, with no power to assert his own desires.
>
> It is pathetic that few realize the actual purpose of the attacks upon the female as a sex.

This excerpt suggests that the actual purpose of the attacks on the female is *not* to get rid of the female or to attack the female, but to attack the male—as a matter not simply of broad philosophic implication, but of deliberate intent. The argument does not hold, however; the second and third paragraphs do not prove the initial assertion. In each case the author says, "They show that the female does such-and-such, and that leads to such-and-such a negative about the man." Yet in neither case does the author *show* that it is something negative about the man; he supposedly *deduces* it. For instance, take the second paragraph. If all females are treacherous, the writer says, then what does that say about the men who love them? The clear-cut structure of the argument is, If a man loves something treacherous, he must be corrupt. If women are treacherous, then a man who loves a woman loves something treacherous. Therefore, if women are treacherous, men are corrupt.

That little capsule of an argument is a clear example of rationalism, because it is a deductive structure omitting a single question: Does the deduction correspond to the actual facts? Suppose it were true that all women were treacherous, to confine ourselves to that example. Would that show, or even suggest, that all men who love them are therefore self-destructive or corrupt? Absolutely not, because even if it were true that all women are treacherous, that is compatible with the men's not knowing it. After all, judging other people's moral character is not a self-evidency. Maybe men are so innocent, so noble and pure a species, that they cannot imagine the degree of female corruption. Or maybe a man might think to himself, "Well, look, if that's the way women are metaphysically, it is a tough life, it is a difficult world, but I still have certain needs; and after all, since she is human, however treacherous, she has to have something good, so I will focus on the better thing, and what can I do?" In short, you simply could not conclude from an argument such as this that men are necessarily no good. Moreover, if the intention was to say, "Men are really rotten," it is a very roundabout way of doing it to say, "Women are really rotten." It is a deduction in a vacuum: "If you love somebody treacherous, then you have to be treacherous, and if you are treacherous, then you are no good, and therefore, if women . . ."—and so on.

Essentially the same type of criticism would apply to the next paragraph. The author cites the attackers he criticizes: "The presence of a woman . . . is the cause of such behavior. In other words: Women are responsible for men's actions," thus implying that men are helpless. In fact, going from "the woman is the cause of the behavior" to "men are therefore merely determinist reactors" is an equivocation on "cause." "Woman is the cause" can mean either that she *necessitates* a certain reaction, or that she is the stimulus or the object that *evokes*, in some cases, a reaction. But the author is intent on his deductive chain: "If this, then this; if this, then this; therefore man is no good." Again, this is a rationalistic argument.

The next author is discussing free will, and the excerpt certainly is very abstract. That is not an indictment in itself, although it might give you a clue as to what is wrong.

> The conceptual faculty cannot be deterministic. There is no way man could automatically conceptualize without some means of selectivity. The field of what concepts could be formed is too wide. If a man were automatically programmed to form all the concepts suggested by the things he saw and heard at every waking moment, he would starve, because every new thing would launch his brain into overdrive in a continuous rush and he would never have time to act. And he could not be programmed only to think and act in a pro-life way, because a concrete action that might be pro-life in one instance might not be in another, and he has to have the capacity to choose in each instance. There is no automatic way of thinking that could be programmed into the species: Each man's conceptual experience as he goes through life will be different.

If you read something and you think it is very, very abstract, the next question to ask yourself is whether it floats without being connected to reality. Then, if you can see one further element in it—namely, a step-by-step structure—that combination will tell you right away that it is rationalism. In this excerpt, there is a definite structure: "This could not be, because this; if you say this, the answer would be this; and if this, then this; if this, then this; therefore, this." That structure per se is fine, if it is connected to reality. But if you combine a very abstract content with a deductive chain, then the chances are you have rationalism, and here you certainly do.

To begin with the very first sentence, there is a difference between saying that the conceptual faculty *cannot be* deterministic, and saying that the conceptual faculty *is not* deterministic. What the author is saying, by implication, is that he is not content to say man *does* have free will. He is going to give a special proof to show that man *has to* have free will, that you cannot get around the fact that he has free will, and that it would be impossible for him not to have free will. The actual Objectivist argument on this point is that man *does* have free will, and ultimately that it is an axiom, validated by the same method as all axioms, namely direct perception followed by an abstract statement of a self-evident truth that you can demonstrate to be a primary, a precondition of all knowledge. I go through that validation in my course on Objectivism.* For now, I want to say simply that if you know the Objectivist literature, you know we do not attempt to prove that there *must* be free will by a deductive chain, because we regard it as an axiom. But this author attempts to prove it by deduction. Since it is an axiom, that cannot be done, and therefore the deductive chain floats.

To see how it floats, follow it. The author says that there is no way man could automatically conceptualize without some means of selectivity, because the field of possible concepts is too wide; if man were automatically programmed to form all the concepts possible, he would starve, because every new thing would launch his brain into overdrive and he would never have time to act. If our method of argument is simply to speculate aloud, meaning that I can reorganize reality and project whatever I want, then in answer to, "If man were programmed, he would never

---

* See *Objectivism: The Philosophy of Ayn Rand*, pp. 69–72.

have time to act, so he would starve," I can program in an evaluation: If a thing interferes with life-sustaining functions, you should not do it. Therefore, I can hypothesize that man *is* automatically forced to conceptualize, but his system has evolved such that his brain will simply lose interest if he forms concepts that interfere with his life. So that takes care of that line of argument.

The next sentence reads, "He could not be programmed only to think and act in a pro-life way, because a concrete action that might be pro-life in one instance might not be in another." True enough, but we could reply that this is very special programming; the members of the human race who could not discriminate the pro-life actions died out, so only the ones who have the really good discriminations remain. Then the writer says, "There is no automatic way of thinking that could be programmed: Each man's conceptual experience will be different." Could I not say, then, that every animal's perceptual experience will be different? If the fact of difference means free will, then all animals have free will. Indeed, every plant encounters in some respects a different environment, so if that proves free will, then plants have free will.

There is actually no argument here at all, but simply a mental projection in a vacuum—"If there were no free will, then this would have to be the case; and if this, then this; and if this, then this"—all of it ignoring the obvious fact that if we are simply going to make things up, we can come up with answers to all these points. Like the previous excerpt, then, this one exhibits a rationalist approach. I deliberately put two examples of rationalism together to show the different forms it takes. You have to become attuned to the combination of very abstract discussions with the appearance of a deductive structure, all of which collapses when you say, "Why?" at a crucial point. That is the infallible sign of rationalism.

As a final example, consider the following excerpt on the foundations of morality.

> Let us assume that there is a society with no moral concepts
> (assume, for instance, that this society is a generation that was

brought up in isolation, without any "moral training" by parents). A philosopher from our society confronts them and tries to get them to accept an explicit morality; he tells them they need a set of rules to guide their actions. The spokesman for the amoral society asks: To guide our actions *toward what*?—and *why*?

The moralist has three possible lines of reply. (1) He points to some actual goal of the amoralist, which moral rules would help to foster—e.g., "If you give up smoking, you will not contract cancer; therefore, do not smoke." Or: (2) He points to a goal which, he claims, the amoralist *should* hold—e.g., "If you give to charity you are helping others, and you should always help others." Or: (3) He merely repeats his claim that men need moral rules, with no further elaboration.

Obviously, (3) would be dismissed as no answer by any rational man. If (2) is chosen, the amoralist will now repeat his question about the new claim (e.g., "*Why* should I help others?"), thus facing the moralist with the same three choices again. Eventually, the man who chooses (2) will be forced into justifying it at some point with an argument of type (1) or (3). But (3) is invalid. Hence, any rational morality must be based on values that human beings already hold.

Morality cannot tell people what they *should* value. It has no way to prove its start. It has to start with what people actually want or desire.

Here we have a seemingly convincing argument that morality has to start with what people actually want or desire. This would, then, be a proof of subjectivism in ethics. The writer has presumably proved it by saying that there are three theoretical possibilities, and possibilities one and two are out, so it has to be number three. If you can do that, you win, because that is a valid argument.

There is a certain problem, though. The author assumes right off the bat that there could be a society without moral concepts. But by implication, if you *could* have a society without moral concepts, then morality is obviously not required to live. Once that is true, then it does, in fact, come down to asking what your choices are. Morality, on this assumption, is a useless luxury, or it is whatever you feel like arbitrarily, because reality does not require it. The argument begins by conceding at the outset the whole issue of why morality is required.

This is another clear example of rationalism. There is a certain assumption, unknowingly granted in this case, that morality is not, in fact, necessary. Then the possibilities within that framework are listed and refuted one at a time, and you are left with an unavoidable deductive conclusion. But the whole question is: Where did this society with no moral concepts come from? How could it exist? What kind of actions does it take, and what does guide its actions, if not moral concepts? By asking these questions, you are going to find out either that this is a self-destroying society, like Jonestown or some version thereof, in which case it obviously needs some moral concepts to guide it to survive; or that it *does* survive, and it does survive because it follows certain rules, and by identifying them, you see what the society's moral concepts are. In this example, then, the author makes a certain assumption that concedes the whole case, and then follows it up with a deductive structure based on that concession. The argument is, therefore, definitely rationalistic.

CHAPTER 7

ANALYSIS OF STUDENT PAPERS

IN WHAT FOLLOWS, we will be taking up some written papers. We are concerned with them, in part, as examples of the presentation of ideas in written form. We want to know about the methods of presentation, how these papers do or do not live up to the principles we have discussed pertaining to presentation of ideas, and specifically to written presentation. Partly, of course, we are also interested in the philosophic content as such—are the points correctly presented, are the essentials there, what can we learn about the topic—because these are all important. It is thus a twofold concern.

"The Primacy of Consciousness: Some Manifestations" (Appendix C)

Using both of those criteria, method and content, let us turn to the first paper. Overall, there are a number of good things about this as a paper. I think it is definitely an interesting paper, and that is an achievement on this topic, because such a title as "The Primacy of Consciousness: Some Manifestations," suggests a very heavy, abstract topic that could cause one's mental set to creak. If you can read this and have your interest held, that is in itself a very good thing. Other virtues of this paper include the author's ability to concretize. The use of concretes and examples is extremely critical in this type of paper, because the topic is so extraordinarily abstract. If you are doing the primacy of consciousness, it is virtually mandatory to give an example before you go into a discussion of it. If you give a definition first, no matter how lucid and simple your definition, it settles on the reader's mind like a weight, because it is so enormously abstract. If you can give a good colorful example first, one that is relevant and newsworthy and yet paves the way for your abstraction, you have done wonders toward getting things started. You have fulfilled two crucial requirements right off the bat: You have motivated the reader, because you have intrigued him by using something pertaining directly to the news (an important example, in fact), and you have paved the way, cognitively speaking, for his understanding. You have given a concrete, so that when you get to your abstraction, it is not so heavy. The opener of this paper, from that point of view, is therefore extremely good, with one possible qualification we will get to shortly.

From the point of view of organization, this paper is very clearly structured and purposefully written. If you can have the sense in reading a paper, even if you do not agree with any given formulation, that you know what the author is talking about and why he is doing it at that point, that is already a great achievement on the author's part, particularly in a philosophy paper. This paper is also well written. The sentences are clear; even in the ones that I think are false, I know what the author is trying to say. There is no equivalent of legal boilerplate in the paper, in the sense of empty rhetoric or deliberately woozy space-filling; the author definitely has an idea that he wants to communicate with each sentence. In all these ways, then, I would certainly say the paper is good.

In terms of the negative, generally speaking, there is a certain confusion in this paper on the primacy of consciousness itself. That would be my main reason for giving a mixed verdict: that there is a certain significant confusion on the content, on the topic being presented. But I want to show that as it comes along.

Let us go through the paper in order. I have already commented on what I think are the virtues of the opening. It is conceivable to me, though, that one could raise a certain objection. In fact, as worded, and given the full context of what we know about Edward Kennedy, this is a good example of the primacy of consciousness. But since Chappaquiddick was a horrible tragedy, the question can be asked how literally Kennedy actually means what he is saying here. Is he simply saying metaphorically, "Oh, God, I wish it hadn't happened"? If you wanted to start a paper on religion, you would not say, "Peikoff just had a tragedy and he just said, 'Oh, God, I wish it hadn't happened,' and that shows that he is religious." In other words, is Kennedy just speaking loosely, or does he mean it literally as a viewpoint? Most people would probably be inclined to think, in a case like this, that when he says, "I hope and pray," it is just a loose way of speaking. This opening might, therefore, put them off a bit. From the aspect of stressing the primacy of consciousness, the best sentence of this whole quote is, "I really willed it in my mind that she survived, and really forced myself to believe that she had." There, Kennedy means a little more than, "I wish it hadn't happened"; he is actively trying to exercise his will to erase the fact.

In the third paragraph, the author asks, "Why would a man think this way? What is the cause, the basic philosophic principle involved, that made possible such a course of action and thought?" That is the transition from the example to the theory. The connection is to say, "The theory that I am going to present explains this behavior; it represents the cause that made him act this way." There is, however, a problem with using "Why? What is the cause?" as the way to get to this principle from that example. You have to think of the context of the reader, and what he will be able to understand on the face of it. The primacy of consciousness is a heavy, abstract metaphysical theory about the dependence or independence of basic constituents of reality, whereas the event that the author is trying to explain by reference to it is that a tragedy occurred and this man wished it had not happened. Most people will think, quite understandably, that you do not need a whole complicated metaphysical theory to explain this. The man wants to be president, and he thinks this is a disaster, so he wishes it had not happened. You do not want to evoke, so to speak, an anti-philosophic response on the part of your reader. You do not want him to feel, "Who needs philosophy to explain this? Horse sense is enough."

There is another aspect involved here. If you asked Senator Kennedy, "Do you believe in the primacy of consciousness?" he would say, "What the hell is that?" So it is certainly not the cause in the sense of being his explicit viewpoint. If Kant did it, it would be more plausible. But in Kennedy's case, it is only by implication of things that he *does* believe. The primacy of consciousness is not per se the conscious thing that is motivating him, and that makes it somewhat dubious to talk about it being the cause. You could make a case, if you had a whole paper, that it is the cause indirectly or by implication. But then you would have to say that the real cause, in the obvious, direct sense, is all the constant attacks on reason and reality—not necessarily the primacy of consciousness as a specific theory, but all the ideas like, "There are no facts; who can say what is true; reason is subjective; it is all a matter of opinion; we all live in our own reality"—that whole torrent of stuff you get from the time you are young, all of which, by implication, adds up in many people's minds to the idea, "In an emergency, you can make things whatever you want just by wishing them." But those people do not necessarily hold that as an explicit viewpoint. It is simply the license they are given as a result of a whole stream of attacks on reason and reality. In that sense, you can say that it is the license to the primacy of consciousness that permits Kennedy to rationalize this behavior, state it explicitly, and defend it. You need, though, a long explanation to make that intelligible. If you just say to an unprepared audience, "What would explain this?" and then give them a weighty theory right away, they do not see that this kind of explanation is necessary, and consequently, you subvert your motivation; you are supposed to be intriguing them with your theory, and instead you made it seem unnecessary.

This point would apply wherever this author makes reference to cause. For instance, in the fifth paragraph, he writes, "This principle . . . is the cause of our cultural disintegration." There, for the same reason, I think it is too simplified a statement. You could say it is an essential part of the cause, but it would still require a discussion. The point is that what really is the cause is the overall attack on reason and reality, of which the primacy of consciousness is merely one aspect and one implication. There is one further causal formulation near the end of the paper, where the author says, "The dominance of the primacy of consciousness produced today's culture." Do not oversimplify in that way. No one philosophic idea can ruin a man or a whole society, certainly not an idea as specific as this.

A better transition in that third paragraph, then, would be to say, "This illustrates," or, "This exemplifies," or, "This is an example of a very widespread attitude or viewpoint." That phrasing would enable you to make use of the opening example in a way that does not raise implications you cannot deal with.

The author's actual presentation of the essence of the theory, his summary of the primacy of consciousness, takes up the rest of paragraph three, from "A clue to the answer can be found" to the end of the paragraph. This is the technical definition on which the whole paper is going to rest. If the author had said it this way in a speech, I would think it an excellent job. But in writing, you have a chance to think about what could be misinterpreted and what should be put slightly differently, what is essential and what you can get rid of, and so on. Therefore, I want to hold to every implication of these statements, as an exercise in the kind of precision that is possible in writing, but not in speaking.

The beginning is excellent. The author starts by saying he is going to talk about "the relationship between man's mind and the external world, between consciousness and existence." If he simply started by saying he was going to talk about the relationship between consciousness and existence, the terms would be too abstract. "Consciousness" and "existence" are very general terms. If you know Objectivism, of course, you sling them around at the drop of a hat. But in writing, you have to make your terms clear, and it becomes painful if you have to say, "By 'consciousness' I mean this, and by 'existence' I mean that." Thus, the much better way to do it is the way this writer did it—say it in a simple way first, and then right after that, in apposition, give your more technical statement. You thereby make clear what you mean very economically and briefly. So we have introduced our terms painlessly and intelligibly, and that is a very sophisticated thing to do.

In the next sentence, the author lists some assumptions, the first of which is, "If existence is not what one wants it to be, one can try to change it." (The semicolon that follows means, "Stop there and digest this; it can be understood on its own.") You have to read a statement like, "If existence is not what one wants it to be, one can try to change it," objectively, not from the framework of feeling that you already know the theory and get what the author means. Suppose you are an outsider who knows nothing about this theory, and somebody tells you, "This bad idea that Senator Kennedy exemplified amounts to the idea that if existence is not what one wants it to be, you can try to change it." The problem with this formulation is that there are conditions of existence that you can not only try to change, but change. In fact, from a certain point of view, all of life consists of changing existence in certain ways. We do not have any food, so we grow wheat. You have a disease, so you go to the doctor and he gives you medicine. Anytime you enact a cause to achieve an effect, you are changing something in the world. But by putting the point in this generalized way, the author of this paper makes it sound as though the alternative is Kennedy or passivity. That is, either you wish existence out of existence, or you just take the kind of Hindu-Stoic attitude, "I am going to change nothing." Obviously, we do not mean that. It is a very bad suggestion to put in someone's mind here, because he will confuse activity with subjectivism, and therefore he will be lost right at the start.

So before the semicolon, in order to cut that implication out, you would have to say that the assumption is that one can try to change existence by solely mental means, or solely conscious actions, or solely feeling. This is the essence of the primacy of consciousness. It is not simply that you can change things if you do not like them; it is that you can change things exclusively by what goes on inside your mind, without any reference to physical action. If you could simply say—the way God was supposed to have said, "Let there be light"—"There is no wheat; let there be wheat," and wheat sprouted, that would be the primacy of consciousness, because that would be an act of consciousness producing a fact or a change in reality. By omitting that, the author dropped the essence of it and threw us off. He did correct it in what follows by giving different examples, but it was really a shame to need a correction there, because when you are doing this kind of complex, abstract theory, you do not want even for a minute to leave a wrong idea and confuse the reader. Here, the idea more or less emerges, but it is a bit mangled because of the way it is put.

The author then says that the second assumption is that you do not need to look outward to know existence, but can look inward, at your own mind. It is certainly true that this is connected to the primacy of consciousness. You could call it the epistemological corollary or implication of the primacy of consciousness. The only question is, Do we need it at this point in the presentation? Remember that the heavier the theory, the harder it is to grasp. The question of the primacy of existence versus the primacy of consciousness is essentially a metaphysical question; it says whether existence is independent of consciousness, or dependent on consciousness. Is existence out there and you have to adhere to it, or can you make it what you want by a wish? That has implications for every branch of philosophy—for how you acquire knowledge, for how you define ethics, for how you define the good in politics, for how you judge works of art. It redounds throughout an entire philosophic system. But in a brief paper, where space is at a premium, the best thing is the bare minimum. On this abstract a topic, and with so little space available, why put in the epistemological implication if you can get along without it?

One of the things you have to learn is when to restrict yourself to a certain formulation and when to elaborate. Given the abstractness of the subject, it is best to get in the basic idea, "consciousness controls existence," let it sink in for a moment, and then later, if there is space at another point in the paper, bring on the further details. I would do that based on the crow epistemology; there is just too much for people to take in. In other words, I am not sure that people would understand the difference between the first and the second assumptions here. If they do not already know the difference between metaphysics and epistemology, I am not sure that they would grasp the difference between "consciousness creates existence" and "consciousness should look inward." The author would have to say, "In the second case, I am talking about how you acquire knowledge," and give some kind of argument to distinguish the two cases; and there is not enough space for that.

Let us assume, then, that we have clearly stated the idea that existence depends on human consciousness, with the few amendments just mentioned. Is anything else either necessary or highly advisable to include in order to make this idea clear right at this point? We have had an example, and now a definition. But there are a couple of things that would be advisable to help clarify the idea and take the curse off its excessive abstractness.

One is to use the example in a different way, in order to set off in complete relief what you are talking about. Contrast is vital. I cannot emphasize enough the importance of contrast in presenting abstract ideas, and the more abstract, the more urgent it is. If you simply say, "You can change reality by an act of consciousness, and facts can be created by one's will," and the reader or listener does not know the theory, then your statement is not fully clear. The immediate question will arise, however implicitly: "As opposed to what else? How else would you function? What could be different?" You may not want to go into the whole theory of the primacy of existence, but at a minimum you should take the Kennedy example and say, "The opposite would be the recognition that facts are what they are, no matter who feels or thinks what, and they are outside of our power to change by an act of will. So if you drown someone, then you have drowned her, and no amount of wishing will alter it." Just that much would let people make the connection; people would say, "Oh, then the primacy of existence is the commonsense idea, and the primacy of consciousness is some kind of awful aberration." If you do not make the contrast, they may conceivably take even your exact definition—that you can change things by an act of consciousness—to mean, "Thought is required to change things, so maybe you are just saying change things by an act of thought; and do we not have to think to change things?" To get rid of those misinterpretations right at the outset, state your contrast as eloquently and briefly as you can, either in broad theory, or at least in the one example. As a general strategy or technique of writing, I cannot over-emphasize the importance, when you introduce an abstraction, of immediately saying, "I mean *this* as against *that*."

There is one other thing that could be done with regard to clarifying this passage, although whether it should be done here is a different question. The author defines the primacy of consciousness as "the relationship between man's mind and the external world," and then goes on to say, "between consciousness and existence." Where does God fit in here? The theory that God created the world—because God is not man's consciousness—is definitely part of the theory of the primacy of consciousness. The author did not want to raise the question of religion, so he restricted himself to man's consciousness, which is understandable. On the other hand, though, he then does not really get the full theory across in its essence, because religion is perhaps the best example by which to understand the primacy of consciousness. Religion is kind of a cosmic version of the primacy of consciousness, and it is the easiest to grasp. People can grasp human forms of the primacy of consciousness much more easily by seeing that it is the same policy ascribed to the human mind that religious people ascribe to God's mind. It immediately conveys the nature of the theory to them. It also shows them how it is all over the place, in ways that are blatant.

For instance, the simplest way that I have of presenting the primacy of consciousness to a class is to ask, "Who created the universe?" The very fact that they think such a question is self-evident and important implies that, to them, existence cannot possibly be a primary, but has to be produced by a consciousness. That question ("Who created the universe?") is a classic expression of the primacy of consciousness, and a beginning class can grasp right away what the theory is and even see the extent to which they have been influenced by it. In the case of the present paper, I would go out of my way to include religion, simply on pedagogical grounds. The audience would understand the point much better, and the

essence of the theory would be expressed more clearly. Even just parentheses, something like "Thus, consciousness (human or other) has metaphysical primacy," would leave a certain suggestion.

The next division here is the example of the antitrust laws, to which
the author devotes three paragraphs. In terms of what he has to do in the
space that he has available to him, that is excessive. The various quotes he
provides all make, in effect, the same point—that these laws are arbitrary,
nonobjective, undefined, and so on. If the author needs that point for his
purposes, any one quote is sufficient. If the reader needs to be convinced
of it, though, then the example is out, because then it is more controversial than the primacy of consciousness, and you cannot possibly go into
it. You cannot have an example that raises more questions than the theory you are presenting. Either you have an audience that can grasp right
away that the antitrust laws are filled with nonobjective formulations, or
you do not. And if they do not grasp it, you cannot use it. Three paragraphs is thus much too long. One is the most the author could use here,
because he needs the space desperately.

He does need the space desperately, because this is where he is finally
cashing in. We have been waiting for three paragraphs to learn what the
antitrust laws have to do with the primacy of consciousness. The author
now writes, "Thus the government official wants *law*—the reality within
which the businessman functions—to remain fluid, dependent on the
government officials' minds' formulations and interpretations." That is
his application of the theory that reality depends on consciousness.

But on what theory of law could law be independent of government
officials' formulation and interpretation? Law is not a fact out there in the
world, intrinsic to reality apart from us, like atoms or planets. It is a conceptual product of an advanced civilization, one that already has a government, that sits down in some form of consultation, formulates rules to
govern behavior, and then establishes judicial agencies to interpret what
they mean and how to apply them. There is no other way to have such a
thing as law. Therefore if the author says, "The antitrust laws illustrate the
primacy of consciousness because they make law dependent on our for-

mulation and interpretation," I am completely stopped. If this is a valid statement, then *any* law has to be the primacy of consciousness, and then what is the use of arguing against the theory? We may as well just say that Senator Kennedy is right, because what he did is obviously essential to any form of law. No law can be independent of man's mind, in the way external reality is. This is the essential error here.

The problem in that sentence is that the author is equivocating on the term "reality." In the first section of the paper, he used "reality" to mean the external world, physical existence. Here, though, he uses it to mean anything that affects human existence—in this specific case, a code of principles formulated by the government. Those meanings are related, but not interchangeable. You cannot say, "This exemplifies the primacy of consciousness," and save that statement by calling anything you want "reality." If I desire a certain woman, I would have to say that the "reality" that is my desire depends on my consciousness, so that is the primacy of consciousness. But obviously, that has nothing to do with the primacy of consciousness, which pertains to the relation between consciousness and physical reality. The author has here gone off the track completely.

It is true that nonobjective law does involve the primacy of consciousness. But it would be fairly time-consuming to show that. In essence, you would have to show how the primacy of consciousness makes the arbitrary possible in the realm of *values*, of which law is simply one form or one example. You would have to say, "The primacy of consciousness has implications for values—for ethics, politics, law. Some theories hold that God creates right and wrong by a sheer declaration of his will; others say society creates right and wrong by a sheer declaration of its will. Both agree with the idea that values are dictated by an arbitrary act of consciousness—as against the view that value judgments have to be derived from the facts of reality, objectively, without reference to any whim or any arbitrary desire at all."

It is important to grasp the connection between values and physical reality. Why does the idea that consciousness controls values imply the primacy of consciousness over physical reality? Values have to be enacted *in* reality. On any theory, you have to live on your values in reality; you have to act in the physical world. If the rules by which you should act can be validated arbitrarily, the implication is then that reality will adjust itself accordingly. Physical reality, in other words, will adapt to whatever God or society decrees. It is thus not an accident that God is held to be the moral lawgiver as well as the creator of reality, because if he were not the creator, he could not be the moral lawgiver. Suppose reality were independent of God, and he came in and said, "You have to do such-and-such," and he did not obey reality—all of his followers would be wiped out. The only reason God can get away with his moral laws is that he is sure that reality is going to follow him, because he is in charge of it.

In other words, control over values by your arbitrary will is possible only on the premise that your consciousness has control over the physical world. That is also why Kant, who was the real source of the idea that society creates right and wrong (although he himself did not hold that), began by saying that the human mind creates the physical world. But there is a connection there that you would have to spell out. Before you say why an arbitrary declaration of law amounts to the primacy of consciousness, you would have to make clear the difference between an arbitrary declaration and a valid derivation of morals (and then laws) from the facts of reality. That is a long, difficult thing to do. The important issue here is to see how the author switches the point. Even an objective law depends on the mind, but there are two different senses of "depend." One sense is that the mind has to try to *discover* the facts out there, including the facts to serve as the value standard; the other is that the mind arbitrarily decrees something, and reality snaps into line. This is a very big omission, and the result is that the presentation is just not plausible.

There are a number of confusions caused by the fact that the author very much missed the point of the application of the primacy of consciousness to law. To take one example, he asks, "What possible courses of action and thought would such a businessman take?" saying that one possibility would be to simply obey the law. That is a very unfortunate thing to put in here, because it seems to imply that if you do not accept the primacy of consciousness, you will defy the law. Civil disobedience is not inherent in the primacy of existence. When and how to break with society is a whole separate question, one that should definitely not be raised if the paper is to be self-contained.

As the second possibility, the author tries to show that the businessman enacts the primacy of consciousness given these nonobjective laws. He does it by saying the businessman looks inward at his own consciousness and his desire to produce and trade goods. The author goes on to imply that the businessman is on the premise of the primacy of consciousness, because instead of looking outward, he looks inward, and then he "tries to create the reality that is dependent on *his* consciousness: his desire to produce and trade goods." Such wording suggests that introspection is the primacy of consciousness—that anytime somebody looks inward and finds some important desire that he wants to act on, he is accepting the primacy of consciousness. That is completely untrue. All self-knowledge, all knowledge of your own motivation, requires you to look inward. It is absolutely wrong to say, "He looked inward before he took this action, and that is the primacy of consciousness."

When is introspection the primacy of consciousness and when is it not? It is if you look inward as a means of acquiring knowledge of reality. In other words, if a man looks inward and says, "I have this desire to produce, and I feel that this desire would best be served by keeping both hands in the air for twenty-four hours in the direction of Mecca," then that is the primacy of consciousness. It is not just that he looked inward; he looked inward and decided that what he found there dictated what reality would have him do. That is the primacy of consciousness: the dependence of reality on what you find when you look inward. Yet there is nothing in what the author says here about the sheer fact that the businessman *feels* that is going to make reality snap into line. All the author says is that the businessman has a desire to produce and trade, which he discovered by looking inward, and he decides to do something about it. But if he decides to do something about it by acting in reality and according to its laws, then that is not the primacy of consciousness.

Here again, the author got thrown off by his idea of the primacy of consciousness. To illustrate the problem: If a robber points a gun at me, and I offer my wallet to appease him, I am not guilty of the primacy of consciousness. I have consulted my desire, decided that I want to live, and said, "He holds the whip hand and sets the terms, and if I do not live up to it, I am going to be killed." That is completely consistent with the primacy of existence premise on my part. I introspected, and I capitulated (if you want to put it that way) to somebody else's arbitrary declaration of consciousness. But I did so in light of one fact that very much mitigates the circumstances here: He was holding a gun on me. It is a fact of reality that I am going to die if I do not do it, and I am respecting facts accordingly. When would it be primacy of consciousness to pay over the money?

The same principle applies also to bribery, which is the author's example here. Two different attitudes can lie behind paying a bribe. One would be simply self-defense, and the other would be primacy of consciousness. What would make the difference? It is self-defense if you simply say, "This guy demanding a bribe is a swine, a bastard, a killer," which is your way of saying, "He does not control reality; he is not the moral authority; he is defying reality, but he has me in his power." That is still recognizing reality. It is completely different if you say, "Well, they all say that he is right, and they must know what they are talking about; right is what society or the government or the robber says." That is the primacy of consciousness. You may pay a bribe, as some businessmen do, on that latter method. "The government must know; who am I to know; they are elected by the public; there is no right and wrong; whatever they say is valid"—that is the primacy of consciousness. But the sheer act of paying is not—not if you protest in your own mind.

So the author has here confused the situation badly. The confusion is caused by the fact that he tried to short-circuit the application of the primacy of consciousness to values; he tried to go straight from "controlling reality" to the application to law, and he could not find the reality that was being controlled, because it is done through values, which imply physical reality. But since he did not identify that, all he could find was desire, and he ended up in the position that it is primacy of consciousness whenever your desire has to mesh with somebody else's desire, regardless of what that is. And that is not true. I would not say a lobbyist is per se operating on the primacy of consciousness.

You also must not oversimplify the point about looking inward and looking outward. It is certainly possible for an advocate of the primacy of consciousness to look outward. How else does he discover his victims? He has to look out and see all these people, all this wealth that he wants to seize, the jails he wants to build, the torture instruments, and so on. He does not just dream those up. He follows reality to some extent, if only in order to enslave people. You have to follow your definitions exactly. That is why it is dangerous to introduce "looking inward" and "looking outward" to a beginning audience in this short a space. People have to think in essentials, and if they are just getting the basic idea of where you should look to acquire knowledge, they will simply think for short, "Inward is bad and outward is good," and then you will lose the essence of the point.

In the last part ("What is the fundamental error . . ."), the author goes into the proper viewpoint and the errors of the primacy of consciousness. Those are essentially done correctly, although the primacy of existence should have been mentioned earlier, as indicated above. One point, though, is not too clear. The author says that the primacy of consciousness holds that A can be non-A, and that is true—the essential problem is that it is a repudiation of the Law of Identity. He gives the example, "A dead woman can be alive if one forces oneself to believe so." That is a good example, because it is a direct A and non-A. It was also mentioned at the opening.

The next example, though, is not so clear: "Businessmen should look outward when producing steel, but let us not define 'restraint of trade' . . . there is no problem in never defining concepts . . . consciousness decrees it to be so." That is a big mouthful, and it would not be too clear to a beginner why it is A and non-A. Even a freshman can understand that the idea that a dead woman can be alive when she is dead is A and non-A. In the second example, though, it is unclear where A and non-A come in. It would be better, in a brief presentation, to stick to something the reader can understand right away. Otherwise, something as complex as, "Non-objective definitions are a violation of the Law of Identity," takes so much time to explain that the point gets lost. The last sentence of the whole paper puts it well: "Businessmen cannot produce under conditions of existence which make it impossible to produce." To say they have to produce under conditions that make production impossible is a direct contradiction, a straight A and non-A, and it would have made another good example if the author had explained it.

To summarize, this author got the main idea correctly, but with a certain vagueness in his own understanding of it, a vagueness that came out in his discussion of antitrust and caused him to go off the tracks. I would have taken a different option. If my goal were cultural manifestations of the primacy of consciousness, I would have focused primarily on three things: psychological manifestations, such as evasion (the idea that you do not have to accept reality); religious manifestations, such as the belief in miracles and the question of who created the universe; and evaluative manifestations, meaning the idea that God or society creates ethics, the good, and so on. Then the reader would grasp the scope of the acceptance of this theory and see that it really is everywhere. Then, if there were enough space, you could go on to one specific type of law as an example of a cultural manifestation. But law is so far down the hierarchy that in a limited space, it is a tricky thing to get in.

"Life, Liberty, and the Pursuit of Happiness" (Appendix D)

The next paper we will analyze is on man's rights. There are certain types of problems that run through it, and it would be a good paper if it were not for one type of problem, albeit a problem that takes a big toll.

First we should consider the paper in general. The author starts off with an easily digestible, conversational tone that attracts and motivates the reader. That is easier to do on this topic, because talking to people about rights requires much less motivation than talking about the primacy of consciousness. People have heard about rights, and they know that it is a big and controversial issue of politics; that is not the same thing as some weighty metaphysical abstraction. Therefore, much less motivation is needed. The author's opening is effective and intriguing; it amounts to, "You talk a big game about liberty, but you do not know what it is, and I am now going to show you." Given the space available, though, a motivation of this length would not be required. When you say to an American, "life, liberty, and the pursuit of happiness," by the very fact of what this author says in her opening paragraph, he is already interested—as opposed to when you say, "I am talking about the primacy of consciousness." But leaving aside whether she carried it out fully, she tried to show that our foreign policy and our domestic policy and the future of the country depend on understanding these issues, which is a very proper intention.

This paper is also clearly written. The reader knows what is intended; there is no rhetoric or padding (a very important thing in a philosophy paper), and the author is working on the laudable premise that every sentence should say something, that the writing has to be purposeful and not just fill up space.

When it comes to the organization of the paper, however, there is something that is defective about its structure, and that is that the theme of the paper is not clear. The theme means the point she is trying to establish, or the topic she is concerned with. Is she trying to illustrate rights, correct a misconception of rights, show the moral basis of rights, or something else? It cannot be a theme just to talk about rights in general; you have to have some specific thing you want to say about them. In fact, the theme that was assigned was to validate the claim that man has certain inalienable rights. As the paper is written, though, the reader might have some question about that, because some of the validation was skimped on at the expense of more space being given to an elaboration of the idea, or some of its more remote ethical bases, or some of its opposites. The author spreads herself pretty thin, so that when she comes to the real essence of what the validation of rights is, the point goes by much too quickly. The paper leaves the reader with a slight feeling that certain more or less appropriate things have been said, without really settling on the issue of the validation.

One might protest that to an American audience, the validation of rights does not have to be any more than indicated. That is debatable. An American audience is very sympathetic to the idea of rights, but the validation of rights was not even discussed in the eighteenth century, when the Declaration of Independence was written. The Founding Fathers held it to be a self-evident truth that man is endowed with certain inalienable rights. "Self-evident" means that no validation is required; you just open your eyes and see it. The Enlightenment theory of epistemology was that there are self-evident axioms in every field of knowledge, like "A is A" in metaphysics, which you just look at reality and see. The Founders thought that rights were the self-evident axioms of politics. That is a big mistake, and they were helpless because they were actually implicitly relying on a certain philosophy without acknowledging it, something still true today. So one could make a case that Americans above all need to stress that rights are *not* self-evident and that they *need* a whole validation. That kind of introduction would be good, but then the author would have to give a real validation.

Let us turn to a step-by-step analysis of the paper. The intention of the opening, as we have said, is good. In the second paragraph, the author says, "At the center of the idea of liberty is the idea of political rights, and here there is confusion." Then she gives us three choices: "Should we respect the public's right to unbiased news, or the publisher's right of free speech? Does a worker have the right to a job, or does his employer have the right to fire him? Are rights always more important than other considerations—like providing for the poor?"

There is a confusing switch here, which obscures the point being made. On one hand, the author could have said, "the right to news versus the right to speech, the right to a job versus the right to fire a worker, the right to your wealth versus your right to a livelihood"; that would be three sets of alleged rights in conflict, and then the theme would be what rights really are. The other way of setting up the conflict would be to highlight rights versus something more important than rights. For instance, the right to free speech versus an educated public, the right to fire versus employment, and the right to one's own wealth versus the needs of the poor—in other words, in each case, rights conflicting with something that supersedes them. The author, though, switches in the middle, creating some confusion. It would be easier to take one tack or the other, saying either, "There are two views of rights, and here I am pitting them one against the other, in three cases," or, "There is the issue of rights versus nonrights, and here are three examples." It is really just an issue of wording, because the wrong view of rights is really the negation of rights. But when it is presented in this confusing way, the parallelism is lost.

The third paragraph begins, "We can evaluate political rights only by evaluating the underlying moral code," followed shortly by, "Americans cannot judge between two radically different ideas of rights because they have two different moralities." In content, the author's point here is correct. It is true that you can evaluate rights only by reference to morality, and it is also true that there are different approaches to rights and that they reflect different approaches to morality. The question is, Does this paragraph make that point objectively clear to an audience that does not already know it? I would say not. It is suggested, but too briefly. It is a key point, but it goes by so fast that you would not be able to take it in.

What kind of elaboration would be necessary for this to be clear? First of all, why do rights need morality at all? The author does not tell us. She *says* we need morality, but what about rights makes them based on morality? Why can they not be discussed without any reference to morality? As a simple explanation, you could say straightaway that by "rights," we mean a moral sanction to a certain kind of action. That is neutral enough to be true on anybody's theory. A right is a moral concept; it says that in a social situation, a person has the prerogative of doing such and such, whatever it happens to be, and that this is right and anybody who interferes with him is wrong. If you just spell out that much, then it is comprehensible that your theory of morality, which is your theory of right and wrong, would obviously be relevant to your idea of rights. But without spelling that out, it is unclear just why we have to go into morality.

The author gives a parallel to a physician, saying the physician has to have some standard by which to judge a given drug, and she refers to "his code of ethics: to heal the sick." But "to heal the sick" is not a code. A code is a whole constellation of values organized systematically by certain principles, which tell you what to do in a whole bunch of situations. "To heal the sick" is not a code; it is a purpose, an ultimate goal. So if we want to show the reader that we need a whole code of morality, this is not too clear an example. All it shows is that we have to have some purpose if we are going to judge our actions. A person could say, "Sure, we have to have some purpose—we want individuality, or we want freedom, or we want Americanism, so therefore we should have rights. Why do we need a whole elaborate code of morality?"

It is not enough simply to motivate people by way of starting your discussion. You have to motivate them at each step. Here, the author wants to plunge us into morality, but we are not prepared yet to see why it is really necessary. She would have to say something explaining that, since rights are moral concepts pertaining to how human beings should relate to one another in all kinds of different circumstances, rights obviously depend on a whole way of life, and we have to see what that could consist of. The analogy to the doctor is not convincing here.

Nor is the reference to two radically different evaluations of rights based on two mutually exclusive codes. We are given just the faintest example of some differences, without summary. The author did not say, in that preceding paragraph, "There are two basically different theories of rights; the first half of my sentences represent one, and the other, the other." She just said questions that an ordinary person would hear and say, "Well, yes, those are questions." How many different theories there are may not be clear, particularly since the author did not keep the wording parallel in that paragraph. The reader has just gotten the intimation that there are different approaches to what rights are, but whether there are two radically different approaches or four, he does not know. Then, right at that point and without further elaboration, the author plunges into, "There are two mutually exclusive moral codes," and it is simply too much to be convincing. The reader has kind of half grasped that there is a variety of views on rights, and half gotten that rights have something to do with morality, and suddenly there are two mutually exclusive views resting on two mutually opposite codes, and it is too big a structure. The thing collapses; it is too much and too vague.

Organizationally, then, it would be better to say, "There are two different theories of rights," and immediately elaborate: "Theory one says this, and theory two says that; now, how can we explain these?" Then you could go into how they rest on two opposite moralities. Another way might be to say, "Let us forget about rights; rights, after all, are a moral concept, so we have to go into morality. There are two different theories of morality; let us look at those first, and then I will show you how they lead to two different theories of rights." Here, though, the author tried to combine both these approaches together in one paragraph, and did not quite do either. All we end up with is the net feeling, "There are a lot of theories of rights, and they are somehow connected to morality, and I am not going to go into morality"—but it goes by so fast that none of it is established, and the author is defeated by the crow epistemology.

Let us now look at the first moral theory as it is presented in paragraph four ("The man who upholds the first of these two moral codes . . ."). That paragraph is, in effect, the author's overall validation of the proper theory of rights. Imagine someone who does not know this material, and is hearing this as a moral code that leads to one theory of rights, as opposed to the other, which comes in the next paragraph. The author writes, "The man who upholds the first of these two moral codes holds as his supreme value—as the primary value against which all else is measured as good or evil—his own life, its furtherance and fulfillment." This is similar to a certain wording in the paper on the draft discussed in chapter 4, and has the same type of problem.

That first sentence could be interpreted as hedonistic. It could be interpreted to mean, "anything goes." Saying, "The primary value against which all else is measured as good or evil is the furtherance and fulfillment of your own life" raises the question: Do we mean your life at any price and by any means? Can you do anything you want to others? Is fulfillment whatever you feel it to be? Remember that when you go into anything pertaining to selfishness, you have to bear in mind the way that term is understood today. Today's intellectual context is enormously hostile to it, and "selfishness" is fraught with implications such as whim worship, cutting other people's throats, and all that kind of stuff. You cannot go into a whole song and dance every time you bring up the term, but you do have to say *something*. In a paper on the validation of rights, I would try to get away from life as the standard and selfishness as the means, because there is no time to explain all those things. But if there were no other way, I would put in parentheses, "By selfishness I do not mean cutting other people's throats; I mean acting according to reason, surviving by your own mind." Say something about each man as an end in himself, as not sacrificing others, simply to make your terms clear. That is absolutely indispensable.

In the next sentence, the author does say *rational* selfishness, but that does not really clarify the issue, because without a definition, you could say it is rational to be anything. It is very common to say that bank robbers are rational, because they have to think in order to figure out how to crack the vault; they have to know science and study safecracking. Obviously, that is not "rational" as we mean it here—but these things are not self-evident. So up to this point, when the author says "all else" is measured by your own life, without further definition, that does convey that it is deuces wild and anything goes.

Next, the author says, "The man who upholds this moral code *must* evaluate political rights as a necessity—for without political rights he does not have the right to take the actions necessary to support and further his life." But *which* actions are necessary to support and further his life? This passage could legitimately be read as follows: "Rational selfishness, whatever that means; so I am going to be selfish and get whatever I can to survive. Therefore, I need rights. Well, that means I have got to have information, or I will not know how to act; therefore, we have to have a law that there should be unbiased news. It also means I have got to have a job, or I cannot support myself; my own life is the standard by which all else is determined, and if I do not get a job, I do not live. I am going to use my mind on my job, so I am going to be rational. So therefore, the government has to legislate jobs. And if I am too poor to eat, what is the use of talking about my life? So, I can see I agree with this, and therefore she means to say that 'rights' means the public's right to news, the worker's right to a job, and providing for the poor."

It is not that this author wrote poorly; she did it as clearly as she could within what she tried to do. But she tried to do the impossible. She tried to condense a whole code of ethics into a paragraph, and it simply cannot be done. Therefore, when writing on a subject like this, you have to decide for yourself: "Instead of trying to give a little précis of a whole code of ethics—life is the standard, your own life, by the means of reason, etc.— what one point could I bring out that would be understandable on its own terms, and on which I could then hang rights if I want to show their moral base?"

The problem here is this: The author wants to show that rights depend on a certain moral theory, and she has not got the space to give the whole moral theory, so she wants to say something that will suggest a moral code that will contrast with the other moral code she is going to describe shortly, yet without committing herself to a full-scale presentation. She also wants to contrast it later with the idea of service to the public good. Therefore, the obvious thing to put in here, the moral peg on which to hang rights, is something on the order of, "Man is an end in himself." In a sentence or so, say that one moral code holds that each man is an end in himself, that he may properly pursue his own happiness, neither sacrificing himself to others nor others to himself. If that is so, then he cannot be sacrificed to others, and he has a right to his own actions and to their results. That is not a complete case, of course, because it does not say *why* man is an end in himself. But what it does do is put it in a formulation that does not raise a host of negative connotations that you will have no chance to answer in a way that is plausible and understandable. It also contrasts easily with the point made in the next paragraph, in which the author says the only other alternative is that you hold as the highest value not your own life, but the public good, and therefore everything has to be judged by how well it serves the public good.

A clarification is necessary here. The author says that regardless of whether the highest value is God or whichever, if it is something other than man's life, then his life is potentially expendable. Note that she says "*man's* life" here, whereas in the preceding paragraph she said "his *own* life." Ayn Rand makes a distinction between those two points. Man's life she calls the *standard* of ethics, his own life the *purpose*. Those are not the same thing. The standard is the broad abstraction, which is the same for everyone. When we say, "Man's life is the standard," then, we indicate that there are certain objective principles that apply to everybody, independently of whether you want it or not, whether you like it or not. The standard is simply inherent in man's nature and in the requirements of his life. Then, to achieve that standard, you have to pursue *your own* life by following the rules of what is required for man's life, meaning that your own life is the purpose of ethics. Thus, in the course of validating an ethics, you first show that man's life is the standard, and then you show that that, in itself, necessitates egoism as the form of implementing it. But those are not the same, and the author of this paper has a tendency to equate the two.

At this point we come to the author's analogy of the physician and the altruist. The author states that the physician who holds the advancement of medical knowledge as his primary has to sacrifice his patients if it advances medical knowledge. There follows a long paragraph essentially trying to show that if you have two different goals, they are going to have to conflict, and one is going to have to be sacrificed to the other. That is an inappropriate procedure here. It is not necessary to go at such length into this analogy and the elaboration of why altruism and egoism are incompatible with each other. It is true that the primary error is that Americans today try to support both man's rights and altruism. But the cause of that error is not that they do not see that altruism and egoism are incompatible with each other, not if the terms are defined. It is simply that they do not connect morality and politics. They think you should live to serve others—that is a moral issue, and then when it comes to politics, they think that each person should be free. They do not give full meaning to altruism.

There is no problem per se in showing that altruism and egoism are incompatible. It is obvious from the definitions, if the definitions are put in terms of essentials. Egoism says that man is an end in himself, that he should live for his own sake. But we need to be very exact here. Although the author says that altruism is the only other possible alternative, the antithesis of egoism, in the strict sense, is not altruism. The *essential* opposite of the idea that man should live for his own sake is not that he should serve others, but that he should sacrifice himself. And that is not altruism.

This point requires elaboration. The essential opposite of egoism is the idea that man is a sacrificial being, a being who should put something above himself and surrender himself or abnegate himself to that thing. What that thing is, though, is wide-open. One possibility is God, who was the collector of sacrifice for a long time. The main idea was that all of mankind should sacrifice themselves to God, and the contrast was self-ishness versus service to God. And if you tried, in the medieval period, to say, "I am going to forget God and just serve my fellow men," that would have been blasphemous and criminal. True, there was a certain element of altruism, because you were supposed to love your neighbor as one means of serving God. But it is still true that the primary moral antithesis was to place God above yourself. After the Renaissance, God fell out of favor, as it were, and little by little your neighbor took over. And it is really only in the nineteenth century that this came to full fruition, when the term "altruism" was invented by Auguste Comte. He explicitly said, "We need something like God to which man will sacrifice himself, but people do not believe in God anymore, so what will we substitute? Let us call it le Grand-Être, the 'great being' of society, humanity." Comte is really the one who formalized the conversion from God to altruism, in the sense of making society the moral primary.

But there are many other possibilities. There are those, like Schopen-hauer, who say everyone should be sacrificed neither to God nor to soci-ety, but to nothing; we should embrace nirvana, nonexistence, as an end in itself. When such people go out and writhe in self-torment, it is not because they think they are going to make their neighbor happy, and not because they believe in a Judeo-Christian God; for them, the worship of nirvana is part of an out-and-out assault on existence as such. Or take Kant, for instance. He is certainly not an altruist. His ethics is organized so that everybody should sacrifice themselves to the categorical impera-tive. It is sacrifice for its own sake.

These are all, in effect, variations within one essential ethical view-point. It is true that the version most common in the West is a secularized religious version, which is altruism: You should live for others, serve the public good, and so on. But in presenting a theoretical argument, it is wrong to introduce altruism as the only possible alternative to egoism. The alternatives are man as an end in himself and man as a being who should sacrifice himself to something. Then, in the context of politics, either he sacrifices himself to the government or the government is the representative of that something, in either case implying that man has no autonomy. If it is presented that way, there is no need for any analogies to show why these two are inherently opposed, because it is obvious that there is no possible way of combining them; they are opposed root and branch from the very beginning. But by not going to the essence of the contrast, the author of this paper put herself into a position as though there is something tenuous about this contrast that she has to argue.

Now look at the problem with the analogy she uses, which is presented at some length. How often is it that there is an inherent clash between the advancement of medical knowledge and the advancement of a patient's health? Those two are by no means fundamental opposites. In the great majority of cases, the physician learns as he treats the patient, and the patient benefits from his knowledge. One could construct a situation in which a mad doctor would sacrifice a certain patient in the name of ex-perimental knowledge, but then such a doctor is perversely dropping the whole context of medicine. The analogy here is thus not very convincing, because it is not a close analogy at all. It involves two things that, most of the time, coexist perfectly well, whereas sacrifice and egoism are complete opposites at root, in every respect, and across the board. The reader may get the idea from this analogy that "Egoism and altruism are like the doctor's dilemma, which means that in a few cases we have to be careful. So let us have egoism and altruism, just like the tension between advancing medical knowledge and patient care, only we will have a principle in our Constitution that wherever it interferes with the welfare of the person, of the individual, we will have to have a vote before we do it. It is a rare thing anyway, so what is the difference?" You must not leave the possible implication that something so profound is a kind of rare, esoteric conflict. The very fact of introducing an analogy already undercuts the point, because if the case were properly presented, the clash of the two opposites would be so naked that no argument would be necessary.

When and when not to argue is an important point of strategy. There is such a thing as gilding the lily. If your point is to pit two nakedly opposed ethics against each other, it is a mistake then to go on and say, "Now I am going to give you an argument showing why these two are opposed." The reader stops altogether, thinking he must have misunderstood, since it seemed so obvious before. Then he hears an argument that is not too good and says, "I do not see it now, and she told me I did not get it before, so I do not get it, period, and I do not agree with it." You therefore have to be careful when you argue this type of point, and here I think it is very ill-advised to argue, certainly by this analogy. If the point in your mind is, "The trouble is that Americans do not see something here," you must define exactly what they do not see. It is not that they do not see that two fundamentally opposed ethics cannot be combined. It is that maybe they do not see that altruism *is* fundamentally opposed to egoism. If they do not see it, then make that point. Stress that the essence of this idea of serving the public good is that you are a sacrificial being; you do not exist for your own sake, and therefore the state can do with you whatever it wants, as opposed to your having autonomy. Then you can say, right on the face of it, that you cannot combine the two viewpoints, and it is obvious why not.

Turning now to the seventh paragraph, consider the first sentence: "The results of the moral code of altruism, regardless of what value-standard is chosen as 'higher' than man's life and the rights that make his proper survival possible, have been demonstrated in China and Russia." The problem with that wording is the questions it will raise in people's minds. To most people, the term "altruism" conveys generosity, kindness, helpfulness, and so on. The author has not given any definition to counter that impression. Just like "selfishness," "altruism" is the kind of term that has to be explained. You have to say, "By 'altruism,' I do not just mean kindness; I mean the theory of self-sacrifice for the sake of others." I would avoid the term and just refer to the idea that man is a sacrificial being.

The author also writes, "The rights that make man's proper survival possible." If she had explained that, the validation of rights would be complete, because the validation is precisely to show that certain rights are necessary to make man's proper survival possible. But that is what she has not yet shown us. It is like begging the question: The author passes over the essential point as though she has covered it. She then says the results of altruism have been demonstrated in China and Russia. Most liberals, though, have a standard comeback when you tell them that Communist countries exemplify altruism and sacrifice, a comeback you have to know exists so you can either answer it or avoid it. They will tell you that China and Russia are the most selfish countries in history, because they are each ruled by an oligarchy, a small group of people who have higher living standards than the rest of the country and who are motivated only by material wealth, power lust, and their own glorification; whereas America is a democratic country in which everybody sacrifices himself for the majority. That is all wrong, but that is a very widespread line among liberals. You have to say something to cut that out. Of course, the motive of the rulers is not what determines the essence of a country, but even counting that, the rulers of Communist countries can get what they are after only by counting on people's willingness to sacrifice themselves. They do not dare preach selfishness. The point here, though, is simply that you cannot just toss out a comment like this. This is the issue of keeping the paper self-contained, especially when you are not yet familiar with what people will say.

In that same paragraph, the author goes into the results of trying to mix two different moral codes, and it is hard to follow, because neither code has really been presented. Without an explicit statement of what altruism is, or what rational selfishness is, much of this would arguably be unclear to the reader: Why would a mixed economy result from a mixture of moral codes, and why is that unstable? Why do we have a mixed concept of rights when we do not yet know what rights really are? What does it mean to hold man's life as the *consistent* value standard when the author has left open how you live by it? Above all, how is our foreign policy "the result of the attempt to consistently defend liberty without first defining what it is"? Our foreign policy is arguably not the result of any purpose or viewpoint at all. It is, in fact, debatable whether we even have a foreign policy, in any sense of the term, as opposed to simply reeling from obstacle to obstacle.

The author then turns to an elaboration on the moral code at the base of rights. This is a little better, because she gives some content, albeit briefly, to what she means by the mind, the proper method of survival, and freedom. The problem, though, is that this is an essential elaboration of the preceding, which is necessary to make the preceding even grasp- able. Even the elaboration is quite brief; she says, "The moral code of ra- tional selfishness acknowledges . . . that his survival requires his freedom to act on the judgment of his mind." The key question, though, is: Why does it? That is the entire essence of the validation of rights—that man's survival requires the freedom to act on the judgment of his mind. Rights are conditions of existence required by rational beings. Since this paper is on the validation of rights, the explanation of that point should be the essence and theme of the paper—why a rational being has to have free- dom to survive. Then you would go into why it is mind versus force, that is, why force is the destruction of the means of survival; you would show that man has to have his mind preserved from force, and that means liberty and rights and the pursuit of happiness. But if you do not elaborate on that, your whole validation is simply an arbitrary declaration.

You need a whole code of ethics if you are giving a detailed validation of rights. If I were to give a full validation of rights, I would say that rights depend upon four different pillars, each one an essential of the Objectivist ethics. Rights depend, first of all, on life as the supreme value, which is the clearly necessary basis of the right to life. They depend, second, on the fact that man survives by reason, and reason can function only if left free; that is the right to liberty. They depend, third, on the fact that man has a right to pursue his *own* life—in other words, ethical selfishness— and that is, in politics, the right to the pursuit of happiness. And fourth, rights depend on the fact that mind and body form a unity, and therefore man cannot survive simply by thought, but by the union of thought and action, including the production of physical goods; that is the basis of the right to property. Thus, if you were going to validate rights, it would have to be on the basis of an ethics that holds life as the standard of value, thought as the means of achieving it, selfishness as the ultimate purpose, and physical action and achievement—in other words, productiveness— as the form in which thought has to be expressed. That is the whole Objectivist ethics, and that is what then leads to rights; it translates directly to life, liberty, the pursuit of happiness, and property.

Just a few last comments. The first line of the next paragraph ("A consistent definition of political rights as freedom from force by any man or group") is missing one critical word: freedom from *physical* force. "Force" is another term that is used very loosely, as in, "I am forced to take this job, because I can't find a better one." If you are talking about rights, you have to be very clear that you are speaking only of physical force (you do not even have to bother with fraud in a brief paper). If you do not put that in, the term "force" is left wide-open. Anybody can then say, "Yours is a utopian theory. Everybody is forced to do things he does not like—you are forced to sit there and listen to me go on and on when you are already bored out of your mind." In a certain usage, you are; you are forced by politeness, because you are bored but you cannot go home. Only that is not what you are talking about, so that clarification is crucial.

On the whole, I think the rest of that paragraph is clear and accurate. It would have been a little better if the author had shown how the altruist or self-sacrifice approach led to the opposite interpretation, because it would have made clear why ethics is so essential to this topic; but even so, it is essentially well-done. The sentence on the right to own property ("The right to own property guarantees the continued possession and right of disposal of whatever a man possesses by purchase, gift or inheritance"), though, does leave out one very big thing: What about *production*? What about actually achieving wealth? What about creating it instead of just getting it from somebody else? It is important to be careful on those formulations.

In sum, then, I would say that the author's intention was certainly good, and she did try to get the moral basis of rights in. What threw her off was not knowing on what level to pitch the approach to morality, as well as doing too much and too little at the same time, resulting in a kind of hit-and-run presentation of the morality involved. For this reason, the paper did not come across very convincingly.

"The Moral and the Practical" (Appendix E)

We are going to look at the next paper, as we did the previous two, from the aspect of its ability to present philosophic ideas objectively, interest the audience, and present the material clearly and in a self-contained way. I would not go so far as to say this paper is essentially negative, because I think there are good things and good intentions in it, but I think there are some real problems.

As far as motivating the audience is concerned, the virtue of this paper is that the author ties his material, or attempts to tie it, to all kinds of actual issues. He does not just discuss the topic in a vacuum; he brings in, right from the outset, inflation, the energy crisis, and the Soviet Union, just to pick a few. (The second paragraph seems repetitive, it should be said, because the author is elaborating on problems we already know.) He then says, "There are answers to these problems, and my answers depend upon my view of the moral and the practical, and I am even going to tell you what my solutions are." He has certainly taken care to tie this subject, which people might be afraid is a floating abstraction, to all kinds of real, practical things.

In that regard, note that the author is still giving motivation in the eighth paragraph ("To provide some motivation . . ."). So he has devoted approximately a third of his paper to motivating his audience, which might suggest to you that there is some error involved. If the topic were the primacy of consciousness, I could see that the author would think, "Everyone in this audience, except graduate students, is going to be turned off completely by this material, so I really have to lay the motivation on thick or they will tune out." But the moral and the practical is not that esoteric a subject. If you see that the author has used up almost a third of the paper and is still trying to get the reader interested, the question arises whether that makes sense.

There is, though, a bigger problem than that. The positive aspect of the attempt at motivation is that the author did try to tie it to the real issues that people would be interested in; the problem is with the way that he did it. The introduction continues on for a number of paragraphs. The author does not actually start to give his answer on the relation of the moral and the practical, which is the theme of the paper, until paragraph twenty ("Many alternate values and actions are possible to man"). And the length of the actual presentation of the moral and the practical, which is the nub of this paper, is about two paragraphs. The rest of the paper is an extended introduction and then an extended example, which already suggests a question of strategy and of approach here, because this is not such a complex issue requiring that much motivation or that much elaboration.

What is the problem with that long and detailed a motivational introduction? It is not simply that it is too long, because it is not repetitive; the author does not keep saying the same thing. He tells you, "Look at all these real-life problems. There are solutions. You may think that there are no solutions, but that is because you have a certain theory of the moral and the practical. Before I tell you what my theory of the moral and the practical is, here, in brief, are my solutions to these problems. On inflation, I would say this, on the energy crisis I would say this, on Iran I would say this, and so on. You may object that this violates so-and-so, but that is because you have a wrong theory that goes back to ancient Greece. . . ." As this continues, what is happening to the mind of the reader is that the crow epistemology is asserting itself. The author is pouring it on, and the reader does not yet have anything to attach to. Someone who does not know the answer, and is just trying to read it, will feel so many unanswered questions piling up in his mind that he will tune out under the growing pressure. The main objection to the introduction, then, is that the author chose a motivation that would really be interesting if he were writing a book. Then he could say, "I am going to answer everything by reference to this, and I will dedicate one chapter to showing you all kinds of questions and historical background and so on. Take your time, go out and have coffee, go to bed now, and tomorrow we will come back." But as written, it overwhelms the reader.

An alternative approach to motivation for this subject, one that would not put that type of pressure on the reader, might be to give a few examples. But I do not even think a few are necessary. In fact, I am not convinced that in this case even one example is needed as a motivation, because everybody knows the issue of the moral and the practical. Everybody has heard, and most people have repeated: "It may be moral, but it is not practical; the two are opposed to each other." The essence of this paper is therefore a frontal attack on a bromide that most people accept. They know that it is an important issue; they know that they preach things as moral that they would not dream of acting on and that they would be in real trouble if they had to live by. Therefore, they think: "This is an obvious truth, so it is certainly intriguing if this author says that my whole viewpoint is wrong." In other words, on this type of well-known moral issue, when your position is so revolutionary, very little is needed to motivate an audience. You just simply have to come in head-on and say, in effect, "You think you can say that something is moral but not practical, and you live by that. I say that that viewpoint is flat wrong, it is leading to disaster, and the moral and the practical always go together." Putting the point intriguingly, virtually that briefly, will pick up anybody's interest.

Another possibility would be to give one example—just one, such as inflation or socialized medicine—where people think the moral and the practical diverge, and then to say they do not diverge. Even that would create a certain pressure, though, because the reader would have to hold the example in mind until you went through the theory and then came back to how your theory resolves the apparent conflict. You would have to choose the example well. But if you try to make your paper convincing by giving example after example of domestic and foreign policy, as this author has, you have to show that your theory provides the answer to *all* of these examples, which is impossible. This author does not, in fact, even try to do it. He simply says, in effect, "Here is my answer to all of these. It does not convince you? If you saw my theory, it would convince you." He then takes a quick shot at the theory and says, "Let us apply this to capitalism"— which itself is a gigantic, controversial issue. But he cannot even begin to undertake the arguments to defend capitalism as a tail-end example of the moral and the practical, so he asks the reader to do it. That, though, is the kind of thing the *writer* should do, namely apply his abstraction.

In short, then, the opening of this paper, while well-intentioned, is just prohibitive. It undertakes such a massive assignment that even the most brilliant writer in the world, one who knew the theory inside and out, could not do it plausibly in this space. One positive aspect, though, is the sixth paragraph, the one that ends with the reader thinking, "Oh, I thought he meant *practical* solutions." It is very effective if you can make the reader experience for himself, "Oh, yes, I *do* believe there is a dichotomy between the moral and the practical," because then you have really hooked him. But it should be possible to get him to grasp that there is this problem right at the outset, without such a lengthy discussion.

Let us now turn to this sentence in the paragraph that follows: "In other words, the moral and the practical are identical." That statement is unclear, because if those two things are identical, the immediate question is: Why have both concepts? Is one of those terms superfluous, or are they synonyms? If you are going to discuss the relation of the moral and the practical, somewhere or other you have to indicate the actual connection between the two. Simply stating outright that they are identical leaves a lot of unanswered questions. The moral and the practical certainly do not clash with each other, but not clashing is not the same as being identical.

Four paragraphs later, the author writes, "The view that there is a dichotomy between the moral and the practical is more widespread than any particular moral or practical philosophy." At minimum, that is a debatable proposition. The idea of a moral-practical dichotomy depends so overwhelmingly on one particular philosophy that it is misleading to say that the root is more widespread than any one moral philosophy. In point of fact, the root of this idea is in some form of altruism or self-sacrifice. Some form of self-sacrifice, whether to God or society, has been people's idea of what constitutes morality for thousands of years, with only occasional, vague elements of a more Greek, pro-egoist ethics. If you hold the former view, then you are necessarily doomed to a moral-practical dichotomy, because self-sacrifice is not a way of living on earth, but an attack on everything required to live on earth—the sacrifice of the mind, of independence, of wealth, of happiness. Therefore, people who hold that code are necessarily put in the position that what the code re-quires is one form of existence, and what actual life requires is another (which, in fact, is true). Insofar as they try to live, then, they have a fun-damental inconsistency built into their viewpoint: There is that which is required to be good, and that which is required to live. Nothing other than that truly and persistently underlies the moral-practical dichotomy. Both sides of the argument in this paper are examples of this. The people who think that capitalism is moral but not practical do so because of a warped view of selfishness—they think big companies will run wild and gobble up the consumers, and everyone will starve because of the rapa-cious greed of the capitalists. That is simply an altruist projection of what egoism would consist of. The other side, of course, explicitly says that capitalism is immoral because it ignores the need to sacrifice for the sake of the needy. So both sides, whether they call capitalism impractical or immoral, do so on the grounds that the good is self-sacrifice. On this author's own example, then, I think that the source of the moral-practical dichotomy is clearly that one moral issue.

The author now goes into the mind-body dichotomy as the source of this view, providing a certain history, as it were, on the metaphysical level. But the reference to two worlds, two realities, and so on at this point in the paper raises a certain problem. As yet, we do not know the correct view on the question of the moral and the practical. The reader, presumably, still thinks it obvious that there are many cases of things that are moral but not practical, and vice versa. The author has just given him an example regarding which he will probably ally himself on one side or another. The reader thinks, "This is very plausible; obviously, there is a clash between the moral and the practical. I would like to see how he is going to get out of that one." The author then says, "Now, the source of this is a profound metaphysical view that goes back to Greece." To the reader, that will not be plausible. He will think, "Who needs a big metaphysical view to explain this? It is just *right*—the moral and the practical are obviously in conflict with each other. We do not need Platonic Forms or whatever to explain that; just look around." The general rule, therefore, is: Do not bring in philosophy as an explanation until your reader appreciates the *need* for an explanation. There was a parallel to this same problem in the paper on the primacy of consciousness. The introduction cited Kennedy's behavior as an example of the primacy of consciousness, and then right away made it look as though an avowed issue of metaphysics in Kennedy's mind was the cause. That is simply implausible, because people would not see that you *need* that kind of complex explanation. The same is applicable here.

Ultimately, if you wanted to explain where altruism and anti-life ethics come from, you would have to say that they come from an attack on this world and on man's life in this world, an attack that has to rest on some supernatural dimension. Therefore, these ethics do rest on a certain metaphysics without which, directly or indirectly, you could not preach self-sacrifice. But it is not clear to people that that would be so, or that that is necessary, if they still are at the stage where they think a given ethical issue is obvious. Consequently, first you have to come in simple and say, "You think that this issue is so obvious, that there is a conflict. I take the opposite view." You do not even need an example. Then you present your view and make mincemeat of their original view. They then get to the stage of thinking, "This is a really fantastic mistake on my part; I wonder where this mistake could have come from." Only then do you say, "Now, if you want to know where you got that viewpoint, you are, in effect, the unconscious product of Plato," and so on—at which point, hopefully, the reader will be horrified and rush out to de-Platonize himself. But much of this is an issue of placement, and that is why the author of the present paper has inadvertently created a countermotivational element. He is giving his readers material that they will not really see that they need if they do not already understand his view.

We now get to the essence of the theory, so let us leave aside the author's introduction and take this as he presents it. " 'Practical' means something that works to achieve a specific goal. It implies a goal or a standard by which to judge if something works." That is certainly true, but how is that related, then, to the term "moral"? "Moral" also implies some standard by which to judge. We are back to the question that came up when the author said that the moral and the practical are identical, namely: What is the actual relation between the term "moral" and the term "practical"? That is a very important thing for you to know in your own mind, even if you do not put it in your paper. Without that being clear in your mind, you are not clear as to whether morality and practicality are two independent realms, or whether they happen to coincide, or whether they are actually two words for the same thing, or whether one is the cause and one is the effect, or what.

If I were to answer that question, I would say that the concept "practical" is much broader and more general than the concept "moral," because "practical" simply means "that which works or succeeds, that which leads to a desired goal or result." You could, therefore, apply the concept "practical" in cases where the term "moral" would not even come up. For instance, the wheel is practical. That does not mean the wheel is moral (or immoral), obviously, but it is a practical invention—if transportation is the goal, the wheel is a very good means toward that end. On the other hand, a perpetual-motion machine, or the attempt to create one, is impractical, because it will not lead to the end in question. Similarly, physics is practical, but astrology is impractical. That is to say, if the standard is knowledge and control of the physical world, one leads to that end and the other does not. So the author is right that the practical is that which works to achieve a specific goal, but it does not necessarily yet come down to anything so specific as human action.

When we get to morality, though, we are talking about a specific code to govern human action in those matters that depend upon human choice. We do have to say that some codes of morality would be practical, in this sense, and others would not be. In the present context, "practical" means efficacious, successful, able to achieve one's goals and values; that is, by any theory, what a practical man is. Some moral codes, then, would enable man to achieve his goals and be efficacious, and others would not; some would be like the wheel, and some would be like the perpetual-motion machine; and, therefore, some codes of morality would be practical, and some would not. Suppose, for instance, that you hold a code in which the primary virtue is prayer. You can thus hold certain goals, like wealth and health and so on, and whenever they are threatened, or whenever you want to take action, you should get down on your knees and simply face Mecca and wait. Now, there is a certain moral code that recommends hope and prayer and faith as very high virtues, but that is obviously not practical. It is not the means required in order to achieve human values, namely a certain kind of thought in action, a certain kind of use of reason. Obviously, then, if you are going to have a moral code that is practical, one that enables you to achieve your values, that code has to extol, as a serious virtue, the actual human faculty that enables man to achieve values, which is reason, and then some elaboration of that—thought, independence, and so on.

Further, suppose you adhered to the kind of moral code that held this: "It is okay to think how to achieve values, and even to go out and get them, but the instant you get them, you should destroy them"—would that be practical? Or, "The more you achieve your values, the more you should torture yourself, and thereby prevent yourself from enjoying them or achieving any further; you should first want something desperately, and then work as hard as you can to get it—and then, just when you are on the threshold of getting it, you should cut your own throat." You would not call that a practical code, by any definition of "practical," because if the definition is "enables you to achieve your values," a code that counts cutting your own throat as the highest virtue obviously wrecks practicality. There is such a code, and its exact name is *sacrifice*. If you know Ayn Rand's elaboration and analysis of the term "sacrifice," you know that if you are indifferent to something and you give it up, that is not a sacrifice; but if you burn passionately for it and *then* you give it up, so that you feel the knife turning, then that is a sacrifice. That is the actual antithesis of practicality, which is the reason that the dominance of altruism and self-sacrifice has led to this dichotomy.

I am not going to go through the whole of Objectivism here, but what I want you to see is that "practicality" is the broader term, and then different codes of ethics have to establish their credentials with regard to practicality by whether they do or do not advocate those policies that enable man actually to achieve values. In this regard, a moral code that advocated all those things that lead consistently to the achievement of values, and did not countenance any policies that lead volitionally to failure or self-destruction, would be perfect. Therefore, if you determine what those policies are that lead consistently to the use of man's means of survival aimed exclusively at the achievement of values for his own sake, then you have got complete, consistent action on principles that will achieve your values. That is practicality. And that is rational egoism, as against any form of anti-reason or anti-selfishness. So I would say that in principle, the Objectivist morality has to be practical—not all moralities, but the Objectivist morality.

The author of this paper does, in effect, try to say this. He writes that morality is necessary because it is not enough to want to be practical; you have to live a certain way, and "Morality is the theory behind practicality's practice." If the right context had been established, that statement would be fine. In other words, you can look at it as, "You want to achieve values? Morality tells you what is required." But the discussion here is not as convincing as it could be. For one main thing, it is too brief. The author does not do what I, in effect, have just done: namely show us why certain principles are necessary by the nature of what practicality is. Since he did not begin by separating the two concepts, it goes by so fast that it is not very clear.

Aside from its brevity, there is another reason this discussion is not too convincing. What is desperately needed to make this point clear is *contrast*. I cannot emphasize that principle enough. If you want to say, "This theory leads to practicality," it is infinitely clearer if you say, "as against this other type of theory." Then the person can see set up, "If I follow this, it leads there, and if I do not, that leads there." The fact of the difference makes the original much clearer. The author of this paper did draw a certain contrast, in a generalized way. But by having it precede this, and doing it in metaphysical rather than ethical terms, he makes it so diffuse that it does not really serve that purpose.

I want to clarify a couple of points on the philosophy here. When I say Objectivism is practical, does that mean that any moral man who follows the Objectivist code will, therefore, necessarily be practical? In other words, if you subscribe to Objectivism, are you in effect guaranteed practicality hereafter, because that simply is the same thing as morality—something that is implied when you say, as this author has, that they are identical concepts? I want to clarify that they are not. You can be one hundred percent moral and fail. Practicality is a hard question of your existence in reality—did you get your goals or not? If you do not get them, you did not succeed; you failed; you were not efficacious; you were impractical. What could make a perfectly moral man, one who lived up to every Objectivist virtue, nevertheless fail? One possibility is errors of knowledge. Morality tells you, in this regard, to use your mind to the fullest, as your best possible chance of achieving values, but it does not guarantee that you are always going to use your mind correctly. You might make a perfectly innocent error of knowledge and fail as a result, even fail very badly. There is no God, and you are not rewarded for having good intentions. Another factor that may prevent you from succeeding even though you are completely moral is other men. If what you want is a goal that in any way depends on other men, either on their cooperation or on their leaving you alone, it cannot be guaranteed to you simply because you are virtuous. Howard Roark in *The Fountainhead*, for instance, had an enormous struggle, even in a free country, and if he had died earlier, he would have failed. Finally, along with errors of knowledge and other people's irrationality, there is, after all, physical nature. The world does not consist only of our minds and other people's minds. You and everybody can be completely, utterly moral, but if you get hit by a meteor, that is the end. Morality does not do anything about earthquakes and diseases and the like. It may be true that if you are completely rational, you will not be subjected to psychosomatic ailments and so on, but rationality still is not a guaranteed protection against physical reality. The point, then, is this: Nothing can guarantee practical success. All you can ask of an ethics is that it do everything possible, within the realm of those things open to your judgment, to promote successful action. If it does, it qualifies as practical.

The moral and the practical, then, are not identical concepts. If you call them identical, you will have a real temptation to think, "If I am moral, I have to be practical, because the two are the same," and then the next consequence is that you will be disappointed, because you did your moral thing and it did not work. There is even a usage in which you can call somebody practical but not moral—not an Objectivist usage, but still a usage, one that creates still another complication. For instance, suppose you took *The Fountainhead* and stopped reading at the beginning of Part

Two. Roark is thus left at the point where he is at the quarry, while Keating has got every practical goal he claimed to want, including wealth, fame, and prestige. Keating is "practical" and Roark is not, so one is a failure and the other is not. Now, the point of *The Fountainhead* is that these concepts apply long-range, across the whole pattern of a life. But take any short-range moment—a criminal might get away with robbing a bank, and a virtuous man might be frustrated and thrown into jail unjustly. So if you apply those terms in a very narrow, short-range way, there is not even a parallel between the moral and the practical. You need to make clear when you are talking about the short term and when you are talking about the long-range, philosophic view.

Note that you could say, regarding the example from *The Fountainhead*, that Roark is the practical man while Keating is not. You can distinguish a sense of the term "practicality" with regard to possessing the equipment or the capacity or the developed abilities to achieve your goals. In other words, you are in tune with reality, you have self-esteem, you have confidence in your own judgment, you have a developed intellectual capacity, you know what you want—you are, in effect, like a mechanism perfected to be able to achieve its goals. In that sense, you are practical as a potentiality. You have to distinguish that from the notional guarantee that in any given concrete, you necessarily are going to succeed with that equipment. But you could say, for instance, if you mean "practical" in this way, that Roark is a practical person and Keating is not. That is compatible with saying that in any given stage of their lives, Roark has not yet succeeded in achieving his goal and Keating has (leaving aside the question of what Keating's goal is, and whether he ever gets whatever he is really after).

I would not say that all of this has to go into this paper. But enough should go in so that we understand what it is about Objectivism that entitles it to claim the compatibility with practicality, why it alone is the ethics that is practical. Restrict your claims so that you are not implying that you guarantee practical success under all circumstances. To make it clear, you would have to make the contrast to an opposing code, as above.

A good question to consider is how to distinguish egoism of a kind that is practical—namely, rational self-interest—from the egoism of Nietzsche and his ilk, which is not. There is a way of wording it that excludes the arbitrary, whim worship, and so on. You need not come at it headlong, saying, "There are twelve theories of egoism and I advocate theory X for these reasons," but simply say always "rational," "in accordance with facts," "by your best judgment," and so on. Those are ways of indicating, "I distinguish myself from another type of egoism, but I am not discussing it here." You see that this is a really tricky assignment, because you have to discuss morality in a framework in which you have no time to establish it, in the teeth of a completely opposite view that dominates people.

Let us turn to the last part, where the author gives an example of how the moral and the practical go hand in hand. An example would be a good thing to show how they go hand in hand, after the theory has been presented, but there is something wrong with this particular example. An example has one overriding function, and that is to concretize, to clarify, to let the reader grasp your point in the simplest possible way. The simplest way may not be the most interesting way, nor an exciting way. But ideally, you choose an example that is intelligible, self-contained, objective, and also sexy, in the sense of arousing people's interest. But if you just cannot think of an example that combines intelligibility and sexiness, you have to go with the more prosaic but intelligible example, because cognition comes before excitement. The reader has to be able to follow your point. Here, the reader is struggling with this very broad abstraction—the moral and the practical—and the example given is capitalism. That is a mammoth subject; it is not just one aspect of morality; it is the whole field of politics. There are so many confusions on that subject that everything you say, in theory and in practice, raises more questions than anything you might say about the moral and the practical.

This is supposed to be an example of the practicality of a certain morality. But if it is practicality, it is so abstract that it is not very convincing as practicality; it reads more like moral theory. For instance, "What conditions do I need to be confident of success in life?" Surely that is abstract moral theory, indistinguishable from the basic question of ethics, "What conditions do I need for success in life?" Similarly, the author's other questions—"Can I produce what I need? Can I plan? What will happen if I am not allowed to act according to my own judgment?"—are all very broad abstractions. If a person is not convinced by this author's broadest abstraction, namely rationality and egoism as prerequisites of achieving values, it is unlikely that he is going to be convinced on this level, which is just one step less general. The author was forced onto this level, though, because he took as his example such a vast subject as an entire, very controversial political system. He could not deal with it in any concrete way, because that would require a whole book, so he had to deal with it in terms of broad abstractions. He was thus left in the position of confessing that "the compelling practical importance of the above argument might be easier to grasp if the argument is examined in a less abstract light." That is certainly true, but that is the author's mind telling him that he really must concretize this and show its connection to practicality as people would use the term "practical." But then he realizes that he cannot do it, because to discuss the practicality of capitalism in concrete terms is out of the question in an essay of this length. So he says, "The reader should try." In other words, it amounts to, "I cannot really show you that the moral is the practical, but I will give you a few intermediate-level abstractions, and good luck; you work it out."

If you are going to use an example, you want the most down-to-earth, concrete type of example that you can possibly find, to tie the discussion right down to something specific. When you argue that something is moral and then say, "And besides that, it is practical," what you really convey is that that thing actually works in reality, that it leads concretely to certain results. Therefore, the best thing to do would be to take something, some one government law, for instance, and say, "I am going to show that this is immoral *and* impractical." (You could do it positively, but negatively would be a good way to do it.) Your whole point would then be to show that the impracticality follows from the immorality. You would then really convince people, "Here is an actual, concrete case in which people disobeyed a certain moral principle, and here is why that led to actual disaster."

As an example, take socialized medicine. It works out to be a very good example, because you can indicate briefly why it is immoral according to the principles of the ethics that you hold. You can also show that it involves the use of force, the elevation of need above ability, and so on. You can do that briefly, and then show that the very things that make you decide that socialized medicine is immoral doom it to failure in actual reality: The better doctors desert the system because they cannot function under those conditions—a direct consequence of the requirements of the mind, and the fact that this is force, and therefore anti-mind; the worse people, the malingerers and their ilk, suddenly multiply, and there appear masses of patients who cannot be treated because they no longer have to earn what they get, so the injustice manifests itself in the complete impossibility of treating them, and so on. Socialized medicine is, therefore, a simple case in which the very violation of abstract moral principles dooms it to practical failure. Such an example becomes very convincing if it is appended to a broader discussion of the moral and the practical. But even that small sample would take you a page and a half. Capitalism, with everything that involves, would be prohibitively long. That is why I again felt the crow asserting itself at the end of this paper; there is just more here than anybody could take in.

I have just one final comment. The very last sentence reads, "The moral principles and practical conclusions are based on the same premises." The author was, in effect, struggling to connect the moral and the practical, but he did not always word it the same way, which means that, in his own mind, he was not exactly clear on the relationship; at one point they were identical, and then they were based on the same premises, and then one led to the other. That confusion is normal. I do not think there is one philosophic idea that I myself did not go through exactly that process of development in trying to understand. That is, I would try to write it out, and one paragraph would come out saying two points were cause and effect, and the next paragraph that they were effect and cause, and in the next paragraph they were the same, and in the next paragraph one was a concrete and the other was a broader abstraction—and all I knew was that they went together *somehow*, but I did not have a clear idea as to how. Learning was a painful process of trying to figure out which of all these is correct, what actually is the relationship, and why do I think it is a little bit of this and a little bit of that. It was an agonizing process across many, many years, one concept at a time. Nor did I ever find any spillover. That is, if I got clear on the relation between two concepts, it never helped on the next two. It was kind of a lifelong thing. But you do finally get certain basic ideas, and then the others become examples. No one should feel bad about feeling this kind of confusion, because it is unavoidable at the beginning of writing.

In sum, I do think there are definitely virtues to this paper. The particular virtues are the author's intention of tying his subject to what people are interested in, and the fact that he did, in one way or another, get his essential point in. But by not relating the moral and the practical exactly, and by not establishing any contrast, he left a certain vagueness. Finally, the overriding problem is the sheer length of the motivation and the examples, which completely violate the crow epistemology and therefore swamp the reader.

"Racism" (Appendix F)

I think there are a lot of good things in this paper, including a lot of good condensation of complex material.

For one thing, the level of abstraction is good. The author at no point degenerates into broad abstractions; you always know what he is talking about. There were some cases in which he does not use the abstractions exactly correctly—he has a tendency to condense certain issues that require distinction—but on the general level, it is all right in that regard. There is also a quality of passionate reasonableness. There is a definite intensity, a sincerity, a conviction to this paper; and it is also intellectual, because the author defines his terms and connects basic issues to wider moral and political issues. It is thus a union of reason and emotion, an honestly felt and intellectually expressed paper.

One of the best things about this paper is its no-nonsense quality. The author begins with, "Let us start by saying what racism is," and he says unequivocally and very well what racism is. He has a definite structure that you can follow: He tells you what racism is, then says, "Now the question is, is this right? An emphatic *no!*" then asks what is wrong with it at the root, what does it lead to, and so on, and then he goes on to the other aspect of racism, which is collectivism. He has a definite purpose ruling him throughout.

As to motivations, the entire motivation of this paper is the first paragraph, and that is perfectly adequate. You do not have to make a big production about a topic such as racism, because it is obviously a current issue, on everybody's mind, and therefore it is not that esoteric and academic. The only issue I would raise about the introduction is that the author has a tendency in his wording to make it sound like this is going to be primarily a psychological rather than a philosophical paper. That is, instead of saying, "What is racism, and is it right or wrong?" he says, "Why do people hold this idea, and what can we do to stop them?" He thus gears us more to expect a psychological paper about motives and so on—topics he does cover, but only briefly at the end, the main thrust being philosophical. So the opening paragraph is slightly misleading in the direction it points, but that is not a major problem.

The discussion of racism is very well put. It is in the author's own words, it is essentially accurate, and I like the conjunction of the mind and the body ("the content of his mind is inherited and indicated by an aspect of his body"), which I think is implied in any form of racism. A racist may, in fact, be a materialist; he may deny that man even has a mind, or that he holds ideas at all; he may say he simply acts by blood. But from our perspective, since we accept that there is a mind, the racist does imply that you have no choice over the mind, and that your genetic structure determines its content. So the author of this paper is defining racism in a way that not necessarily every racist would agree with, but what it actually is from his perspective, and that is perfectly legitimate and, I think, very well-done. I particularly liked this sentence, which I found illuminating: "By definition, racism is both a form of determinism and collectivism." I knew that racism is, by definition, a form of collectivism, but that it is also, by definition, a form of determinism stopped me for a minute, because I had never thought of that connection. But the preceding paragraph really established the context, namely that man has no control over his mind; and this paragraph explains that his mind, and so on, are all determined by his ancestors, and therefore he really has no choice; and it is really implicit in the doctrine that the individual is nothing, just a fragment of the group. I found that clarifying, and therefore I would like to make a big point of praising this author for that, because I think that's a very economical and intelligent way of making the point. So I give very high grades for this paper's analysis of what racism is.

There is, though, a question about how the author relates racism to collectivism. Here he says it is a *form* of collectivism, which is correct, but later he has a tendency to *equate* it with collectivism, which is not. Collectivism is the broader term. Communism would be a form of collectivism that is not racism. Communists claim that they do not accept blood or skin color or any physiological criterion. They *do* divide men into groups, and they do say that the individual is nothing but a member of the group and that his whole existence is to serve the group. In that sense, they are collectivists. But the preeminent group for communism is not a racially defined group, but an economically defined group, namely the proletariat. You could make a case—and in fact, I think it is true—that every collectivist ultimately will end up as a racist. I do not think it is an accident that, for instance, anti-Semitism is so strong in Russia, that racist feeling is growing in Britain as they get more and more socialistic, and so on. So I think you can make a case that racist doctrines will start to proliferate when collectivism of *any* kind takes place in a society. But that does not mean that the two doctrines are synonymous. Technically and philosophically, racism is one form of collectivism. The reason, of course, that racism would begin to develop wherever collectivism of any kind takes place is that it is the most primitive form of collectivism, as Ayn Rand has explained. If you tell men that they have to huddle in a group, that they are nothing, then on that perceptual-level mentality, which is what collectivism appeals to, the worldwide proletariat is infinitely too big an abstraction and has no reality to them. They are, therefore, going to huddle in the group that is the folks next door, people who are exactly like them, and they are going to be hostile to all so-called outsiders or aliens. It is thus not an accident that racism coexists with collectivism, but it is important to understand that technically they are not the same.

Now, how do you relate the term "tribalism" to "collectivism"? (I do not mean to make this a course in language, but when you start writing, you have to know your key terms and how they are interconnected.) "Collectivism" is broader and "tribalism" is more narrow. All tribes are racial. A tribe is, if you take it in the literal sense, a group of people of the same race in a given geographic area. The two terms are thus similar in that respect. But we can use "tribalism" more broadly than "racism" for a certain kind of mental attitude of belonging to the group and ignoring your own individuality, effacing your own individuality and merging with others, without that necessarily specifically implying racism. Tribalism is really a kind of primitive, pre-philosophic phenomenon. It is simply the phenomenon of a person merging into the group around him without intellectual justification, simply because they are there; they are the folks around him, they are what he knows, and who is he to assert himself or question things? "Collectivism," on the other hand, is the more philosophical term. When that tribalist mentality enters the scene of philosophy and says what is real and what is not, what is important and what is not, and how man should live, and translates all that into an abstract viewpoint, that is what we call collectivism. So the two terms are definitely related, but "collectivism" is the more abstract, philosophical term.

In this paragraph, we should also note that it is not always wrong to use some of these expressions if the context is available for you. For instance, "the Asian mind." If you use that in a racial way to imply that it is an innate endowment caused by their ancestors, that is obviously wrong.

But there are many contexts in which you can talk about "the Western mind versus the Oriental mind," by which you mean the dominant ideas pervading the culture, recognizing that those are volitionally chosen and not racially motivated. Do not assume that every one of these expressions, in every context, exemplifies racism.

Finally, at the end of this paragraph, the author is correct when he writes that a racist would think a man guilty by his birth into a given race, but by the same token, if a man is thought *superior* by birth, that is equally racist. It can work positively or negatively. Whether you judge a person positively or negatively, if you judge him only by race, that is racist. Whether you say the Jews are inferior or the Aryans are superior, strictly by blood and race, that is racist either way.

The author of this paper now asks, "Is man the collectivized product of his ancestors?" Nowhere, however, does he give a definition of what exactly is meant here by "collectivized," or by "collectivism." In terms of the fundamental use of the term, where it is not simply a synonym for some other term that already exists, of the four major branches of philosophy, collectivism *primarily* belongs to politics (with some overlap with morality). Collectivism, in essence, is the view that the group comes above the individual, that it is more important and more valuable than the individual, and that the individual should therefore live to serve the group. That view rests on a certain view of the mind, on a certain view of reality, and, obviously, on the ethics of sacrifice. But it is specifically sacrifice with the group as the beneficiary, with that as the guide to how you organize society. It holds that you should organize society according to the idea that a given type of group is a supreme value, its representatives should be all-powerful, its will should have no limits, and every individual is simply a means to it.

If you understand that, you will see that when the author writes, "Is he the collectivized product of his ancestors?" he is not using the term "collectivized" in its primary sense. He is actually using it here in a metaphysical sense—that is, "Is he in effect nothing but a fragment of the group?" He is using it in terms of *what* man is, whereas the essence of collectivism—including racism, which is one of its essential forms—is an *evaluative* issue. There is thus a slight imprecision. In any event, the author would have been better advised, if he knew that determinism and collectivism were the two areas that he was really going to hit, to define each explicitly. Philosophic terms are very slippery, and all the branches and issues of philosophy are interconnected; you have to be careful that the words do not get away from you. Therefore, I like to hammer down the guidelines in advance. And if my theme is, "Determinism and collectivism are the two big points in this topic," then I want to define each, at least in my own mind, and be sure I make that clear to the reader.

In the next paragraph, the author gives his answer to the determinist argument. But since he introduces it as the collectivized one as well, I was slightly thrown off; I never found the answer directly to the collectivized one. Let us assume, then, that he is just discussing determinism. This paragraph undertakes a difficult assignment, which is to make plausible, in a brief space, that thinking is volitional and determinism is false. That is very hard to do, because it is either common sense or wildly controversial—either you simply state that man has free choice and take it as obvious, or you go into an elaborate argument about how there have been all these determinists, but they are wrong, and so on. This author tried a middle ground, and he came very close to getting away with it. He wants to give some indication of why determinism is wrong. The way I would do it is to bring in the term "automatic," which is something that most people recognize. In other words, if you are going to try this with such brevity, I would say something like, "Man's nature is his ability to reason, which involves the use of concepts. Obviously, concepts are not automatic; they do not just pop into our minds without effort. We have to work; it takes choice." In other words, I would keep the same intention of tying free will to the conceptual nature of man, which is really the philosophic issue, but do it a little more simply and commonsensically, and not rely so much on terms like "integrating his perceptions," which might either scare off or baffle the reader. But this is a very difficult thing, and within the framework of what he could do, this author did quite well.

When he gets to "a man's *character* is self-made and independent of his forefathers," though, he raises a big problem. The point is certainly true, but character is not the same as mind. If he had said "a man's *mind* is self-made," that would have been fine; he could have gone on from there with no problem. But "character," as a term, involves more than simply your mental processes; it also involves your actions and above all your *emotions*—your desires, your feelings, what you want and do not want. It is very difficult to get people to see, in a brief space like this, that the way they act and feel is actually determined by their thought, because that raises the whole question of reason and emotion. Nor is it needed here, because simply sticking to "Your *mind* is self-made" leaves character to implication. The term "mind" will carry the reader to thinking, "This person runs his own life," and only when he finishes the paper will he think, "He did not discuss character," at which point you say, "You can come back for my next paper for that one." Raising it here, though, will cause people to think, "Wait, he never said anything about character."

The last sentence in this paragraph is also problematic. How does the author get to "has certain fundamental rights by nature"? How does it follow, from the fact that determinism is false, that man has certain rights? It does not; that is a non sequitur. Let us suppose that I agree with the author: Man has free will; he is self-made; he is independent. All kinds of people believe that without believing in rights. What is the connection? Is it because man has free will that he has rights, or is it because of something more basic?

The reason free will is such an important issue, as well as the reason we have to have rights, is that the mind is man's means of survival. The importance of free will is simply to validate the mind—to say you really *do* have a mind, and you have to exercise it. If determinism were true, it would amount to the negation of the mind. It would mean we are just like animals: We just sit there; we do not have to think; we have no choices; we are a nonconceptual species. Free will versus determinism is like a skirmish on the side; the main fight is reason versus anti-reason. There are a dozen different ways of annihilating or undercutting reason; for example, "Man has free will, but since his senses are completely invalid, his reason is worthless. So he can do whatever he wants with his free will, and we can do whatever we want with him—we can use our free will to smash his free will, and what's the difference?" You have to keep your eye on the main point here, which is that man is a *rational* being. Determinism is an assault on that, and therefore, you do have to fight for free will. But the reason man requires rights is not simply that he is free; it is that he is a conceptual being who has to think in order to survive.

There is also a certain conjunction in this paragraph that confuses two different things. The author writes that man has certain fundamental rights: life, property, and "to be judged on the basis of his self-initiated actions." That is a mixture of morality and politics. Two of those rights are political—namely, life and property—because they simply mean that you have the right to act a certain way and other people have to leave you alone. But you cannot have a *political* right to be judged by others as an individual. You cannot have a political right to other people's thoughts. They have a right, a political right, to be irrational. Their rights stop when they try to initiate force against you or against anyone else, when they try to legislate or compel other people to agree with them. But you have to make very clear, in a paper such as this, that the only rights man can have are the rights to action and to the products of his action. There can never be a right to other people's thoughts. You can say morally, "If someone views me simply as a racial manifestation, I think that is evil and I think he is evil." That, however, is a different question. You can say he has no right to do it in the same way that he has no right to lie, or no right to drink his brains out, or no right to countless forms of irrationality—*morally*. Politically, though, he has a right, and you cannot mix those two things together.

The author's next paragraph, on determinism as anti-reason, is very good, with only this question: At the very end, the statement "it is worse than irrational—it is immoral" is dubiously worded. Why is immorality worse than irrationality? Immorality, according to Objectivism, is a form of irrationality, so it cannot be worse than irrationality. The reason that morality is desirable is that it is dictated by reason. The superior of those two concepts, then, is "rationality," not "morality"; rationality determines morality. The author's statement is just a little hyperbolic.

The next paragraph indicates the problem that I mentioned before. The author lists some examples, and then says, "Will such events ever stop happening? Can the doctrines of determinism be defeated?"—thereby explicitly suggesting that the main issue is determinism. That is not the only issue, and it is not even the fundamental issue underlying racism; it is one issue. But the author himself said there are two, namely determinism and collectivism, and that the whole matter turns on that combination.

The author has just indicated in what way determinism is anti-reason; in what way is the issue of collectivism versus individualism related to reason? Collectivism subjugates the individual to society, and specifically it subjugates his mind. It tells him, in effect, "Your mind is nothing; its exercise is unimportant; you belong to the state, and you should do only what others tell you to do." Its advice is thus, "Stifle your mind in the name of a superior value." Individualism, by contrast, would say that the crucial thing is that you have to exist as an individual, because you exist by your mind, and the mind is an attribute of the individual. The issue of collectivism versus individualism thus also reduces back, by several steps, to the issue of reason versus anti-reason. So both determinism and collectivism are manifestations, in different branches of philosophy, of the same root issue. And therefore, by concentrating entirely on determinism instead of going to the root of what leads to racism and what explains both of the elements in it, this author ends up doing just a partial analysis. He is not wrong as far as he goes, but he missed the overall theme that would tie it all together.

Several paragraphs later, the author says, "It is, unfortunately, the same thing as discussed before—the race, the tribe, only now these things are clothed in the trappings of government." With this wording, he clearly implies that all statists are racists, something he said earlier he did not believe. There is a tendency in this paper to equate racism with collectivism and statism, which is not correct.

Two paragraphs down, the author is right when he says that collectivism negates the source and purpose of rights. But it negates them not because it is determinism, but because it is anti-mind, as discussed above. So regarding the connection made here between collectivism and determinism, the real way I would look at that connection is like this—determinism says your mind is nothing, and collectivism then comes in and says, "If so, then do not try to live by your mind, but adapt to what is around you and let others rule you." That is somewhat oversimplified, because there are many other doctrines. But you must understand that not everything comes from determinism, that there is a deeper issue. For instance, farther down the page the author writes, "Statism, then, is just another deadly variation of determinism." That is an explicit example of this very mistake. A statist can be an advocate of free will. Statism comes out of politics. Determinism comes, essentially, out of epistemology; it is a view of how the mind operates, and it says the mind has no choice. It is not possible for a political view to be a variation of an epistemological view. The most it could be is a consequence. And as I am saying, it is not even necessary to be a determinist to be a statist. A belief in free will is completely compatible with outright statism, as can be found throughout the history of philosophy. The existentialists, for instance, at least in some of their moods, say that man has free will, but the universe is unintelligible and existence is absurd, so there is no way for him to know what to do with his free will; life is therefore hell, and man is doomed to fear and trembling and nausea and dread, so the ideal thing for him to do is to throw himself at the feet of Fidel Castro, or Jean Genet,* or whoever. The existentialists are certainly classified as advocates of free will, but they are violently anti-mind, and by the same consequence they end up preaching statism, as Heidegger was a Nazi. It comes back to what the basic issue is. It is true that in order fully to capture racism, you have to include determinism. But in analyzing it, always go back to your fundamentals.

---

* Jean Genet (1910–1986), petty criminal turned author, much praised by Jean-Paul Sartre in his *Saint Genet: Actor and Martyr* (1952).

The author writes, "Since determinism dispenses with the signifi-cance of the mind, and since there is no such thing as innate knowledge, collectivism is left with nothing but whim, wish, and mysticism upon which to base a government." True enough, but is that objective? Take Marxism, for instance. Marxists certainly are collectivists, as well as de-terminists, and they not only dispense with the significance of the mind by implication, but say openly that there is no mind, that the mind is a bourgeois superstition. And they certainly do not believe in innate knowledge. So they would grant the entire first part of that sentence, and then say, "We most assuredly do not say government is based on whim, wish, and mysticism. We are based on science, on materialism. Ours is scientific socialism, based on the laws of the dialectic process; this is his-torically inevitable, given the trend of history." In other words, the author of this paper is presenting a view on a question that he has not yet shown is the only possible view on this question, and therefore the collectivists would say that he is completely distorting their position. He has not even tried to cover that type of thing, and he could not in this paper.

If you want to show that collectivism leads to arbitrary dictatorship, what would be a simple way to establish that? You know that collectivism denies individual rights. And if you know philosophy and you know your own philosophy, you know that rights are an expression of man's reason. Therefore collectivism denies rights, and so it denies reason. It has to deal with men by force. All you have to say is simply, "Collectivism denies rights, meaning that it does not have to deal with men by persuasion, but by force, and can override anybody's mind according to the whim of the ruler." You need to try to put these things in a self-contained way, so that you do not bring in other aspects of your view that you do not have time to discuss. It is very hard to do, and it takes a long time. The only way you get to that stage is to write something that you think is really clear and show it to somebody who does not agree with it; he will say, "That does not follow." Eventually you will automatize what will be clear and what will not.

One other thing in this paper requires comment, and that is the fifth paragraph from the end: "When the moral leaders of today call for sacrifice to the state, to any group or anyone, they are, in effect, calling for racism. That is why racism still continues." That is too simple a statement, because it rests on the author's equation of statism with racism. You could make a case that sacrifice would lead to racism, but not as simply as this. You could say that sacrifice prepares the ground on which racism develops. You would have to show that sacrifice leads to collectivism, and collectivism, by the mechanism we discussed at the beginning, engenders racism. But the main thing that engenders racism is anti-reason; that is what leads to sacrifice, determinism, collectivism, and all the rest. This, then, is an oversimplified statement.

My last comment on this paper regards the ending. It is unclear why the author goes into government at this point, unless it is simply that he could not resist the chance to get in a gratuitous plug for capitalism (something I can certainly sympathize with). It would be a more logical presentation to conclude on some note relating to racism, since that is the overall theme of the paper. If he had to get in capitalism, he would have had to end on some note like, "The only way to combat racism is the system based on reason, namely capitalism. For details, see my next book." As it is, he raises a lot of issues that are hard to establish.

In summary, I think that there were a lot of very good things in this paper. The main problem is really with regard to the thinking, not the exposition. It is simply the difficulty of dealing with so many different philosophic concepts and trying to see which is cause and which is effect, and what is concrete and what is abstract. In that regard, it is the same type of problem with the paper "The Moral and the Practical." And that is something that only a lot of experience can help with. You need to work painstakingly with one concept until you get a little clearer, and then another and then another, and after a while it comes to you.

CHAPTER 8

PRINCIPLES OF SPEAKING

IN THIS CHAPTER we are going to focus on oral presentation—that is, the presentation of ideas in spoken form, as against written. You will see that everything that we have learned so far about communication in general applies equally to oral communication, but the form is often different.

By "oral presentation," I mean extemporaneous delivery, as against taking a completely written-out statement or talk and simply reading it aloud. That is oral, in the sense that it is spoken rather than written, but it is kind of halfway between writing and speaking. I will say a few words about it at the end of this chapter, but our main topic is extemporaneous delivery. In this type of presentation, it is all right to have some brief notes or keywords as an aid or a jog to your memory, and I will say something subsequently about the kind of notes that would be helpful or appropriate. But you have nothing approaching written-out sentences. Essentially, in extemporaneous delivery, you are putting your ideas into words on the spot before the audience, rather than reading what you have prepared at home.

What is the value of extemporaneous presentation? There are several good features to it. For one thing, it is excellent practice in your own intellectual development and growth. It is equally excellent practice for writing, because it is practice in one crucial skill, namely putting your thoughts into words as clearly as possible. The essence of communication, if you break it down into steps, is that you first have an idea, but in an inchoate, undefined, unverbalized way; it is, in effect, like a prenatal idea, an idea that has not yet been born, which is experienced almost as a mental pressure in your head—you know something, but you have not yet found the words to state it. Then you grope, you struggle, you hesitate, you pick out a word focusing on your idea, until you finally express it exactly. That is involved in all communication, in any form. And that is exactly what extemporaneous presentation consists of. It is the pure process of finding words for your ideas. In this type of delivery, you have no time to concentrate on higher subtleties, such as style, editing, or polishing. That is out of the question in an extemporaneous delivery. You have just one basic imperative: "There are people sitting there, and somehow I have got to put this mental pressure into coherent words that they can grasp; I have to translate my thoughts into language." When you develop an ease or facility in this, you will find that it is helpful in all communication, including writing, because then, when you sit down, the writing of your rough draft becomes, in effect, like doing an extemporaneous talk. If you have developed the skill properly, the words will pour out of you (other things being equal), and then you can apply the later skill of editing. So it is very helpful to have practice in having to put your ideas into words without knowing the formulation in advance.

Another value of extemporaneous presentation is its sheer practicality. Most people can do much more of this than they can of writing, owing primarily to time. The preparation for extemporaneous delivery is brief. You just sketch down a few notes, and then you take the plunge. The main work is on the spot, rather than in advance. It is also a more practical form of expression, in that most people have more opportunity to use this than they do any other form of expression. There are any number of meetings, forums, gatherings, etc., at which you could spontaneously rise to give a two- or three- or five-minute statement of your views off-the-cuff. You could even do so in a living room or informal setting, as opposed to settings where you would be the invited speaker with the need for an official, prepared talk.

One further value of extemporaneous delivery is that audiences, as a rule, far prefer this kind of talk to one that is written out and read to them. There are many reasons for that, as we will see. But one of them is that there is a certain excitement to live presentation that a prepared talk virtually never equals, comparable to the difference between live TV and prerecorded broadcasts. There is a certain quality when you know it is live. It is not merely, as has sometimes been said, the hope of scandal—that is, the audience's hope that the speaker will go blank or say something outrageous. It is a certain sense that the presentation is happening *now*, and who knows what will come next, bad or good. You see the person actually functioning, right before your eyes, on his feet. It is a present event, as against one that was over and done last week. Among many other factors, it is also the case that in a live extemporaneous presentation, the audience knows that it is the center of attention; the people listening know that the speaker is aiming his comments at them, as opposed to just going on with a preset speech whether or not the audience follows, understands, or even hears him. So extemporaneous speaking is good practice for you; it is enjoyable to an audience, comparatively speaking; and you get a great many chances to use it, even if your field is not the professional communication of ideas.

I can say at the outset that everything we have already discussed about communication applies to extemporaneous presentation also. The similarities to written presentation are overwhelming. Whether you speak or write, it is a conceptual presentation, with everything that that involves. You have to take into account the audience's context; you have to remember the limits of what people can retain, i.e., the crow epistemology; you have to delimit your subject matter; you have to make your formulations self-contained; you have to motivate the audience; you have to have a structure; you have to concretize; and you have to be objective. All of this applies.

What is interesting, though, are the differences, those things that separate oral delivery (as I will call it from here on) from writing. Let me give it to you in the form of several differences.

Pace

Perhaps the most basic difference is that there is a difference of pace between oral delivery and writing. In all communication, as you know, the principle of the crow epistemology applies. The audience can hold only so much. There is always the potential problem of giving people more than they can retain or integrate, leading them to lose you. We have already seen the example of the sentence from Kant, as well as the case of a speaker who started an interesting talk with three tricky examples and then went on to the main theoretical point, overloading his audience. This is always an issue, in every form of communication. You always have to try to economize your units, to reduce the amount that the audience has to hold—whether it is the complexity of your sentences, the number of examples, or other factors. This is a much greater issue and problem in oral than in written communication. The problem of overloading is much more severe if your audience is listening to you. It is a difference only of degree, not of kind, from writing; but nevertheless, it is a big, important difference. *An audience at an oral presentation can retain or deal with fewer units.* This has to affect the whole presentation, specifically the pace or rate at which you offer your material. You have to slow down.

One major reason for this is that in writing, the audience can set its own pace. Whenever the reader needs a pause or a stop, he simply takes one. Even assuming that something is properly written, there are a number of reasons you, the reader, would have to stop and pause. Something might strike you as new. Some connection, for instance, strikes you; you get a side thought, and you want to pause for a moment to make a note of it. Another important reason is that people get tired. They need to rest, not necessarily for a long time, but maybe just enough to catch their breath and remind themselves where they are. You can stop frequently when you are reading somebody else's work. Another reason to pause might be that you come across a striking formulation. It is perfectly clear, it does not suggest any new implications to you, but you need a moment simply for the mental equivalent of saying, "My God!" or, "Gee, I never thought of it that way." The mental gears need time to click, as it were. Or you may get a puzzling formulation—not one that is the fault of the author, but maybe one with several aspects to it—and it takes you a second either to reread and say, "Oh, I see what he meant," or else to say, "I do not see it, but I will put it to one side and go on with the understanding that I do not get this point." Or the author may make a backward reference, such as, "As we saw in the last chapter," and you do not remember, so you have to stop and say, "What did we see in the last chapter?" Sometimes, too, you reach the end of a section, and your mind feels the need to pause and sum up.

These are some of the reasons why perfectly clear, well-organized, interesting writing can still give the attentive reader reason to pause. He certainly does not have to sit over every sentence, but every once in a while he needs a couple of seconds, without which he cannot absorb the material. This, by the way, is why I am profoundly opposed to the speed-reading method as applied to ideas. You may as well not even pretend to read if you use that method in which the finger just goes down the page and you turn the pages every five seconds. Attempting to read Ayn Rand, Kant, or anything in between that way is ludicrous. Reading necessitates the constant possibility of stops. They may be brief ones, but they are essential to enabling the mind to stay on track. The reader has to know where he is and what he thinks; he has to have a chance to monitor his own reactions. Everybody, in fact, does this in one way or another if he is trying to understand, although everybody will stop at different points, for different reasons, and for different lengths of time.

When you read, the pauses are under your own control. In oral presentation, however, the audience is at the mercy of the speaker. The audience may need just a very brief, fleeting pause to square the mental books, but a merciless speaker just goes right on. For one second, the audience's attention leaves the speaker's voice; there was one baffling thing, and the audience just paused mentally for one second to try to get what it was. Meanwhile, by the time people tune in again, the speaker has gone on to the next sentence. They lost the end of the sentence, they lost the point, and, if it was important enough, they lost him. This, of course, would be true whatever the category of reason for the pause. You might attempt to solve this by stopping after every sentence, but you cannot do that, because it is very often unnecessary and you would simply bore the audience wild. Besides, pauses vary from person to person according to their need for them, so that is not the solution.

Another reason that there is a necessary difference of pace between speaking and reading is the difference between seeing and hearing. Most people find hearing ideas much more difficult than seeing them in print. I know I do. One obvious reason is that in seeing, if you miss something, you can always go back. There is a certain basic security; the stuff is always there under your control; whereas in hearing, if you miss something, you are out of luck, because the speaker has gone on. In my view, though, there is a more fundamental issue involved. Sight is the sense that permits us to grasp entities. In that way, it is the basic sense bringing us into contact with the world (or, at least, one of two senses that do so, the other being touch). Sight conveys a kind of reassurance, a solidity, the idea of the dealable-with and that which is within one's control. Hearing, on the other hand, deals merely with a fleeting, transitory attribute—not an entity, but simply the sounds it makes—and therefore, the experience it provides is less solid, less absolute, less dealable-with. In any event, for whatever combination of factors, speaking is harder to take in than writing. The degree of concentration required, of sheer, unbreached focus on the audience's part, is greater.

We therefore have to recognize that there is a certain problem. Listeners are often unavoidably torn between the needs of their own consciousness in regard to the material and the demand of the speaker that he go on, and we have to know how to adapt the presentation of ideas to take this fact into account. We have to know how to reduce the pace of the presentation vis-à-vis writing. "Pace" here means not simply the rate of speaking, but the actual amount of material you cover in a given time to a given audience. The actual rate of data must be less, thereby relieving the audience of the need to concentrate so furiously. Writing can be supercondensed, and often the very condensation is what makes writing good—it makes it purposeful, lean, taut, fast; every word counts, as in a telegram. Speaking cannot be that way; the audience could not keep up with it. For example, if you are writing to your father, you might simply send a telegram saying, in pattern: "Broke, send cash." That would be okay in writing. But in speaking to him, leaving aside now questions of tact and so on, the same information would have to be fed like this, in pattern: "I spent all my money. I have nothing left. I need more. I would appreciate your help." In other words, you give the listener a moment to wander if necessary, to let his attention flag for a second; if he misses that you spent all the money, he tunes in when you say you have got nothing left. He can thus still keep up with you. In writing, however, it is his responsibility if he does not get it, because it is right there unequivocally. The way I look at it is that in writing, the audience is responsible for getting every word; in speaking, you are responsible for getting it into them.

I can give you a real-life example showing how I first discovered this. Many years ago, I was teaching a course that subsequently became *The Ominous Parallels*, and I had finally written out a certain lecture that I had always presented extemporaneously. I thought, "Oh, how terrific; I do not have to do anything now; I will just go to class and read aloud." And it was a revelation to me, because although the content was thoroughly prepared, the class was entirely baffled. I could feel that something completely wrong was going on, and yet the material was very clearly stated in every aspect; I could not figure it out. I will present it to you as is, and then show how I would give this exact same content to an audience orally, as opposed to in writing. This is one paragraph that actually appeared in *The Objectivist* as an excerpt in May of 1969. It comes at the end of my presentation of Hegel's philosophy and how Hegel is responsible for the Nazis. It says:

> While the Hegelian philosophy is the primary modern influ-
> ence responsible for Nazism, no philosopher can produce such
> a cataclysm single-handed. A complex series of lesser intel-
> lectual influences—both preceding and proceeding from
> Hegel—was involved in preparing the climate for the rise of
> the Nazis. The sum of such accessory influences determined
> the specific form of Hegelian statism prevalent in modern
> Germany. Some of the better-known of these influences are
> worth mentioning briefly.*

That is how I presented it in writing. Now, this is how I would say the
same thing orally:

> Hegel is the main influence, the big gun here. But no philoso-
> pher could do it alone. There were lots of others, lesser ones.
> Some came before him, some after. Together they made up the
> climate; they paved the way for the Nazis. Now let us look at
> some of these smaller fry for a moment.

You see that that is exactly the same content, but I have reduced the
pace, lengthened the time per unit, generally simplified, and made it
easier to take in. Later we will analyze the differences and the different
technique involved.

Exactness of Formulation

A second, crucial difference between an oral and a written presentation
is the exactness of formulation. We are speaking now of the difference
from the perspective of the speaker, rather than of the audience. In writing, you can choose the exact word or phrase you need. You can reach

---

* "Nazi Politics (IV)," *The Objectivist* (May 1969): 652.

perfect accuracy, because you have three stages: first your outline, which gives you your basic directions; then your rough draft, in which you blurt everything out onto the page; and then your editing, during which you say, "This phrase is unclear; this is misleading; this is equivocal; this is too vague," and knock the piece into shape. When you speak extemporaneously, your notes function like your outline in writing. Your actual talk, though, is the rough draft. There is no chance for editing. You are thinking aloud, to a certain extent. There is, therefore, a necessary groping for your words, and the best choice will not necessarily come first.

For this reason, in oral extemporaneous delivery, there is a certain amount of what we might call "circling around," in which you say something and then come back and restate it slightly differently. Perhaps the first way of putting it suggested to you a different word that would make it clearer, but the word did not occur to you until you made your first statement. Or, as you are uttering the formulation, a flash goes through your mind that there is an aspect that you missed, and you realize that another, slightly different formulation will cover it. Or you suddenly think, as your lips are moving, "Gee, that could be misinterpreted," so, as you finish, you immediately say, "Or, to put it another way," and then you catch and obviate the thing that was worrying you. In other words, you circle around it; you say it and restate it from different aspects until you get the sense that, "Now I have got it across, and the point is unmistakable."

To show you the difference from the point of view of formulation, here is an example sentence on Thomas Hobbes, from the same article: "Thomas Hobbes [is] the materialist apostle of modern science, who, in its name rather than God's, issues anew the perennial call for unqualified obedience to the state."* Now, suppose I am speaking and my notes reminding me of what points to make said, "Hobbes, materialist, science, state." I might say something like, "Thomas Hobbes was a materialist. He bases his ideas not on God, but on science—what he calls science." Here I have to add in "what he calls science," because I realize that if I say "he

---

* Ibid., p. 653.

bases his ideas on science," it sounds as though I agree that he represents science. So I amend it right there to "what he *calls* science." I go on: "His idea is the age-old idea 'obey the state.' Without qualification, mind you." Note that I would have to add that last comment; otherwise, people would think I am advocating anarchism, because it sounds like I do not think you should obey the government. In writing, that is avoided, because I choose the words so carefully that that problem does not come up. In speaking, there is a little stumbling and self-correction as you try to get the gist across. You try out synonyms, elaborations, and so on, until you are satisfied that the audience gets it. We can call this a process of self-monitoring. It is the closest to editing that you can come in extemporaneous delivery; you are, in effect, amending or clarifying your formulations as you go. It is not nearly as compact as in writing.

This kind of temporary roughness is unavoidable in extemporaneous speech. It is not fatal to objectivity, though, because if you do it properly, you do finally achieve complete clarity. You just do so by a different means. You have to know that this process is involved and then do the self-monitoring, coming again at the same formulation two or three times until it comes out clearly. This takes a certain skill and experience, because it is as though one part of your mind is checking what you have already said ("Is that okay, or could it be misinterpreted?") while the other part of your mind has to focus on the new material, so that if you do not find any correction to make, you do not just sit there with your mouth open; you go into the next point. It is an oscillation of attention. It is not as difficult as it sounds, but it does take experience.

Audiences, I may say, are almost always sympathetic to this problem. They understand. Once they know that the delivery is extemporaneous, they do not listen to the nuances of every word choice. In fact, they could not take it in anyway, because since they are hearing, they have their own problems with absorbing what you are saying. So they get only the gist of the point, and know from experience not to expect more. Thus if you grope for words a bit, that does not bother them, so long as the main point emerges. In that piece on the draft that I wrote, we criticized the sentence

"Money is the main issue involved," and I showed all the dreadful implications it contained. In writing, such a sentence would be really wrong. In speaking, however, it could very easily happen that when you get to that point in your talk (assuming the rest of the paper is okay), you are groping to formulate, and the words that occur to you are, "Money is the real issue here." Then you think, "I had better clarify that I am talking about the practical solution, not derogating ideas." The audience understands this. They know that it is an extemporaneous process, so they are not going to rush out in horror, thinking you are opposed to ideas, when you say that money is the main issue. They know you did not have time to pin it down, whereas in writing, they have every right to judge your every word. For this reason as well, then, the pace has to be slower in speaking.

You can see that there is no conflict, therefore, between you and your audience. They need a slower pace, and so do you. You are groping for words, and they take things in more slowly. If, on the other hand, you could speak like a perfectly edited piece of writing, it would be much too fast for them to take in. Your need to circle is matched by their need for you to slow down. There is thus perfect harmony here, in principle.

The question now becomes, How do we implement this slowing down? What specifically do you do to tailor your presentation to the requirements of oral delivery? Generally speaking, you have to give your audience every pointer you can, many more than are needed in writing, about your structure and content. You have to make it as easy as possible to follow. In basic terms, of course, the method is to reduce the amount that you include in a given time and in a given context. Strip your talk down to essentials. In writing you can cover a host of complexities, shadings, asides, nuances, and integrations, whereas speaking has to be much more single-track. That is the basic issue. Now, though, let us look at some more specific ways to reduce the pace.

1. *Simplify your grammar and vocabulary.* Long, complex sentences can be very elegant in writing, but they are not too good in speaking. Asking your listeners to subordinate complex thoughts makes their job difficult. A sentence that begins, "While the Hegelian philosophy is the

primary modern influence . . ." tells the poor audience listening, "You have got to hold the whole thing that comes after 'while,' and that is going to modify yet another clause." It is much easier to give them two main clauses: "Hegel was the main one," which the audience can grasp and pass by, and then you go on to the next clause: "There were others." This does not mean you should never use subordinate clauses. Generally speaking, though, short, independent clauses reduce the pressure on the audience.

By the same token, simplify your vocabulary. If you use a very big word—even a perfectly legitimate, genuine, exact word—that is not completely routine to your audience, it may stun them for a second; it may cause a little pocket of fog and confuse them even for the moment it takes to realize, "Oh, yes, I know what that means," during which they lose your thought. I would thus tend to be much more colloquial in speaking than in writing. For instance, in that passage on Hegel, I referred to "the cataclysm of the Nazis." Now, "cataclysm" is not exactly a horrendous word, and it is an exact word; it means, in effect, a negative on an enormous scale. In speaking, though, I would instinctively, unless I had a very erudite audience, avoid a word like "cataclysm" and say "disaster" instead. Because an average audience would take it in right away; it would not cause a mental wrinkle; they would take "disaster" as a normal kind of term. Then, if I thought, "Well, 'disaster' is not really big enough," I could say, "It was Hegel who prepared the disaster of the Nazis. Not just the disaster—the catastrophe, the cataclysm." By the time I get to it, it is already prepared; I have dug a trench in their minds, and "cataclysm" slips right in.

Obviously, you must not overdo this point about simplification. It does not mean that you should treat your listeners as though they are babies. As a general rule, though, you shift your presentation in the direction of simpler sentence structure and more colloquial vocabulary, and the more so the harder the subject. If I were talking about concept formation, for example, I would tend to approach baby talk in form, simply because the subject is so difficult.

2. *Anticipate the audience's need to pause.* Sometimes you know that

a given formulation is going to puzzle or impress your audience; sometimes you see it written on their faces. In such a case, just stop for a second and give them the time that they would have taken on their own. This is a very difficult thing for most people to learn, but it is okay just to stand and look. If it goes on too long, the audience does get restless. But it rarely seems as long to them as it does to you, so you can have a drink of water or whatever. It is much more common for a speaker to have too few pauses than too many.

3. *Be liberal about repeating yourself.* This is one of the most important points. In writing, repetition is generally needless and usually confusing, because if you use exactly the words you just used, the reader thinks, "Why is he saying this again?" And if you use similar but different words, the reader thinks, "Is this the same point, or another point?" It is, therefore, generally confusing to repeat yourself in writing; in most cases, writing moves forward very tersely. In speaking, however, repetition is imperative. It is one of the major ways of slowing the pace down. Repetition sometimes means simply repeating the same words, such as important formulations. Most often, though, it means not literal repetition, but circling around, groping, saying something in several different ways: "I have no money. There is nothing left. I need some assistance." You cover your point several times, and one of them gets through to your listener.

A very important aspect of repetition is to sum up frequently for your listeners. "Now we have done so-and-so. We have covered this topic." In other words, you give them a kind of overview of what you have said. That is one of the things they would have had to do themselves in reading; you have to do it for them in speaking. The same is true of repetition as applied to review. Whenever you say, "As we said," you have to decide: Do they remember what we said? If they do not, you stick in a quick reminder. That is another form of repetition. Again, you have to do it, whereas in writing, they can look it up for themselves. You do not do it all the time, but only until you feel that your audience gets it. For instance, when I first introduce the term "crow epistemology" to a class, that is a big mouthful. So the next five or ten times that I mention it, I will say "the crow epistemology—in other words, the point that consciousness is limited." At a certain point you see that they get it and that you do not have to remind them of what it is anymore. But you do have to repeat until you reach that point. So I repeat: repeat in various forms.

4. *Make transitions unmistakable.* A transition is the movement from one topic to another, from one point of your outline to the next. For instance, if I go from one difference between writing and speaking to another one, I have to get somehow from the first to the second. This is true in writing as well as in speaking, but in writing it is not so difficult for the reader, because he can always pause and figure out himself where you are (assuming you are somewhere). In writing, too, there are visual aids to help the reader, such as paragraphs, sequence breaks, asterisks, chapter titles, and so on. So it is not urgent in writing that you stress transitions. In fact, it is very often a virtue to make your transitions so smooth that your audience is irresistibly carried along with you and does not even notice that you have switched from one subject to another. An obvious example of that occurs in fiction, when an author goes into a flashback from the present. A skilled writer will begin a scene in the present, and without your even being aware of what is happening, the sentences will take you into the past, and it will be twenty years earlier and you will read right through it absolutely unknowingly. Ayn Rand is an expert at this. Think of the transition in the scene in *Atlas Shrugged* that begins with Dagny walking to the Wayne-Falkland Hotel to see Francisco; suddenly you are back in her childhood days with him, and it is the most brilliantly seamless transition imaginable. In contrast, imagine an author who would write, "Now let us look at this character's past." That is definitely an unmistakable transition, but it would be just awful in writing.

In speaking, however, you need every aid possible, including an explicit structure. Therefore, as a rule, in oral communication the reverse generally applies: Reveal your skeleton. If you are just starting to speak and you want to be clear, a good rule of thumb is to break your material up into units in your own mind, about ten minutes per unit at most, so that you have, say, five or six units per hour. Whenever you move from one unit to the next, make a point about it; let your listeners know, "We have now finished that, and we are going on to this." The best and the simplest way is to state, "Okay, so much for that, on to the next." Or you can say, "Now I would like to turn to," or something along those lines. Numbering is obviously of value here, because a number signals that you are starting a new point.

Remember also that you are going to lose some of your audience as you go. No matter what their level of motivation, some people are going to tune you out, because there is some extent to which they are not going to be synchronized with you. You are not going to pause quite at the point that each one needs. He is particularly tired that night; she has got a personal problem; you are always losing some. But each transition gives you a chance to get them to tune in again, because you are saying, in effect, "Okay, we have finished that; we are starting again with a new point." It amounts to saying to your listener, "All is forgiven; come back." Very often, you can get them back even if you have lost them, if you make it clear that you are starting a new point.

5. *Use emphasis where appropriate.* In writing, there are many ways of indicating emphasis, besides repetition and degree of elaboration. For instance, you can put a sentence in italics, which indicates that it is really important, or you can take a short sentence and make a whole paragraph out of it, and then it really hits the reader. In speaking you have to do the equivalent, but even more so. If your particular statement is important, you have to signal that to the audience unmistakably. You have to stress important points and throw away lesser ones—not mumble them or make them unclear, but make them unstressed. There has to be a difference, for instance, between the examples you give and the principle that you want your audience to retain. You give the examples, let us say, a bit more rapidly, a little more quietly, a little less intensely, whereas, when stating the principle, you slow down and say it louder, with more emphasis and intensity. Emphasis in oral presentation involves many factors, but basically volume and speed.

Let me give you the same material with and without emphasis. It is a point that we have covered, but I will try to give it to you as much as I can with no emphasis at all. "One of the big problems in oral presentation is too much material for the audience to hold. The crow epistemology, which we discussed many times, applies here also. The audience can hold only so much. Therefore, go more slowly. Pace is an important issue." Now that is exactly the right wording and the right pace; it is geared stylistically to an oral audience. But look at the difference now: "One of the big problems in oral presentation is *too much* material. The crow epistemology, which we have discussed many times, applies here also. The audience can hold only so much. So *go more slowly*. Pace—P-A-C-E."

In other words, in speaking, not only do you have to get the material out clearly, but also, if you think about it, you have to imprint it in the audience's mind as far as is possible to you. You have to give them the signal not only by the words, but by the stress. "*This* is important; remember it!"—as against, "If you have to forget something, forget this." Use any means of stress you can, including spelling out words if necessary. I have seen very good talks—good, I mean, in content and in every presentational device—fail, simply for lack of emphasis. If I were to put it in a slightly philosophical way, I would say: Do not be egalitarian in your delivery. Statements are not all equal; some statements are more important than others. Therefore, they have to be treated that way. And by the same token, lesser points should not be emphasized.

Monitoring the Audience

There is one last, crucial difference between oral presentation and written presentation. In oral presentation, leaving aside radio and TV, you, the speaker, are in direct contact with your audience members. You can observe their reactions as you go, and you can adapt your presentation on the spot according to what you observe. In writing, there is a certain problem, in that you have to project your audience theoretically, without their being present. You have to try to figure out what the reader will understand, what he needs to have explained, and what will interest him. In any communication, you need to know whether you are getting your point across, whether you have projected the audience's context correctly. In the case of writing, you have to do this by sheer theoretical projection. You simply define your audience and try to figure out what will motivate them and what will be clear to them.

In speaking, of course, there is also a certain degree of theoretical projection; you do, after all, make notes in advance. In the actual delivery, though, you have the audience right before you. Every moment, you are being given a torrent of concrete information about the motivation of your listeners (are they interested, or are they bored?) and about the degree of their understanding (are they following you, or are they lost?). You can, therefore, tailor your presentation to the specific needs of your audience. If they are bored, you can do something right there on the spot, including, if necessary, throwing away your notes and doing something dramatic to rescue the situation and bring them back. The same is true if they are lost. Writing is frozen in this regard. Once it is done and in print, it is out of your control. An extemporaneous presentation, though, is continually self-correcting. This is another reason that in writing, every word is calculated, whereas in speaking, you have a certain safety margin, because if your message is not getting through, you can see immediately that it is not.

In order to take advantage of this difference, it is essential that you look at your audience. You have to see their responses, if your eyesight permits it; you have to try to maintain eye contact, rove around, move your head, get a sense of their response. Naturally, most of your mind has to be on choosing your next words, because if you get too involved in the audience, you stop that inner voice feeding you what you want to say. But in quick glimpses, you have to get a sense of how your talk is going over. You may see smiles and nods, and you make a quick mental check, "Fine"; or you see brows knit together and grimaces and contortions and so on, and you think, "Something is not right here." Audience reaction is in no way infallible; I have had classes that smile and nod, and then turn in a disastrous exam. But even if the people smiling and nodding are wrong, it does mean something, because they *think* they are following you, at least for the moment, and so they will continue to listen; whereas if they are frowning and you do nothing about it, they give up and you lose them.

You have to monitor two different issues: your listeners' actual grasp of your content, and their interest—in other words, whether they get it, and whether they care. You should be able to recognize the indicators: yawns; coughs; shuffling; the quality of the silence when you pause; a restless feeling in the audience; whether you get the desired response when you say something, or whether it falls flat; whether people return your looks, or avert their gaze, or glaze over entirely. To repeat, you have to rove; you have to monitor the audience as a whole. You also have to be careful, because in almost every audience, there are one or two extremely expressive faces, and since any speaker desperately wants to know if he is getting across, there is a terrific temptation, when you find a really expressive face, to look only at that one person. Then, of course, you end up tailoring your talk wonderfully to that one person, while leaving hundreds completely baffled. So you have to keep your head moving, however much you would like to focus just on the one responder.

It is also the case that people like to be looked at. Therefore, if you move your head in their direction, that makes a difference to them; they feel they are getting something more for their money than just words. The master of this, in my experience, was Frank Sinatra. I saw him at the Nassau Coliseum, in an audience of many thousands. It was a theater in the round, so his back was always to a good fraction of the audience, and he just kept going around and around. It was uncanny the extent to which, buried in thousands of people, you had the feeling—when his back was not to you—that he was looking right at you. He was a real master in that regard. I am not suggesting that we should attempt to approach the top level of the entertainment profession, but simply pointing out that it is good to keep your head moving and scan as much as you can.

To repeat, you cannot take any one response as probative. If one person yawns, that is not per se a comment on you; he might be tired. If several start to yawn, that is already a bad sign, and you should be gearing up mentally to take corrective action. When you see whole rows sinking under the seats, you may as well quit then; you have already lost, so you have to do something drastic. A proper extemporaneous presentation is an interaction. You are getting constant cues, and you are making continual small adjustments in what you intended to say according to the feedback that you get. That is an essential difference between extemporaneous delivery and lecturing from a fully prepared paper, when you just rattle off your material regardless of the audience's reaction. It is also one reason that a completely written-out presentation is closer to writing than to speaking; the audience reaction does not affect it.

Let us look at some methods to regain your audience if you are losing them, techniques that will help you if you feel that your listeners are confused or bored or both.

1. *Change your pace.* This can mean either slow down or speed up. For example, suppose that you had decided in advance, when you were projecting your talk, "A certain degree of elaboration is necessary at this point, and then I expect the audience to get it." Yet when you reach that point in speaking, everyone looks at you completely blank and uncomprehending. Then your mind should tell you, "I have to throw in something more here; I did not anticipate the right reaction, and they do not get it." You have to do this quickly—you cannot stop to sit down and figure it out. But if it is very abstract material, you might decide that one more example is really what they need; or, if it is a lengthy point and you have been developing it for about five minutes, you can think to yourself, "I did not realize it would go on for quite this long when I wrote it in notes. It is a pretty big amount for them to hold. Maybe what I had better do is toss in a summary at this point, so that they get it and I relieve the strain." Alternatively, suppose your words came out in an excessively snarled form, grammatically speaking; the sentence was so contorted that the audience came to a halt. You had not planned to repeat yourself, but you stop to do so. You might even say, "Let us try that again, a little more simply." In other words, you slow down the pace as necessary, adding material right on the spot according to what the audience requires.

Suppose that you really cannot figure out what the problem is. You think that a given point is clear; you have given examples, it is not that long, the sentences are simple, and so on—it is all prepared, but everybody looks baffled at this particular point. It is not a subnormal audience, either, so you cannot explain it by reference to the audience as a whole. The best thing to do in a case like that is to ask the audience. Say, "I see you are not getting this point. Could somebody tell me why? Is there any question you might ask that would help me clarify this to you?" That helps to enlist the audience on your side, because they become partners in trying to figure out where the communication failed. Sometimes, someone will actually ask a question. However, people in an audience tend to be very shy if they are not warmed up, so if they are baffled, everyone will feel, "Everybody gets it but me," and very few people will raise their hand to say, "I do not see this point." What you might do in that case is say, "I do not see why you do not get this. Let me put it this way: I really was making two points, A and B. How many see A?" Then they raise their hands. "How many see B? Oh, B is the one you do not see? I will explain that." In addition, the fact of raising their hands helps to give your listeners a certain courage—they see that they raised their hand and nothing awful happened, so the next step is that someone will actually speak and tell you what the problem is.

The same considerations are applicable to the need to speed up a presentation. Suppose you are all prepared to launch into a lengthy discussion, but the audience shows signs that they have had enough; they already get this point; they are ahead of what you expected. You then have to throw out, on the spot, your prepared elaborations and just skip right over that point. You may have a moment of regret—you may have this wonderful, sexy example that you can hardly wait to give them—but the audience has already gotten it, and therefore you just drop it. With experience, you get to know what degree of elaboration to include for a given audience, and what not. Almost always, even after many years, I find I need some adjustment. But for each point, there usually comes a moment when you can sort of hear in the room, if you have had some experience,

"This audience gets it; it is clear." As a general rule, stay on the point until that moment comes, and get off it right away as soon as they do. Of course, they will not all get it. There will be some members of the audience who never get it. But you have to get the overview of the total. This is perhaps most crucial in adjusting your pace.

2. *Reestablish motivation.* Suppose your pace is okay, and let us assume your individual points are clear, but the audience is still generally restive and you cannot tie it down to any specific issue. It is not as though your listeners are frowning on one particular passage; they are just generally uninterested, and speeding up and slowing down do not seem to make any difference. You might consider, then, the idea that there is something wrong with their underlying interest in what you are saying. If this happens to you, it is of no use whatsoever to continue with your outline, however brilliant it may be, because if the audience is indifferent, they are simply not taking it in, and you may as well be talking to a brick wall. You then have to stop, just completely stop, and rectify the situation by some means if you can. But it is completely useless to continue with a bored audience. Ideally, you would not reach this situation, because you would have established a strong motivation in advance. But let us say you misjudged; you did not make it strong enough for a given audience, you did not explain to them clearly enough at the beginning why they should want to listen, and now you think you are losing them—not because your pace is off, but because they simply do not care. At that point, stop and say something like, "I do not think it is entirely clear to you why we are covering these points, so let us take a moment to discuss the purpose of all this." Then beef up your motivation right there. It is better to give up the last half of your talk, to spend ten minutes talking your audience into being interested, than to continue when they do not care. So stop and state the importance of the issue to them. Explain why the particular topic is necessary. Or remind them of why you are covering such-and-such topic. Continue up to the point at which, as far as you are concerned, they really do now have the knowledge to understand why you are covering it; they have all the content needed to motivate them, and there is nothing more you can do.

3. *Use humor.* What do you do if your pace is okay, you have established motivation, and the audience is interested, but people are still un-
responsive and restless? That does not necessarily mean that the audience
is bad or hopeless or hostile; nor does it mean that the talk is wrong. It
can come from many factors, including the sheer strain of listening to
ideas, which is always there and always needs relief. There is always that
relentless pressure on listeners to concentrate. They have to listen to the
next thing and the next, and the speaker never seems to stop. Anything
you, as a speaker, can do to relieve that pressure will often help you to get
back an audience that is restless even though the basic content and motivation of your talk are fine.

There are certain techniques you can use that will rest a tired audience, spice things up, and buy you a little bit of interest, assuming now that
the basic pace and motivation are okay. A good one is to use humor. Make
your audience laugh, if you can and if it is appropriate. I visualize an audience's mind as being like a room with a door. When the door is shut, nothing enters, however brilliantly clear; it simply does not go in. When the
door is open, then it goes in and they get it. A laugh temporarily opens the
door. My general rule is that a loud laugh from an audience is worth three
to five minutes of additional attention; a chuckle is worth about one minute; a smile, twenty seconds. In a lecture on ideas, if a person laughs or
even smiles, his inner reaction is, "My God, this is not so bad; I am enjoying it." People today are so incredulous, given what they expect in regard
to education and ideas, that when a speaker makes them laugh, for a moment they feel, "Gee, I like this; I would like to learn." To be sure, it is very
temporary. A few minutes later, they forget; the old context returns, they
come back to the idea that education is grief and boredom, concentration
becomes hard again, and their attention starts to wander. Humor thus
grants you only a limited reprieve. But it is a way to get some life into a
flagging audience, and it can be very helpful. So I would suggest that you
lighten your material wherever it is appropriate. Use a funny example, a
joke, a story—anything to wake them up. Obviously, you have to do this
with a certain taste. If you are in the midst of moral condemnation or

moral praise of somebody, you do not inject a giggle. You would not need it anyway, because if it is a moral issue, presumably your audience would be aroused by the gravity of the issue. Humor is particularly appropriate in the drier, more technical parts of a speech.

How to get laughs is where this course leaves off. That depends on you. Some speakers actually have a fund of prepared jokes, and they just dole them out when needed; as soon as they feel the audience is sagging, they say, "That reminds me of . . ." and they use a joke, or they build jokes into their topics. Good speakers on an audience circuit usually have prepared jokes that tie into their material, ready to inject about every ten minutes, and they feed them as their audience starts to go to sleep. This is fine, if you can do it. It requires that the jokes have some appearance of relevance to the audience, because an audience is offended if you just stop in the middle without any connection to anything. Also, it takes a certain courage; to tell a joke with a beginning, middle, and an end, you have to have supreme confidence, because it is going to come to an end, and if it falls completely flat, you are in even deeper than you were when you started telling it, and you have to get out of that as well.

If you do not want to tackle prepared jokes, you can confine yourself to extemporaneous remarks—ad-lib wisecracks, funny wording, ridiculous examples—anything on the spur of the moment that occurs to you to pep things up. I favor this approach, because I cannot tell a prepared joke. The question, however, is not how you do it, but whether you do it. In other words, it is important to include an element of entertainment. You have to project to your listeners, "It is okay to like this. It is not so horrifying just because it is ideology and theory and philosophy and so on." You have to communicate to them, in effect, "I appreciate that you are trapped in here and would give anything to escape, and I am going to help ease the pain." If you get that message across, your audience will be grateful, because listening is very difficult.

4. *Get the audience to participate.* Another way to get an audience back is to let people speak. Assuming that you have established the context so that they are not afraid of speaking, people like to speak, as opposed to just

listening. If necessary, ask a question, and then try to get somebody to answer it. In part, this will help you figure out whether your audience understands you, because if you ask a question and you get a completely hopeless answer, you know that you have to do something to salvage the situation. Partly, then, it gives you some information. Partly, however, it is motivation, and the sheer fact of taking part, of raising hands and speaking, amplifies the audience's interest. They feel that they are actively participating, not just passively letting your words wash over them. And if they say something right and you can say, "That is very good; that is just the point that I was going to make," then that is reassuring to them, and they think, "Yes, I get this," so they are back with you. But the most important reason to have people speak is to keep them interested.

You can do this in many different ways. One is to stop on one word and ask people to call out. For example, you get to, "We are at the theory of knowledge here; what is that? What is the theory of knowledge?" And there is dead silence. You continue, "One word for the theory of knowledge, anybody? With an E? E-P?" You just bring them to it that way for a minute (it was "epistemology," by the way). You can also ask questions, have people express their views, or something similar. The most drastic technique, in this regard, is to single out specific members of the audience by name and without warning. In the middle of a large lecture audience, just say, "Ms. Smith, what do you say about so-and-so?" That has the motivating effect of a knife of fear through every member, because nobody knows who will be next. So you can keep a whole room on the edge of their seat waiting. But that is a very unfriendly technique.

The pitfall with audience participation is how to keep it in balance. If an audience gets too eager to participate, then you have simply an unstructured bull session, which is a complete waste of time. You have to keep participation limited. You have to remember that the main purpose is to get your ideas across, and participation is simply one accessory means to keep your listeners awake if it is heavy going for them. You also have to remember to spread it around. There are always a few people in a large group who want to speak on every point, who will monopolize the discussion if you throw it open. The rest of the audience then resents that the same person is always speaking, and they sigh and look at the ceiling and roll their eyes. You have to avoid that. Therefore, when the same person responds over and over, you simply do not look in his direction when you ask questions, but look to the other side.

There are, of course, other factors that could be relevant besides the above four. Therefore, what I want to say now is in the nature of an "etc."; we are passing now from content to something more in the nature of oratory.

Just for what it is worth, and in passing, it is very helpful to try to exude a certain enthusiasm and confidence in your voice. Do not just drone on at the sky. There is a certain quality of energy, of commitment, that you can put into your voice, a kind of take-charge quality, when you throw yourself into what you are saying and, in effect, communicate by your energy: "I know what I am doing; this is the most important subject in the world, and I know it thoroughly, and here is your chance to get it." If you can communicate that, that is very helpful in motivating an audience. Sometimes you will have to act this out if you do not feel it spontaneously. If you have repeated something so often, to so many audiences, that you do not really feel that excited in the moment, you can still act enthusiastic if you remind yourself of the audience's context.

One factor that I must mention—and it sounds obvious, but more talks have come to grief owing to this than perhaps any other single factor—is volume. If an audience has to strain to hear you, you are finished. If you say quietly, "It is important to stress enthusiasm in your tone," they will simply tune you out—no one can stand it. You have to be like Ethel Merman and just belt it out. Ideally, of course, you do not scream at the audience, although I myself have a tendency to err in that direction. But be sure your voice is loud enough. This is particularly true for women speakers, because their voices are higher.

There are many other factors to consider, such as mannerisms. The best speaker stands unobtrusive and still. He does not weave back and forth, as I sometimes do. He does not talk with his hands, adjust his tie, have a tic or twitch, or the like. The more motionless you stand when speaking, the better. You can have a talk that is clear, interesting, and brimming with motivation, but if your mannerisms are so obnoxious that your listeners cannot get their minds off them, they will not be able to listen to what you say. The temperature can also do you in. If you have any doubts about the motivation of your audience, lower the temperature—the colder, the better. Better they should really shiver; then they will listen. If it is even slightly too warm, you will find it hard to keep them. If it is too smoky, if it is too dark, if the microphone reverberates—there are a million things of this kind, but for that you do not need me; just consult any professional speech manual. The only last point I would make on these lesser points is that you must remember the possibility that a given audience is just simply tired, particularly in the evening. Give them intermissions, and above all, do not go on for three hours the way I do.

The Role of Notes

A few practical topics now on the mechanics of oral presentation. The first regards note making. I am often asked, "How detailed should a speaker's notes be?" Here you want to strike a balance. If your notes are too brief, they will not serve as a guide, and they will leave you stranded. The worst thing is to get to the end of a point, look down at your notes, see nothing, and think, "My God, what comes next?" You have to have enough detail in order to keep yourself on track. On the other hand, if your notes are too detailed, you are going to revert to reading rather than to extemporaneous delivery. What I would suggest is to make notes to cover two main types of things: the divisions of your outline and your key formulations.

By "divisions of your outline," I mean your structure, your main points. You can sketch them in with maybe just a word or so each; the level of detail depends on your knowledge of the topic and your experience. But whether in a word or a phrase, write down the key divisions, enough to keep you going. If you are not sure, rehearse in advance: Make up your outline, look at a blank wall, and then look at your notes as you deliver it to the wall. If you notice your mind continually failing to know what is coming next, you have not got enough. So stick in what word you would have liked to have had there to remind you, had you actually been in front of an audience. Then try it with that further word there. After a while you get the hang of it. You need to take into account here, though, that if you are not an experienced speaker (and even if you are), you will be nervous at the beginning, and nervousness has the effect of making many people go blank. This is not a disease or an abnormality; this is in the nature of speaking. Therefore, if you are not experienced, you are much better advised to have detailed notes for the first minute or two of your presentation. That helps to counteract the nervousness, because you know that if worse comes to worst and you go completely blank, you are safe for two minutes. You then find, after two minutes, that it is not as bad as you thought; you can speak, the audience did not rise in wrath or roll over on the floor as you had imagined they would, and so you can go on from there. The first public lecture I ever gave was many years ago, in a class at Hunter College. I was petrified, as I had known I would be. Because I knew I was going to go blank, I wrote out the first five or ten minutes of the class word for word: "My name is . . ." "This class is . . ." Then I found that it was not so bad, and I went on from there.

There is a whole spectrum of speaker's notes, from the briefest notes—which might be one or two words for a whole hour—to a completely written-out talk. You need to judge which to use according to the various variables mentioned above.

Let us turn now to specific formulations. I would write out any tricky formulations, any points that it is really important to get exact and that you are not completely sure of. After all, this is the substance that you want to get across to the audience. If you have to grope a little bit on some of the lesser material, that is okay. But on the really crucial stuff, if you know you are not too clear about it, write it out so that you are sure you will get across your main point. Here you have to rely on experience as to how much to write out—not too much, but not too little.

While we are on notes, I might just point out one other thing: How do you combine watching your audience with following your notes? If you look down at your notes all the time, you do not see your listeners, and they resent it, and if you look at the audience all the time, you do not see your notes. What if you look at the audience while you speak, and when you decide you are ready for the next point, you look down at your notes and say, "Where the heck in this pile of paper is the next point?" The solution that I have found is just to keep your finger moving down the outline as you proceed. I never take my finger away from the point that I am on, so that when I look down, I look right to the point where my finger is. Then I just move it to the next point and look up until I am finished with that, after which I look down and get the next one, and so on. I thus always have an anchor. I am not patenting that device, so use it if you find it helpful. But you need some device so you can keep yourself linked to your notes as well as maintain eye contact with your audience.

Another topic that is very important in preparing an oral talk is timing. This can be quite tricky. On the one hand, you may find that you run out of material too soon. The audience is looking at you; they were told to expect an hour-long talk; ten minutes have gone, and you have come to the end. That is very upsetting both to you and to the audience. The other difficulty, of course, is when your time runs out and you still have mountains of material to cover. The audience will not sit there indefinitely; you have to come to an end somehow, but you have run out of time without reaching your main point. To avoid either of these situations, you need experience in translating your outline into time estimates. You have to get to know your material as well as the rate of delivery. After a while, you will get to know that a particular point X—which may be only three words in your notes—is a difficult point, one that audiences have trouble with, and therefore you are going to need a lot of elaboration, examples, and so on, so you give it ten minutes. On the other hand, point Y, which is also represented by three words in your notes, is an easy point, one that audiences grasp right away, so you give it just two minutes. After a while, you get the sense of that. Again, the best thing is to practice speaking to a wall at home. Choose a point from your talk, estimate the time in advance, and then actually deliver it as though to an audience and time yourself. You will be amazed, at least at first, at the discrepancy between your projection and the actual time it takes you.

Professional speakers usually have the time of their talks written right on the notes. I definitely recommend this. The time is usually written in a different color, such as red, so that it leaps right out of the page at you. Wherever you should be at that time is marked right there. That, of course, means that you have to have a watch right in front of you, so that you can always check as to whether you are on track or not. Normally, professionals divide their talks into units of ten or fifteen minutes, and they keep track of the time. So if they start at seven thirty, at a certain point in the notes it will say seven forty, then seven fifty, then eight, and so on. This is a very, very valuable technique, as long as you start with the right time. It is really bad if you assume that your talk starts at seven thirty, and the audience is late and you start at seven fifty, and you have to add twenty minutes to each estimate as you go.

The important thing about timing is to watch it as you go and be flexible in both directions. As soon as you begin to see, "This is overlong," you start to cut, and as soon as you see, "This is too short; I am running out of material," you need to expand. As it happens, the need to expand is not commonly a problem. Speaking usually takes longer than anybody expects, because there is more groping for words than you would project. But it has happened to me once that a talk I gave finished too early, and it is very embarrassing. To avoid that, I now always keep in reserve about twenty minutes' worth of material that I have no intention whatsoever of delivering. That way, if worse comes to absolute worst, I know as a certainty that I have a twenty-minute cushion of relevant material. I virtually never use it, but it is reassuring to know that it is there if I need it.

The much more common problem is the need to cut. You are running long and you cannot go on indefinitely; what should you do? The most important thing I could advise you in this case is a negative—do *not* talk faster. That is the curse of all beginning speakers, and even of some not-so-beginning ones. The idea in their minds is, "I have so much to cover, and I have not got time; I have got to start blurting it out as fast as I can possibly get it out of my mouth." There is no use doing that, because the audience's mind remains the same. The listeners cannot take it in any faster than the norm. It is therefore an exercise in futility to talk faster. Your first instinct, then, should be to *slow down* when you realize you are running much too long. That will cut the temptation to cheat and to try to squeeze in a lot of material very quickly. If you have marked your time estimates ahead of time, as I suggested, you should find this out early; it is very bad if you do not find it out until late. That should help you, because in any extemporaneous talk, you should have optional points, marked as such in your notes; you can put them in square brackets, or draw question marks beside them, or whatever. That would be your shorthand to say to yourself, "If I am running long, leave these out; the talk can stand without them." That gives you an out in the other direction. As soon as you see you are running long, start cutting those points, one after another. If you do not have optional points, then you have to cut extemporaneously, and that is hard to do. Again, it is good exercise to practice at home. Take some point, any point you want, and allow yourself five minutes to present it; then set the timer for two minutes and give the same point in two minutes; then set it for thirty seconds and give the same point in thirty seconds. That is really terrific in teaching you what is essential. But if worse comes to worst and you just cannot cut, and you end up running out of time in the middle of your talk, then simply confess to your audience. Say, "Well, I am sorry. I ran overlong, I did not get to my main point, but at least you got something, and maybe another day."

One final point, and that is about reading aloud from a completely prepared text. You can see that this has one great virtue, and that is exactness. It is like writing—there is no groping or circling necessary. The problem, of course, is that the pace still has to be what is required for a listening audience. Therefore, the sentence structure and the language must be appropriately simplified. And it is very difficult to do this in completely written-out form. When most people write, they tend to *write*, and that implies a certain formality that is very different from that involved in speaking. It is very hard, therefore, to completely write out everything and still keep the pace needed for an oral presentation. A further problem with a completely prepared text is the issue of not being adaptable to the audience. You are stuck with your prepared script, and there is nothing you can do, whether they understand or not, whether they are bored or not.

You can, however, do one thing. (I just want to indicate to you that this exists, but it would come more from a speech course than from this type of course.) One problem of these completely written-out talks is the sense that the audience gets that they are canned, that they are not taking place live. You can fake this to a certain extent by the form of your delivery. In other words, it is possible for a skilled speaker to take a talk completely written out in every word, read it without departing from it in any way, and have the audience swear that this was an extemporaneous performance. The trick is that the speaker reads it as though he is thinking of it for the first time. He reads it not as though he already knows it, but as though it is just occurring to him. So he deliberately hesitates as though he is searching for a word, when he knows perfectly well what the word is. But he stops—and then he says the word. What it amounts to is that he is reenacting the process of thinking as a deliberate performance. An audience always likes this better than just reading, because it gives the sense that it is live. This is a skill that can be taught and learned, and if you are stuck with a written-out delivery, it is very helpful. But I just mention that that exists. Generally speaking, extemporaneous delivery is much easier to do, and the audience finds it much livelier.

CHAPTER 9

ANALYSIS OF STUDENT PRESENTATIONS

IN THIS SECTION we will analyze the first of several presentations by people who were courageous enough and good enough to volunteer to speak. I would suggest you try to focus in part on the content, and in part on the method of presentation. In regard to the content, you should be concerned with questions like, "Essentially, is this true? Is there something basically confused about the viewpoint being presented? Is it riddled with non sequiturs or illogical connections? Is there some vital, crucial point that is being omitted by the speaker?" In essence, it comes down to, "Does this make sense as a basic philosophic viewpoint?" But also, from the aspect of this course even more primarily, I would like you to focus on the *method* of presentation. I am using that term in the broadest sense, to encompass not simply the narrow techniques of oral delivery (although that is included), but all the kinds of points that I have been making since the course began: the crow epistemology, the nature of an audience's context, and all the rest.

Presentation: "Effective Child Rearing"

Can you hear me? All right, I'd like you to imagine that you are parents at a PTA meeting in either a Montessori, a public, or a private school. The topic tonight is an effective approach to child rearing.

How many of you would expect an eighty-story skyscraper to be constructed without using a blueprint prepared by an architect, or without organized human effort provided by skilled construction workers? While few of you would expect a skyscraper to result without rational human effort, many of you do expect your child to develop into a mature, rational adult without your having to use a systematic approach, or possessing the skills or methods necessary to assist your child's development. The role of an architect is to develop a blueprint, to guide construction, and to see that there's an orderly step-by-step process, beginning with a foundation and going into a framework, and, eventually, a skyscraper is built. The role of an adult is to supervise a child's development. The adult should possess a blueprint. That is, he should be aware of the goal and the direction and the steps involved in a child's development. He should understand what are the qualities an independent adult possesses, and how are these developed. Then he should have the skills and the methods necessary to help the child develop these qualities. And finally, he should use a systematic approach to enable the child to develop a broad foundation and a sturdy framework during the childhood years.

Tonight's topic is to look at what a systematic or an effective approach to child rearing is. And we are going to note that it involves four ingredients. These four ingredients are: It should be an *objective* approach, a *rational* approach, an *individual* approach, and an *integrated* approach. By an "objective approach" to child rearing, I mean child rearing must look to the facts of reality and observe children to discover the nature and needs of children, and to identify the exact steps in a child's development. The adult should be aware of the goal, the direction, and the process involved in self-development. By sticking to the facts of reality, you then will be able to develop realistic guidelines, expectations, and rules, so that you'll know what the child can do and when he can be expected to do it, and you will not be expecting or demanding the impossible, or neglecting aspects of his development, or expecting too little. By using realistic guidelines and objective rules, you will find that you will be treating the child in a just and fair manner. The child will soon see that the rules, the same rules and needs and laws, apply to everyone, not just to him.

Secondly, an effective approach to child rearing should be a rational approach. Child rearing must involve the use of reason to develop the understandings of what child development involves. You have to also use reason to apply these understandings to your particular child. The adult involved should trust his mind and trust his ability to think for himself when applying these principles to your particular child. Using a rational approach involves treating the child in a rational manner—not telling the child, "Do this because I say so, or else," but rather, taking the time to explain to the child, "This is what I want you to do, this is why I want you to do it, this is how you are to do it, and this is when I expect you to do it." And finally, a rational approach to child rearing is an approach that will help the child to become a rational person. This involves starting with the child when he's young, to do all you can to help him to understand reality. Eventually the child will realize that reality is knowable, it's orderly, and it's predictable. The child should be able to develop a trust in his ability to learn, and trust his ability to think. And we can do this by actually instructing the child in how to think. This would involve helping a child learn how to make decisions, how to solve problems, what's involved in formulating your goals and how to go about achieving them. It also involves introducing the child to logic, helping the child to develop a code of values that he can use to guide his actions, and eventually helping the child to develop a philosophy that will guide his life.

Aside from using an objective and a rational approach, you must use an individual approach to child rearing. Child rearing is concerned with the self-development of individual children. Now, this involves accepting and treating your child as the individual he is. Each child is unique; they are entitled to their own thoughts, their own feelings, their own interests, and their own needs. It involves comparing the child to himself and his development, not to others. And it also involves helping the child to understand himself as the unique individual he is, so that he will become aware of himself as a valuable person, as a person competent in certain areas, and as a person able to develop competency in other areas. And finally the child will realize that he possesses a potential for human greatness that we are there to help him explore and to develop.

Finally, an effective approach to child rearing is an integrated approach, rather than a fragmented, haphazard, hit-or-miss approach. We are dealing with a whole child, and all these different aspects of child development are related and integrated. We can achieve an integrated approach to child rearing by using the child's life as the standard to which we relate all we are doing, all that we expect the child to do, and all that he does, so he will see that everything he does is related to his needs, his interests, and his goals. He will see that certain of his actions are either going to help him grow and develop and achieve his goals, or that other actions will not let him grow and develop and they will hinder him from achieving his goal. An integrated approach to child rearing will let the child know that he has an active role in his self-development. He's basically a self-made individual; our role is just to be there to guide him in his self-development. He will realize that he is responsible for all he does, all he becomes, in life.

Now in summary, we discussed three points tonight. The first was the importance of using an effective approach to child rearing. Secondly, we looked at the role of an adult in such an approach, and we found the adult should possess an awareness of the goals and the steps of human development; they should possess certain skills and methods and use a systematic approach in guiding the child's development. And third, we looked at what this systematic approach would be, and we found that it would be an objective approach based on the nature and the needs of the child, a rational approach involving the use of reason in dealing with the child, an individual approach based on the self-development of your child, and an integrated approach which uses your child's life as the standard to relate all of his actions to. Just as it is up to an architect to supervise the entire process of constructing a skyscraper, it is up to you, the parent, to supervise your child's development. By using an effective approach to child rearing, you will help your child construct a foundation and a framework that will enable him to achieve his life's goals and his individual greatness. Thank you.

COMMENTARY

This presentation is an excellent demonstration, because it definitely has virtues, as well as certain problems. The speaker did certain things extremely well, and if you are sufficiently enthusiastic about the things she did well, then you would not pay as much attention to the others.

Let us first of all establish what was done well in this talk. It was a very organized presentation, something that is always a pleasure to hear.

The audience always relaxes when a speaker says, "We are going to cover this subject. I have four points: one, two, three, four. Now here is my review." In other words, he explains to the audience why he is going to cover each point, and then summarizes it at the end. That way we always know where he is; it is easy to take notes within certain limits, but we know where he is. Leaving aside now any questions about the content, then, on the point of organization this presentation was easy to follow and straightforward.

The speaker also had a good, strong opening with her reference to the skyscraper and the blueprint. That comes under the general heading of motivation. She motivated the audience by giving them an analogy, something they understand—there is such a field as architecture, and that requires a certain kind of knowledge and approach, and she is going to do the same thing with regard to building the character of children. That is an analogy, but a very apt analogy, one that an audience can get. It is, moreover, a good analogy for a completely raw audience, because even if they know nothing, it invokes in them the idea, "Obviously, you have to do something to produce a certain kind of effect, and there is a certain way in which I am forming my child the way you would form a skyscraper." Per se, that does not necessarily convince people, but no opening is going to convince them; it might, though, intrigue them and give them a motivating framework. So I would say this presentation was very good with regard to motivation.

Another positive aspect was that the speaker spoke loudly. I like the fact that she started by saying, "Can you hear me?" That is a good thing, because it is urgent that you be able to be heard. Therefore, by the speaker's sheer act of starting that way, an audience thinks, "She's not going to drone on; she is aware that we have to hear her." That is a forthright opening, and there would be many speeches highly improved if the first words were, "Can you hear me?" So I regard as a definite virtue that it was loud and unequivocal. She did not whisper her words or drop them; you could definitely hear her.

Similarly, the titles of her various sections—"objective," "rational," "independent," and "integrated"—were a little louder and set apart from the content. In that sense, the emphasis was correct; you could tell that there are four main concepts operating here. She made her structure clear to the audience. I have questions about emphasis in another way, but let us leave that for the moment.

I did think that the speaker could have done with less reliance on the notes. I had the impression that she had overprepared this presentation, that it was not completely extemporaneous. While she did not have it all written out, she admits that she had, in fact, practiced in a mirror more than five times, and that definitely came across in the presentation. If you are going to do that with a talk—if you are going to go over it so many times that you effectively commit it to memory—then you have to counteract that with some kind of technique that will give the audience the impression that this is extemporaneous. But in this case, what the speaker never did was stumble; she never paused to grasp a word; she never gave the impression that she was thinking of her material as she was presenting it.

In the ideal extemporaneous delivery, you do not want to pause so often that the audience gets lost, but you also do not want to just zip through the material. The people listening want to feel that you are getting to it as they are getting to it. This speaker definitely communicated that she had rehearsed the material thoroughly, and that she knew exactly what she was going to say when, and then she just went right on. There was some eye contact with the audience, but I, at least, did not have the impression that if people had frowned, it would have stopped the speaker in her tracks and made her add something. She had her eye on the notes and the time, and she was going to make it to the end, and she was just kind of looking at the audience with the idea, "Well, I will give them a glance." That is very understandable if you are nervous. The best way around that is actually to jump in at some point and simply lecture to an audience without that much preparation. Have more fragmented notes, and take advantage if your mind goes blank. For example, you get to, say, the middle of "objectivity," and you do not have it prepared. You look at your notes and it says "objectivity (explain)," and you cannot remember what the explanation is—you go blank. You can make an asset of that by saying, "Now, the next point we want to cover is the role of objectivity in child rearing. What do you think that would consist of?" That is actually helpful, because if you need the pause, the chances are that your listeners need the pause, too. (True, in the act of doing that, you are losing time, so you have to make a mental note, "Good-bye to 'integration' then, I suppose," and you would then have three points instead of four.) Then somebody from the audience will say, "Well, objectivity, that has to do with facts rather than emotions," and that might jog your memory. Meanwhile, you have also had your listeners participate a bit, and you have also slowed it down somewhat.

You do have to risk something for this. In other words, if you want a true extemporaneous quality, you have to go up with just a few notes, with the idea that if you go blank, you are going to have to think on the spot. But that is correspondingly a more effective presentation than just rattling right through it. That was one of my criticisms of this presentation. The positive side of that, however, is that the speaker was terrific with regard to timing; she came out to the minute.

One more virtue of this presentation was repetition. I liked the fact that the speaker stated in advance what she was going to do. That is the classic three-part lecture—"I am going to cover these four points; here are the four points; I have covered these four points"—and that is always a perfectly valid way of giving a talk. The transitions were also clear; she consistently said, "Now let us go to the next point." Another positive is that there was no rhetoric in this talk. By "rhetoric" I mean, in this context, not the ancient Greek sense of the term, but empty verbiage, such as the way politicians speak; they go on and on, not simply uttering floating abstractions or the like, but saying nothing at all—just clacking their uppers, so to speak. There was none of that. This presentation was condensed; it was taut; the speaker had her points and knew what she wanted to say, and she just kept pouring the material out.

There were, however, some aspects in which this talk could be improved. A very important criticism is that the talk was too abstract. We kept waiting for it to cover specific issues and problems that would arise in the home and in daily life. This is the essential reason I would regard this talk as mixed rather than positive; I do not believe that an audience could take it in. The material was organized, and the speaker definitely motivated her listeners, but she pitched it on a level of such abstractness that it is questionable to me how much an outside audience—that is, one that does not already know "objectivity," "rationality," "integration," and all these complex philosophic concepts—would get out of it. For instance, I tried to put myself into the framework of that type of audience, and I started the first point, but I could not take down the definitions (I am not a fast writer, but I did get through many years of college). The speaker zipped through them without a pause, and thus did not give us time to digest them or illustrate them. Consequently, I had the experience as though she was, in effect, giving a definition and then saying, in a generalized way, why it would be helpful, rather than actually concretizing it.

Take, for instance, "objectivity." I wrote down in my notes, "facts of reality—too fast," meaning I could not keep up with it. The speaker's definition of "objectivity," in this context, was: "Look to the facts of reality and observe children to discover the nature and needs of children, and to identify the exact steps in a child's development." On the face of it, that definition is too unwieldy to be graspable. By "objectivity" we mean: Look to the facts of reality and of children in order to determine the proper approach. That is the essential concept, and it is very, very abstract. The questions immediately arise: What facts about reality, and what facts about children, and what would be a contrasting policy?

A beginning audience does not know the alternative to looking at the facts of reality, nor even necessarily what you mean by "the facts of reality." Sometimes, they might take you to mean by "reality" some superdimension beyond us. The same difficulty arises when you invoke the "facts about children." Does that mean, for instance, that it is a fact that my child does not want to go to bed, and therefore I should respect that fact whether or not it is his bedtime? A term such as "objectivity," then, creates a vast chaos in the audience's mind. Just saying simply, "Look to the facts of reality and of children to know what to do," is, in itself, too abstract. It is okay to tell a beginning audience to look to the facts of reality, but then, to make that point clear, you have to give a contrast and a concrete example.

Presumably, the point the speaker means to make here is, "Look to the facts of reality, as opposed to your arbitrary emotions." If you put it that way, then what you really mean to convey is, "Look to the facts of reality, as opposed to merely acting arbitrarily," and to an audience, that sounds like you are repeating, in a generalized way, your introduction. If your introductory point is, "We have got to be organized and systematic, just like in building; we cannot just do this helter-skelter," then when you come to point one, it has to be something more specific than, "Do not be arbitrary," because that sounds like a mere reiteration of what you said at the beginning. For instance, you might say, "You made a promise to your child that he could see this movie, and now Saturday morning comes and you do not feel like taking him. There is no good reason that you can think up; you just do not feel like it. So you tell him, 'I do not feel like it,' and you are not going to go. That is a case of putting your emotion above the facts. You made a certain promise; you led the child to believe that reality would be a certain way, that this would be the fact; he counted on it, and now you are letting your emotion override it."

I do not say that this is a brilliant or captivating example. But it does pin down the abstract idea. You know, in pattern, what the speaker is talking about, as against what, and how it would come up in daily life. You need a couple of such examples, and the homier, the better, because the more abstract your abstraction, the more familiar and daily must be the concrete. Ideally, you would want to give several concretes—one to say, "I do not mean anything frightening; I mean something really everyday that you can understand," and then, after the audience gets it, another, more intriguing concrete so they get the idea that there is a broader issue here that they have not thought about. That is what is sometimes called "chewing" an abstraction: putting it before an audience and saying, "I mean this; I do not mean that; here would be a simple example; here is a more important example; this is how I differentiate it from this other point," and so on. At a certain point, the audience grasps it.

Obviously, to do that, you have to move at a certain pace. If you have ten minutes, one of the four points is all you could really "chew," given that your talk has a beginning and an end. But it is interesting that this speaker attempted to do the four, because she was put in that position throughout. This same problem, of not concretizing, ran throughout all four points in this presentation. Not counting her introduction and wrap-up, the speaker had about two minutes per item, of which about twenty seconds would be just uttering the abstract definition. So she had a minute and forty seconds, and that is just impossible—the greatest genius of presentation in the world could not do it in that time.

The speaker's second point was "rationality." How does "rationality," even in this speaker's special context, differ from "objectivity"? When giving the audience points, the important thing is that you have to make clear the difference between the points. According to the speaker, "rationality," in this case, means going by reason. How does that differ from accepting the facts of reality, which was the operative definition of "objectivity" in the first point? You might say "objectivity" would be looking at the facts about the child and putting them to use, and "reason" would be trying to understand the facts and use them. But that is not much of a distinction, because what is the use of looking at them if you do not use them, and how can you use them without looking at them? Philosophically, too, objectivity is an aspect of rationality. So really, it is the same one point.

In order to keep these points distinguished, I would suggest that the key point here is "rationality," which should be defined first. Then, when you get to "objectivity," you can say, "This is an application, one form of rationality, and it arises in this type of context." The same would then be true of your other points. It is okay to have four points and say, "First is my broad point; second is an application." But always remember that your structure will not hold if your audience does not see the interrelation of the points. Because this speaker was forced to be so abstract, the points kept falling, particularly points one and two.

Point four, integration, was also somewhat unclear. Here there is an issue of objectivity of formulation. By "integrated approach," the speaker obviously did not mean racial balance or anything of that kind. Given the way the word is commonly used today, though, a contemporary audience will hear the word "integrated" as having nothing to do with mental processes, but rather with ratios of minorities and so on. Since you do not want to set up an expectation that you do not intend, that word would, therefore, not be advisable; perhaps "organized," or "interconnected," or "systematic." Even so, the point about being "integrated" was not clear. The speaker contrasted it to being fragmented or haphazard. But that is, again, the same issue that was raised in the introduction, namely that we want a systematic approach. You cannot call for a systematic approach, and then have one of the elements of the system be, over again, that it has to be systematic. The speaker actually meant something more specific by "integrated" here, just as she meant something more specific by "objective." But because of the generality of her definitions and her discussion, she did not have a chance to make it clear.

What might "integrated" specifically have meant here, in a way that differentiates it from merely "systematic," "objective," and so on? You might say, "By 'integrated approach,' I mean that every aspect of your child's life has to be seen by you as part of one systematic plan, including his homework, his dancing, his piano lessons, his parties, his movies, etc." Then you say, "For instance, some parents tell their child, 'Do your best,' and then they tell him, 'It's okay to cheat,' and then they give him a similar contradiction in another realm," and so on, and then you say, "That's going to ruin him. You have to have one consistent approach." (In that case, it is really consistency that you are talking about.) Then you could say, "Now, what will unite all these things? How will you know what to do to be consistent?" Then the audience says, "Well, I guess you need something to guide you." And you say, "You decide according to a certain idea of how you want your child to develop, and that has to be the standard," and then you have to give us some idea of what that is. (I am here myself guilty of being a little abstract. But I want to indicate the level on which you have to pitch it.)

You always have to do the following with broad abstractions: contrast them with their opposites, distinguish them from other crucial abstractions you use, and give the most concrete examples you can of their application. This speaker did not do any of these three things. There was a certain amount of concretizing; for instance, in connection with rationality, she mentioned, "Do not say, 'Do it because I say so.'" That was fine; that would be a recognizable example, but more of that was needed. Many fewer abstractions, much more detail. For that reason, I thought that the pace was off; I thought too much material poured forth in a way the audience could not digest. But that is really a derivative problem, caused by the lack of concretization.

This speaker was trying to say, in effect, that you have to bring a child up in contact with reality, with reason, and with his own values. Yet it is not clear that she got those points across. There was a certain indefiniteness about the talk; it was slightly unclear whether it was about how to bring up the child, or how to think about bringing up the child. I believe she was focused on the first. But one of her central points was that you have to know how to think about bringing up a child in order to bring it up. So she was trying to, so to speak, give epistemological guidance on top of child-rearing advice. That is too much to attempt in ten minutes, because those are two distinct topics. One is, "what to do when," even in broad philosophic terms; the other is, "how to get clear in your mind about this whole subject." One is the content; the other is more the parents' thinking method. The speaker had a certain tendency to combine the two.

A related criticism regards emphasis. I do not believe this talk was completely satisfactory with regard to emphasis. This is what I would ideally have liked: "The first important point I want to cover is objectivity—*objectivity*—and that is very important. By 'objectivity,' I mean that you have to pay attention to the facts of reality." And then the speaker could go on. With an important point, you pause; you stress it. The speaker, though, sped right on through, so that even if she did give, let us say, a perfectly appropriate definition, and even if it was loud, louder than the rest, it still went by too quickly. Remember, too, that many people try to take notes, and there is nothing more frustrating—as students have told me bitterly—than to get down the first four words of somebody's definition, only for him to move on to the next point; you throw your pen down and say, "Oh, hell!" and lose the whole thing. When giving any definition, it is crucial to pause, and it is particularly important when giving four heavy, abstract definitions of the kind this speaker was presenting. Go slower; stress the word; wait; repeat. Always repeat a key word. Say, "Objectivity—*objectivity*—O-B-J . . ."—whatever you have to do to hit your listeners over the head with it. Then you can zip through it again if your material is light enough to allow it.

One thing that struck me in this presentation was that the speaker would have been better off concluding somewhat differently. She had already milked the parallel to architecture, and therefore it kind of fell flat when she used it again at the end. You want to have a dramatic ending, because the ending sticks in people's minds. The beginning and the end of any presentation are the most crucial, because the opening determines whether people will listen, and the closing determines whether they will remember. An effective ending to this talk might be what the speaker could not do in the beginning, because it would be arbitrary there: At the end, if she had concretized her points sufficiently, she could briefly depict a maladjusted or neurotic child in terms that the audience would recognize, and say, "This is going to be the product of irrational, dogmatic, arbitrary, nonobjective parents, as opposed to"—and then a few glowing words of what they could have instead. That would be a motivational conclusion. It would not be as arbitrary as it would be at the beginning, where there was no explanation of it, and it is a better, more effective ending than just using the architecture analogy over again, because there is no more mileage to be had from that.

The last content point I want to mention is that it is very important to realize that when you talk about individualism—"Treat the child as an individual, stress his self-development, compare him to himself and not to others," and so on—there is always, particularly today, one blatant way in which that type of thing will be misheard. It can be interpreted as the attitude of, "Do your own thing," or, in philosophic terms, as subjectivism. You have to take cognizance of that interpretation and, either in your choice of wording or explicitly, set yourself apart from it. This would not be true in a better world, but it certainly is true of even completely innocent and honest people today. A lot of people take "individualism" to mean "doing whatever you feel like." Particularly, therefore, in the context of a talk in which you have just stressed objectivity, when you say, "Treat the child as an individual," you need to indicate, "And I do not mean that I am contradicting everything that I said before." So you have to say something like, "This is completely compatible with treating the child objectively and going by facts. But the fact is that in certain respects, your child is unique, and that is a fact that you have to respect." You need merely put in something like that so that the audience understands that this is not the standard line of, "Do your own thing." As a general point, this is the issue of the audience's context. You have to take into account how you can be misheard, within limits.

To summarize, the main problem in this presentation, as I see it, was the pace of treating abstractions. It was not concretized enough; it was too floating, and that was consequently a big problem. The main virtue is that it was forthright, motivated, and organized, and we therefore knew exactly what the speaker aimed to do and how to criticize it.

The second talk has as its topic the Objectivist ethics. The speaker is presenting his talk to an audience of conservatives, that is, people who are already advocates of or sympathetic to capitalism, but who know nothing about Objectivism or the need for philosophy.

Presentation: "The Objectivist Ethics"

Good evening, ladies and gentlemen. (Can you hear me?) Do you have trouble defending capitalism? Do you wonder why the noose of government control is tightening around our necks while the polls indicate that people, that public opinion, is swinging to the right? Do you wonder what these questions have to do with my topic, which is the Objectivist ethics? The answer is contained in a single sentence: In order to defend capitalism, you must do so from a proper moral base. That moral base is the Objectivist ethics. I'm not going to speak to you tonight about capitalism, about economics; I'm going to talk to you about the Objectivist ethics. Given the short amount of time, I'm only going to make three points. But I will illustrate each of those points with some examples to point out the trouble that you might have defending capitalism from some other base.

Okay, the first point that I want to make is that ethics is necessary; that is, you need ethics. What is ethics? Ethics, or morality, is a code of values to guide the choices and actions of man's life. Ethics, let me repeat that, morality, is a code of values which will guide the choices and actions of your life. You can think of ethics as being a road map, except instead of telling you where you are going to go, it will tell you what you are going to be. So at each point of your life, it helps you make your choices; it helps you decide; it helps you move, act. It tells you, for example, if you want to be a success, if you want to be happy, then you should produce; you should work for yourself. If you do not mind winding up being a shiftless no-good, then you do not have to produce; you can steal, etc.

Now, no human action is independent of ethics. Everything you do depends on ethics. Now, in particular, economics is not independent of ethics. The relationship between ethics or morality and economics is very much the same in one regard as the relationship between biology and nutrition. By that I mean morality sets the standard for economics, and for nutrition it is biology which sets the standard. For example, if you were to study nutrition, or to make nutritious recommendations, without respecting the standards of biology, without respect to life or death, you would not know whether to prescribe protein or poison. And economics without reference to morality, the effect that you get is you will have some conservative economist advocating free trade and claiming that that means free trade with communist Russia, taking and selling planes to Red China. Ethics is necessary for you; it's necessary for all human action. So that's the first point that I wanted to make.

The second point is that the Objectivist ethics holds that the highest value is your life. Remember, I said ethics is a code to guide you and your actions. And the highest value of that code is your life. For example, in the economic realm, when you produce, you own the product. This is the answer that you need to answer, this is the—I guess I said it right—this is the answer you need to answer the welfare statists who are claiming that you should be sacrificing your product, that you should work and earn, and that somebody else should dispense your earnings to other people. In order to say that is wrong, you need morality; and in order to say that that is wrong, the standard by which it is wrong, the value, has to be your own life. So the second point that I have made is that you have to be selfish.

But you ask, "How can you defend such a term as 'selfishness'?" The answer is that you need a standard, and this is the third point that I want to make. The trouble that you get into in economics is exemplified by those people who claim that a mugger in Central Park is acting in his self-interest. Now usually, the term is not put quite so boldly as that. You may get it put to you as, "Wouldn't you steal a million dollars if you thought you could get away with it?" This makes me think of Oscar Wilde's put-down of a very snooty aristocratic lady, and he said, "Madam, would you spend the night with me for ten thousand pounds?" And she said, "Yes, I believe I would." And he said, "Well, would you do so for a shilling?" And she said, "Oh, heavens no, what do you take me for?" And he said, "We've already determined that. Now we are just dickering over the price." In order to make that determination, you need a standard. In order to call the mugger a thief, you need a standard. Objectivist ethics holds that the standard is man's life. The difference between the mugger and a man is that he is not surviving at the human level; he is surviving at the level of the brute; he's surviving by purely using brute force. The difference between men and brutes is that men possess the faculty of reason. I cannot say more about that, however; I'm sure I'm running out of time; I forgot to set my watch at the beginning. But the point is that, the economic point with respect to this, is that production is good; that is, this is a combination of an economic and a moral point; production is good, and theft is bad. The way that you know that is the standard of man's life. Production is the use of reason; theft is not.

Now, if I was really so fast that I have the two minutes left that Dr. Peikoff indicated, I'm now running short. Nonetheless, I'm going to sum up. With a long enough pause for laughter, then I will come out just right. Okay, I have illustrated my topic by examples from the field of economics. But the real point is that ethics applies to all of your life, not only to economic matters. So you need ethics to live your life. So let me sum up the three points that I have made. I just repeated the first one—you need ethics. The second point, the purpose of your life is you; the thing at the end of the road map will be your life. And the third point is that in order to guide yourself along that road map, you have to use reason. What you need for yourself, not only what capitalism needs but what you need, is rational selfishness. Thank you.

COMMENTARY

There were a number of virtues to this talk. The pace was excellent. This was an oral presentation; this was not a written presentation that you felt was going on no matter what and that you had to struggle with. He slowed up when he gave a definition; he paused; he repeated—you definitely had the feeling that he was monitoring the audience. It was a very good example of extemporaneous delivery, because you could see in many cases that he was thinking on his feet. I think a very effective touch, one that really helps to win an audience—and I do not believe he was diabolical enough to plan this, although some speakers do so—was that one where he hesitated halfway through a sentence and said, "I guess I said it right." That was purely extemporaneous, and he was perfectly straightforward with the audience. You could see, therefore, that his mind actually was operating and thinking as he went, circling around and correcting. This was very good; he let you in on his mental processes, and that is what gives a talk the aura of an extemporaneous presentation. As far as I could see from where I was sitting, too, he was looking at the audience, aware of their requirements. Therefore, with regard to pace and the monitoring of the audience, I think this talk was excellent.

The only one sign I could see, in the speaker's actual delivery, that he was not experienced was that he was nervous, as indicated by the timbre of his voice. That is something that a beginning speaker cannot do anything about; it is automatic. But this speaker did exactly the right thing; that is to say, you just go on no matter what. If an audience is at all disconcerted by that, they take your estimate of it, and if they see that your nervousness does not stop you, they just set it aside and stop paying any attention to it. It is not distracting, and it goes away across time as you see audience after audience and give talk after talk; you automatize the skill and all the "what ifs" vanish ("What if I forget," "What if the audience revolts," and so on). Then you relax and just do it normally.

The use of humor was very good, with one question. The speaker had a nice, dry humor, which came to him when he needed it and livened things up. He did, though, have one prepared joke, the one about Oscar Wilde. He got a polite laugh from that, but not the laugh that he got from his extemporaneous ones. That, by the way, is why I do not do that. He did, in effect, what I do when giving a prepared joke: He said, "That reminds me," and then started telling a story that he had obviously thought at home would get a laugh. If you do it that way, an audience gets nervous, because they know they have to laugh, and they wait for it, and the thought goes through their mind, "Is this really relevant?" I must say it was a little bit stretched here, because he was going to talk about how a mugger thought it was in his self-interest to steal a million dollars; I could not get the connection to Oscar Wilde's put-down of the woman losing her integrity. It was in common that they were doing something bad for a sum of money, but that is very broad, so broad that it was slightly disconcerting. The problem with a prepared joke is that first, it has to be relevant, directly perceptible, not obvious to the audience that you have got this prepared; and second, you have to say it with complete, consummate confidence, which I cannot do. If you can do it, fine. If not, and you happen to have a good, dry sense of extemporaneous humor, I would tend to rely more on that. Generally speaking, though, this speaker did make an effective use of humor, and the audience was definitely sympathetic and attentive to him.

The repetition was good, especially because the speaker used different words. For example, he said, "Ethics is necessary; you need ethics." That kind of repetition is what I call circling around. He said it two different ways, not in the exact same words. He brought out two aspects—"It is necessary to man, and that means you"—and he got to say it twice for the same price, which served to emphasize it.

In general, then, the speaker's repetition was good, his emphasis was good, he was loud, his timing came out fine, his transitions were perfectly clear, he knew what he was going to do, his structure was very straightforward. As a method of presentation, he did not overload the audience, and in that respect I think he handled the technical requirements very well. He also had good concretization. The intention to concretize, to give examples, ran throughout his presentation, such as the analogy to the road map. You did not have the feeling that this was a bunch of floating abstractions; you could see in each case what he meant concretely.

In general, to summarize the positives: The pace was excellent (and under "pace," I subsume all the things that go to make a good pace—pauses, repetitions, and so on); concretization was fine; the structure was clear; humor was a valuable element; and he did give it extemporaneously, which held his audience.

The motivation in this presentation went by a little too quickly. Right at the beginning this speaker asked why government controls keep getting bigger even though there is a swing to the political right. I would have slowed that first part down a bit. Even if your content is okay, you have to set that motivation firmly. You would just have to elaborate with a couple sentences more. For example, "You know capitalism is the best system; I do not have to convince you of that. But it is failing. Why? Why do you have trouble? The public is with you, logic is with you, economics is with you, but you are losing—why?" Just that much, and then they will listen. That is not much more than the speaker said, but it is just that little extra bit to pass from a kind of dutiful motivation—"You have trouble; I am going to give you the solution"—to emphasizing it so that the audience is gripped.

One criticism of this talk is that the speaker made it clear why one would need ethics in general, but not why one would need specifically the Objectivist ethics, as opposed to any other ethics. Now, he did say something about the Objectivist ethics. After all, he said the highest value is your life, and he tied that to economics by making the point that you own the products that you yourself create, as opposed to the need to sacrifice them, and why the Objectivist ethics stresses production, which is essential to capitalism. Further to this criticism, then, what is it that this speaker did not do to emphasize the need for the Objectivist ethics, as opposed to ethics as such? There are clearly two different topics here. One is: Why should an audience with an economic viewpoint care about ethics at all? Then, more specifically: Why should they care about this particular ethics? Given the subject, you have to do both. This speaker did, in a general way, cover why you cannot get around ethics. But he did not do so well with the question of the Objectivist ethics.

Remember that the intended audience knows nothing about Objectivism or philosophy; they are simply advocates of capitalism, just typical conservatives. What, then, was the problem? The speaker actually ran out a minute early, so he had nine minutes, and let us say he took about four of those minutes on his introduction and the role of ethics. So he had approximately five minutes to speak to this audience on why they need Objectivism in particular. And in that five-minute period, he tried to cover the points that life is the standard, that this involves selfishness, that selfishness involves production as opposed to surviving on a subhuman level, and that this means the use of reason. The question is, can you do that in a way that is convincing in that amount of time? In fact, you cannot.

In this type of assignment, you have to decide whether you are going to try to give a kind of a contour of Objectivism, four big points (life, reason, selfishness, production) with one quick tie-in of each to capitalism ("It has to be life, otherwise you cannot keep your property; it has to be reason, otherwise the mugger can run wild," etc.); or whether you will give a more in-depth analysis of a few essential points, given a limited time. This speaker tried the former approach, and for reasons that we will illustrate shortly, it was not really convincing. It had the effect that the formulations were so generalized that it did not really hit home.

In a case like this, you have to pick your spot. You have to decide breadth or depth, a whole survey or one dagger to the heart. In a ten-minute speech, you take the dagger approach. You do not have to pretend that that is all; an ethics consists of a great many different theories. But because of the time required to grasp these things, it would be a much more effective strategy, in terms of conviction, if you said: "You need ethics in general, but you need specifically the kind of ethics that makes capitalism possible. Now, what does capitalism consist of? People left free to pursue their own profit, to make money by trade on a free market. Under capitalism, does the government have the right to control you? No. Does it have the right to control you even if that would help the needy? No." And so on. Give it just on the terms of what capitalism is, terms that the audience can recognize. Say, "The government under capitalism cannot do this even if . . ." and then give various situations in which altruism would say the government can and should do it. Then you say, "But in fact, today in the world, the government is doing all those things, and what is it appealing to for justification? It says, 'So-and-so needs it, so-and-so needs it, we have to sacrifice,' and so on. Now it should be obvious to you. If you know nothing else about ethics, you have to know this: If sacrifice is the imperative, capitalism is out. Therefore, if you want to advocate capitalism, give up sacrifice." Finally, you tell them, "But then how do you live? Then you have to have some other approach—say, be selfish. But what does 'selfish' mean? That is a big question; there are many different theories, and you need an ethics to tell you. That is what Objectivism would tell you. Read such-and-such. Thank you."

In both types of talk, you can give your listeners only a hint. But it is a question of pace. I speak now not of the pace of your oral delivery, but of the content of abstractions that people can take in who do not know them. The hardest thing for people without experience to grasp is how slowly you have to go in terms of the amount of content. In ten minutes, the most you can do is to say, "Do not sacrifice." You say it, and you say, "I mean by that so-and-so, as against such-and-such, and here is an example, and this is why it is important," and your ten minutes are gone. You have to rid yourself of the idea that you can say, "Reason, point one, one minute; no sacrifice, point two, one minute; production. . . ." You cannot hit those things that way. If you could, the world would be in a completely different state. It would mean that those terms are familiar, the context is familiar, what you want to say is familiar, and you are more or less reminding the audience. You always have to decide about a point: Is this new to your audience, or are you reminding them? If you are merely reminding, you can throw it away. You could say, "As we all know, man has rights" to a conservative group. But you cannot say, "As we all know, man should be selfish," even without the "As we all know."

Let us now look at some of this speaker's formulations just from the aspect of the questions that he raised. They were not floating abstractions, in the sense that the speaker did what was possible within the limits of ten minutes. When he got to the Objectivist ethics, though, his first point was, "The highest value is your life." The question that would raise, in an audience that does not know the rest of your viewpoint, is: Can a criminal then say, "It is my life"? In other words, does "your life" mean anybody's life at any price? True, as the speaker went along, he did ultimately indicate that he does not approve of muggers and sacrifice and so on. But if the standard is "your life," the question is, Why not? All he said, at a later point, was that a mugger is not surviving on a human level. He did not say anything about why man has to use reason if life is the standard, or if he did, it was only by implication. But that is an essential point.

If the people in the audience do not see that reason is man's actual tool of survival, if the extent of the message they get is, "Your life is the standard, and you have to do things in a human way, and a human is rational," then what is "rational"? The speaker has said that he does not like muggers, but if "life is the standard," what if the mugger gets away with it? In the beginning the speaker said, "Either you produce and work for yourself, or you can steal, if you do not mind winding up being a shiftless no-good." That, perhaps, was simply an appeal to the fact that the audience would, obviously, disapprove of stealing. But we hear this now as a total presentation. We are told at one point, "It depends; do you mind or not?" Then later, we learn that the standard is your life, and the reason you cannot do certain things is that it would not be human—but we do not see why it would not be human, since human beings do it, and he has not told us what human faculty has to be employed if life is the standard. If you then throw in, "You have to be selfish," with only the briefest indication that you need a standard, and that the standard is man's life—the net effect that comes across is that it is some kind of subjectivism.

It is not that the speaker's formulations were bad. The audience's context, as it would have to be today, combined with the density of points he was trying to make, forced him into that position. So even though he went out of his way to try to exemplify and define, the assignment defeated him. He ended up giving the net impression, "I need some kind of values, but I do not see why I need this particular code, or why I need any code as such—it is whatever you do not mind, or whatever fits your sense of the human." It is the same type of problem, in a way, that the presentation on child rearing had. When presenting ideas in today's world, the problem is always how not to fall into one or the other of two false views: assuming objectivity at the price of saying there is nothing in it for you (in other words, of being disinterested), or falling into subjectivism when stressing selfishness.

Even within the framework of the way this speaker approached his task, he would have had to give a little more emphasis. Remember that his point here is why advocates of capitalism need Objectivism. Therefore, he would constantly have to make his emphasis follow his theme, rather than just throwing his points away, as he tended to do. For instance, he said, without any further elaboration, "The highest value is your life. For example, when you produce, you own the product." As far as I could follow his reasoning, it was, "I gave them the application to capitalism, and now I have to get on to new material." But given that audience and that theme, this is the point that matters. You would at least have to pause and say something to the effect of, "Private property is essential to capitalism. How are you going to defend it if you do not have a private life?" It is more important that the listeners understand why they need a certain type of ethics, than that they grasp what it is. You do have to tell them something about it, because otherwise they will not know what you are talking about. But if you are going to present your case scattershot, one point after the other, you must consistently stress the theme of why they need this to defend capitalism.

The same goes for the way the speaker treated sacrifice. He mentioned it, but he said, in effect, "You need the kind of ethics that recognizes man's rights, as against the kind that tells him to sacrifice for others," and then he went right on. That, however, is a big point, a bombshell; that really is the essence of the whole issue, as far as politics is concerned. Therefore, when you get to that, you have to stop. You have to look at the audience after you have elaborated on it and say, "The choice is capitalism or the ethics of sacrifice. It is either-or. If you see that, you see why you need Objectivism, because every other ethics tells you otherwise." This speaker covered it, but his emphasis was completely off—not in the narrow sense that he raced over it or swallowed it linguistically, but in terms of its centrality to the presentation. He did not take that point and stun the audience with its impact, yet that is really what you would have to do in this type of talk. (You also need to be careful when throwing out a term like "sacrifice," which the audience might hear as a good thing.)

The problem really comes down to the question of how much an audience can take in of what they do not know in advance. My general advice is: If in doubt, reduce the number of abstractions; give more emphasis, more contrast of your view with some other view, more examples.

To summarize, this presentation was definitely good in its mechanics, but it had the problem of too much content, which had to be too vague. Therefore, in its net effect, the talk was not convincing. But it was very helpful, and I think it helped illuminate issues for us.

This next speaker is addressing just a general audience, one unfamiliar with philosophy or Objectivism, and her subject is the defense of Romanticism in art.

Presentation: "Romanticism in Art"

Ladies and gentlemen, I'm going to speak on the state of contemporary art. And I may say, to start, that it is rather hellish. We find that within the avant-garde, we have examples of artistic works where an artist nails his own body to his Volkswagen. We have art in which John Cage takes a dead fish and slaps it on the string of a piano. So you see, Francis Ford Coppola may be right—artistically, at least, this may be apocalypse now. Audiences still seem to want to go to the movies and have a good story, however. Audiences still seem to want portraits of beautiful things. They still seem to want music that has melody. Intellectuals laugh. They cannot imagine why people still want that kind of art. Well, what can we do as a general public?

I suggest to you that what we can do is combat art by identifying the kind of art that we want. When we go to an artwork, what we seek is a refueling experience. We work through the week, and then on the weekend we seek to go to a film in which we can, in a sense, be refueled, be recharged. We go to a museum and we seek to enjoy ourselves. What we need to say is, we do not want mindless entertainment; we want entertainment that will stir us emotionally and that will stimulate us intellectually. I suggest to you that what we want is Romanticism, the kind of Romanticism that maybe is best shown in *Cyrano de Bergerac*, a hero fighting for what he believes in; maybe best heard in the music of Tchaikovsky, a music of powerful melodies; maybe best seen in the sculptures of Rodin, in which man is shown as powerful with any struggle. Romanticism seems very mixed, though. When you try to define it, it seems to have such a wide variety that many people consider Romanticism undefinable. It is that that is our task. We must define "Romanticism"; we must identify its premises in order to defend it. Let us look to the roots of Romanticism.

If we look at the German Romantics or the French Romantics, like Friedrich Schiller, like Victor Hugo, we find that they said that "Romanticism" was defined as being emotional. And that makes some sense, yes; Romantic works do have very powerful emotion. However, what happened to Romanticism was the emotion became so strong that eventually it lost its contact with reality; emotion became so strong that Romanticism became irrational. So to find the definition of "Romanticism," let us look deeper into this idea of emotion.

What is the root of emotion? In the twentieth century, we've come to the idea that emotion is rooted in values—that when we value something, we feel positive toward it; when we do not value something, we feel negative toward it. So our emotions are tied to the kinds of things that we value. Now we are getting a little closer to what might be the root of Romanticism.

How can we value something? The whole idea of values, you see, is on the premise of free will. Without free will, values make no sense. If you cannot choose to value something, then you have no values; your values are merely insignificant. You must have volition or free will in order for the idea of values to make any sense at all. And what I'm suggesting to you now is that now we have reached the root of Romanticism, and that is volition. It is volition that makes values possible, it is values that make emotion possible, and that's why Romanticism has such a strong emphasis on emotion—because it has a strong emphasis on value, and therefore has a strong emphasis on free will.

So we can get a better, clearer idea, I think, of emotion if we look at some specific people again within Romanticism. If we say that Cyrano then *chooses* values in the form of his white plume (if you remember that symbol); if we say that Tchaikovsky is struggling to maintain values within the music; if we say that Rodin is showing people trying to hang on to their values, then we are beginning to make some sense out of free will in terms of Romanticism.

I'd like to go back to this idea of Romanticism dissolving into irrationalism. The early Romantics were tied to reality. Later on Romantics became kind of pie-in-the-sky—you know, Romantics got the idea of escapist entertainment, some guy riding off on a white charger, and so on. Romanticism has to be tied to reality and how do we make choices, how do we attain our values, but only through reason. So I'm not talking about a Romanticism in which *reason* is not included. Obviously we are talking about emotions that are based in some sense on some *reasonable* premises.

Let us look at Romanticism and contrast it with a few other

kinds of theories. The most obvious one in literature is Naturalism. The basic premise of Naturalism is deterministic; that is, it is fate that determines what will happen to you, whether your fate is from social circumstances, whether you have inherited it, whether you had a psychological problem when you were five years old that made you an ax murderer—whatever that is, it determines the outcome of the story in the case of literature. If we look at art, we see Romanticism replaced by abstraction. That is, figurative art is totally out the window, subjectivism is in, and when we look at art we no longer see, say, Rembrandt, but we see Picasso. We see total irrationalism where, you know, if you want to paint somebody with a blue nose, you paint somebody with a blue nose because that's what you feel; that's how you perceive it in your subjective state.

Let us look at music. What has replaced Romantic music? Well, to a certain extent, in popular music we've kind of forgotten about melody and in popular music gotten into a beat idea, a primitive beat, so that the waltzes of the nineteenth century are replaced with a disco thump.

As popular audiences, what we are calling for is a Romantic vision. We want exciting plots where heroes act upon their values. We want paintings with a clear vision of reality that does not give up beauty. We want melodic music that stirs our emotions. Who does this? Not many people today. We have some people who have Romantic values, but they are so mixed that it's difficult to cite a Romantic artist. I suggest to you that if you look at the works of Ayn Rand, you will find both romance and realism united. Rand was the person in the twentieth century who discovered that the premise of Romanticism is free will. She also mentions that reason is the thing that ties free will to reality. If we look at her work called *The Romantic Manifesto*, you will see this brought out in detail.

However, I think what we have to do as audiences in general

is encourage the Romanticism within future artists. We have to say to filmmakers, "You can be as clever as Hitchcock, but you do not have to be horrible. You can paint like da Vinci, but you do not have to be naturalistic about it. You can compose as brilliantly as Sondheim, but you do not have to write *Sweeney Todd*. You can perform with the joy of Astaire, but you can do it on the stage of the Met; you do not have to do it in a disco." Reason is on the side of the artist and on the side of the audience; reality is on the side of artist and the audience. We can say to artists now, "You can uphold Romanticism because we've identified its basis." And its basis is volition, and now we can defend it. Thank you.

COMMENTARY

It was a very difficult assignment to define, discuss, and defend Romanticism, which is a highly abstract artistic category, in ten minutes. In fact, it is impossible as an assignment, and we cannot ask whether it was completely successfully done.

In terms of overall introduction, the good thing about this talk was that it used vivid examples. The speaker's purpose in bringing in nailing bodies to Volkswagens or slapping fish on pianos, obviously, was on the premise of motivating the audience. That is a very reasonable motivation, if you assume a decent audience. Most people, if they reach the stage of coming to a talk called "Defending Romanticism," would know what kind of nonsense goes on today under the name of art, and presumably would not be too sympathetic to it; they see this horrible stuff, and they need something from art that they are obviously not getting. It might be a way of intriguing your listeners to let them see that they are missing something, and you are going to fill the void. (One might object that the extremity of the examples made it sound exaggerated, but the speaker might counter that objection by just giving a one-sentence survey to indicate that this sort of thing, while extreme, is indeed representative of the whole nonobjective trend in art.) There is a caveat, though. Suppose you have an audience of people who do not necessarily agree with you, or who like modern art; if you keep saying "we," as this speaker did, they can very reasonably object to that. You can simply alienate them. Moreover, it is a kind of crutch on your part, because it amounts to saying, "I cannot prove all of this, but I am assuming you believe it, too." It would be better to say, "A rational audience would want such-and-such," and then, if your listeners do not like it, let them argue it. But to ascribe it directly to them potentially creates a certain difficulty.

The motivational element was undercut by the speaker's manner of delivery. The talk desperately needed pauses. The speaker wanted to be sure that she finished within the time limit, and that is desirable, but it is much better not to do it by the method that she used, which is to go full speed ahead, nonstop. It is much better to pause and let something sink in, if you can. You should always have a cushion of points that you can dispense with. If you feel, as you are delivering a motivation, for instance, that you need a beat for the audience to take it in, a beat you did not anticipate, you stop right there and just let your listeners mentally digest what you have said. As they are thinking, you say to yourself, "Well, there goes one of my dispensable points," and you just let it go. By that means, you keep a certain pace.

By way of increasing the motivation, one intellectual point to include would be, "There is a reason for this kind of art. There once was a different kind of art, as a result of two different kinds of philosophy that dominated the world. I want to tell you what an alternative would be and depend on, and then you will see why today's art has come to be what it is." If people do not get the idea that there is some deeper significance to it, that there is some basic issue involved, then they can hear it as, "She does not like this kind of stuff, and I do not either—but it is all a matter of taste, and there is no disputing about taste." It leaves a certain subjective cast, not by what is said, but by the cultural implication that aesthetics is completely subjective and arbitrary. Whenever I am discussing aesthetics, therefore, I try to stress, "There is a right and a wrong answer.

It depends on the kind of philosophy you hold. We see this stuff today because of a certain kind of philosophy. There once was a different one." That way, you derail it from the subjective track in the audience's mind and onto a cognitive track. Then they think there may be something to learn, there may be some objective points here, and even if they do not agree, they go on the premise of listening, rather than thinking, "It is her taste, my taste; nobody can know; it is all a matter of opinion." In art, it is important to counter that at the outset. But I do think this speaker definitely did intend a good motivational approach, one that could work with just a little of this other element injected.

From the point of view of monitoring the audience, the speaker gave the impression that she had her talk all prepared, and she was going to deliver it no matter what the audience did. I did not notice any stumbling or circling; she went ahead like a speeding truck. That definitely detracts from any extemporaneous presentation, because you leave the audience out of it. They do not have time to digest or question anything. You do not tailor your presentation to what they seek, so you achieve safety at the price of a canned quality, which I am trying to urge you not to do. Just take the risk of giving the talk, not being fully prepared, and falling flat. You will find, probably, that you will stumble, and it will be a more agonizing experience for you, but a more interesting one for the audience (and not simply because they are sadistic).

The speaker was definitely good as far as her level of volume; that was good; she could be heard. She had a brisk delivery. She made a few stabs at a kind of unobtrusive humor, enough to give the audience a little titter that kind of eased her over an edge here and there. Her sentence structure and vocabulary were simple. I could definitely have done with more repetition—but that will get me to the major problem running through this presentation, namely the crow epistemology.

There was definitely more material than could possibly be grasped in ten minutes. This is a common denominator in the presentations we have been discussing. You have to overcome the idea that because something is clear to you, you can just rattle off an enormous content to an audience of people who do not know it, and they will be able to understand it. The essence of objectivity, of a self-contained presentation, and of the crow—of all those points in this context—is that you have to figure out how much your listeners need in order to grasp a given point. The present speaker's main problem throughout her talk was that she gave the audience many points, any one of which could have been grasped if she had paused for a minute, repeated, given an example, given a contrast, summarized it, and then said, "Okay, hold that and let us go on." But when the points come one after the other after the other—assuming that we do not already know the points—it is not graspable. In part, it is too abstract without examples, and in part it is simply too fast to know what to do with. There is no way to assess it all. You have a limited time, and after all, even if you have a two-hour talk, it is limited compared to what you could do in a ten-hour talk. You have to decide between two different strategies: a whole bunch of points done hit-and-run, or a few, more essential points done more slowly and in depth, and the second is always a preferable strategy.

What I suggest you do, in general, is make a list of all the points that you would like to cover if you had lots of time on a given topic, and then cut out everything that you think is optional. Then look at what you have left, that which you regard as indispensable, and estimate reasonably how much time it would take you to explain each point to a raw audience. Finally, add up the times. You will find that you exceed by far what can be done in ten minutes—in which case, then, you simply have to be more ruthless; after you cut the flesh, you have to cut the bone and the vital organs. The only way you can justify it in your own mind is this: If the universe were coming to an end, and your listeners were going to hear this and then die, you might be able to say, "My God, I just have to cram it all in." But if they are going to be around, and they have agreed to come to a ten-minute talk (or whatever it happens to be), then they must know that you cannot do the impossible. Therefore, the way to get around it is simply to say, "This topic would take hours to cover. I am going to give you a couple of highlights, which I will try to explain, and I will say a few things that I cannot even explain, but will give you the general drift; and then I refer you to so-and-so." That is a much better way than trying to do the impossible.

Let us get to some examples. The statement that emotions come from values is an example of a statement that per se was okay, but that there was no time to digest, illustrate, elaborate, or develop. If you have to inject that topic, you are already lost, because that emotions come from intellectual content is already more controversial than Romanticism versus Naturalism. By "values," you mean some intellectual conclusions that you have come to, as opposed to reflexes caused by social conditioning or your heredity or your genes or glands or whatever, or as opposed to simply inexplicable primaries. That in itself is a very revolutionary theory. You cannot take a theory like that and say, "We in the twentieth century have come to the idea that emotions are rooted in values." Only a very small minority in the twentieth century has discovered any such thing. The great majority, including the major schools of psychology, such as the Freudians or the behaviorists, would say that that is a fantastic notion.

This speaker retained some plausibility because she kept her statement very generalized. She did not specify that by "value" she means an intellectual conclusion that a person reaches. As a result, the people listening could say, "I guess by 'value' she merely means what you like and do not like, which is a synonym for 'emotion.'" They thus hear her as saying, "Emotions come from emotions," or, "Some emotions come from other emotions," both of which are acceptable. In other words, they can accept her point on emotions at the price of collapsing her next connection, which was going to be where values come from. Then she went right to, "If we cannot choose, values are insignificant." Now, why is that? It is not very clear unless you can give some kind of elaboration. If "values" are simply a name for certain kinds of feelings—which is how the audience is hearing this—why do we have to choose them? It seems plausible that you are just born, and grow up, and develop, and start to feel titillated at certain points, and you like certain things and you hate certain things, and that is it; that is the way you are. So where does choice come in?

The speaker was not too clear about that, because she said, "If you cannot choose, there are no values," which she then amended to say, "If you cannot choose, values are insignificant." In other words, she was not very clear, and she could not have been, given her structure. Suppose "values" were conclusions that the mind came to—why would they, in fact, require choice? Why could not there be such a thing as values that are determined, built into the mechanism? Why do values necessitate free will? She is counting on this kind of contrast: "If man were a helpless puppet, completely a product of factors outside of his control, then he would just be buffeted by fate, in which case he would have no decisions to make, no choices to make, no goals to select, no values to choose, meaning he would be effectively indifferent. As against the opposite." But she did not have time to give us all this. It is so generalized and so vague that by the time you get to free will, it just kind of leaves the audience with, "She believes in free will, but why this is connected to emotions is completely unclear." Which means that the whole definition and defense is gone.

There were other cases of this in this presentation—that is, the attempt to cover too much, and therefore being reduced to a very abstract, floating presentation. Consider the discussion of free will. There is a certain problem here—if you are going to give the Objectivist defense of Romanticism, the defense does depend on the fact that it is based on the actual facts of human nature, namely free will. Free will would be a whole topic in itself, so in the context of this talk you would have to cover it in a brief, commonsense way. But you would have, at least, to give one level of elaboration.

You have not got time to say, "By 'free will' I mean the mind's power to think or not to think," because that will raise ten thousand questions, and you will lose everyone. But you also do not want simply to say "free will" and let it go so fast that the audience does not know what it is. One way of doing it briefly would be to say, "Are you responsible for your own actions, or is something outside of you the cause of what you do?" In other words, do not just use the jargon term "free will," but take some familiar terms applicable to free will. "Are you the master of your fate?

Are you a puppet pulled by destiny? Are you responsible for what you do; do you select it? Or are you just dragged by forces beyond your control wearily to your fate, with no say, no input, no choice, no control?" It does not take much longer; just by doing it, say, twice, in the kind of language that people would recognize, you make the point clear. (Note that it is obviously slanted language. A determinist will have apoplexy at hearing his position described that way, but that is okay—you are presenting your view; you never said you were arguing against determinism.) In short, you indicate what you are saying, and since it is so crucial to you, you repeat it. That is essential emphasis.

You also include its opposite. It bears repeating that you really cannot make philosophic points clear except by contrast. To make clear what you are talking about you have to contrast your central ideas with their antonyms, with what they exclude, so people will know what you are saying, as against what you are not. You cannot make "free will" clear except by saying, "As against determinism." You cannot say, "Emotions come from values," clearly unless you say, "As against the view that they come from chemistry or from God, or that they are inexplicable." You always have to set a contrast. Philosophy is made up of such broad abstractions that one absolutely indispensable means of clarification, in writing or in speech, is to say, "I mean *this* as against *that*."

This same type of problem came up at another point, when the speaker, in discussing how Romanticism dissolved into irrationalism, stated that Romanticism has to be tied to reality and to reasonable premises. She is trying to exclude escapism from Romanticism, saying, in effect, "If somebody sets something in a fantasy world, that is not Romanticism." But isn't it? Romanticism is not exclusively what Ayn Rand calls Romantic Realism. Romanticism is a very broad category. You can be wildly irrational and still be a complete Romantic in art. In fact, this was true of a great many of the leading Romantics. Dostoevsky, to take an example, is hardly an apostle of reason; in terms of the content of his views, he is an ardent Russian Orthodox religious maniac. By his own statement, the values that he espouses are completely separate from reality. Therefore, you must not restrict Romanticism to one particular philosophic interpretation of it; it is a much broader category.

On the other hand, what the speaker wanted to do was to cover the philosophical point. She was trying to say, "Do not think that because I am for emotion, I am therefore against reason." What left that question open, and prompted the need to clarify it, was the point made early in the presentation about traditional Romanticism. The speaker said that the emotion found in the works of figures like Schiller and Hugo became so strong that eventually the whole movement became irrational. In oral presentation, you cannot be held to exact wording, but that one is pretty extreme—it contains the obvious implication that emotion is appropriate only up to a point. It implies a view of emotions as nonrational, not to say irrational, elements in the personality. Plato would be quite prepared to accept that particular formulation (not that this speaker agrees with him, but simply by inadvertency). Plato held that emotions are like a roaring beast within you, ready to spring and take over and topple the reason.

Romanticism, in the minds of most people, is associated with strong feeling, emotion, passion. People therefore have two different reasons, in today's cultural context, to want to associate Romanticism with irrationalism: because it is emotion, and because it is art. If you know that context, the first thing you have to think in defending Romanticism is how to avoid suggesting to your listeners that it is completely irrational. That is tricky, because you cannot go into what emotions are, and you cannot go into the idea that art is really rational, because both of those are more controversial than Romanticism. This speaker, though, sabotaged herself at the beginning by confirming the original opinion her presumed listeners came to the talk with. They would say, "Yes, that is right—emotions get too strong and make you irrational." Then the next step will be, "Well, then, modern art is really a continuation of Romanticism, because the artists got so emotional that they went over into the nonobjective; the fish on the piano is just what the artist felt like doing, completely irrationally. But we were already told that emotions lead you to irrationality, and we know that, so what is really the difference?" If the speaker then invokes free will, they will reply, "Well, he was free to decide whether to slap the fish on the piano or not." You just lose them completely.

The speaker's very definition of Romanticism, the subject of her talk, suffered from the same problem as her other points: She tried to take in so much territory that she necessarily had to leave it unclear. This arose from the fact of putting in Cyrano, Tchaikovsky, and Rodin, all in one shot, and then later bringing in Hitchcock and Fred Astaire and so on. Take just those initial three. What is the problem if you try to introduce Romanticism by including literature, music, and sculpture all at one time? True, the term does apply to all of them. And the advantage you get is that you show the total range, so if people are not interested in literature, you are also giving them music, thereby motivating them. But there is one enormous problem with including all these branches of art. In part, it is that the differences among them are so outstanding that the essential is hard to identify. But that, in turn, is partly because some of these cases are extremely treacherous to define in their own terms.

Romanticism is a specific term standing for a very distinct school of art. If you wanted to talk about Romanticism in sculpture, for example, you could not equate it with any type of heroic sculpture.* As for music, I always avoid it in lecturing about art, because there is no objective vocabulary to discuss it; you say you hear the swell of aspiration in Tchaikovsky, and somebody else says, "Well, that is just what I hear when I hear some modern stuff"; or you say disco music sounds primitive, and he says, "I hear the pulsing beat of the man of achievement." So you cannot say those things are self-evident. Literature is the easiest art to discuss, because it is a conceptual art, one actually expressed in words. You can therefore identify what the author is after, what his message is, and what his means are. Painting and the visual arts are much harder to do on this count. You have to have slides and a really excellent knowledge of the field

---

* Ayn Rand admired Greek sculpture, for example, but did not regard it as Romantic. See *Ayn Rand Answers: The Best of Her Q&A*, ed. Robert Mayhew (New American Library, 2005), pp. 224–25.

to point out what a given piece of sculpture means, for instance, and what about it conveys that meaning. But the way this speaker approached Romanticism, bringing in all those art forms at once, all that comes across is a very generalized "something aspiring" or "something positive." Precisely because it is so generalized, though, it could apply to anything the viewer or the listener happens to like. Therefore, at the end of the talk, all he knows is, "You want the kind of art that is going to make you feel good"—but what, specifically, does it consist of? This presentation fell down in explaining that, partly because the speaker set her scope of examples too broad, and partly because she put in too much theory.

To summarize, the broadest criticism of this presentation would be that the speaker was basically off with regard to the crow epistemology. More specifically, it was the issue of pace again—too much material attempted in an impossibly short space. If I were going to do this assignment, all I would attempt to do in a ten-minute presentation would be to say, "Romanticism is a very broad school. It is completely opposed to anything you know about from today. Let us take just an example of it from a couple of plays, just that much. The general application and the other things I will have to leave for another time." And I would cover, let us say, one or two plays, but from the aspect specifically of something like plot and characterization, because that is what gives you the real content. If you simply say, "Aspiration and the positive and refueling," people can take it to mean anything. But if you say, "A certain progression of events, and a certain type of character, as against what you see today," they get a more specific idea. The whole thing here is to try to specify within a delimited time. So this presentation was helpful, because it gave us an idea of what complexity you have to choose from in order to undertake such a difficult assignment.

CHAPTER 10

PRINCIPLES OF ARGUING

BY "ARGUING," IN connection with this course, I do *not* mean formal debate—in other words, formal presentations, rebuttal, counter-rebuttal, and so on. That would not introduce anything new over and above the methods of oral presentation that we have already covered. In this context, I mean by "arguing" an informal process as it takes place in a drawing room, in an office, or at a party—a kind of unstructured back-and-forth exchange between two people; no speeches, no lengthy statements, just a conversation about some idea by two people who obviously disagree.

Obviously, if this is regarded as a form or method of *presenting* ideas, it has major drawbacks. It is not nearly as effective a method as either a formal written presentation or a formal oral presentation, because in this kind of informal arguing, you have virtually no chance to lay down your context, or to structure and organize your presentation. One obvious reason is that the other person chronically injects his ideas just when you get started, and it is always a point that you do not want to cover right at this moment because you have not laid the basis yet, but he raises it. The subject changes all the time in accordance with the other person's desire to persuade you; he keeps introducing new objections, and the thing sprawls all over the place. In addition, the other person may be antagonistic or cut you off; you may have no time to develop your point; you may have just launched into topic A, when suddenly you find yourself on topic B, and so on. In other words, this kind of arguing is more or less chaos.

Granting all these drawbacks, however, there is one thing you can say about arguing: It is basically unavoidable in some form or other. The great majority of you are going to be doing it anyway, whether you really want to or not. You will make some remark, or a person with you will make some remark, and another person will say, "I disagree," and you innocently say, "Why?"—and the next thing you know, a back-and-forth discussion involving momentous issues is taking place. The only way that I can think of to avoid argument entirely is to remain in a completely insulated environment of people who agree with you entirely on everything substantial—a course that would require you to withdraw from the world altogether. The alternative would be for you to simply sanction by your silence whatever you hear, however heinous. According to Objectivism, though, the proper policy is that you do not have to argue with people with whom you disagree, but you should not sanction by your sheer silence some horrendous remark; you should say that you disagree. Since most of you are, to some extent, going to engage in argument anyway, the better you do it, the better all around.

There are two general goals that you can hope to achieve by arguing. You cannot give a good formal presentation of your viewpoint, but you can suggest to your listener a new idea or a new approach. The chances of converting someone in argument are minimal, not to say nonexistent. To get a person to change his mind, particularly on a philosophical topic, you need an organized presentation, he needs time to digest it, and so on (unless it is an extremely delimited question). What you *can* do in argument is indicate, "Look, there is a new viewpoint here worth your looking into." This is especially true if you have any onlookers, such as if the argument takes place in a living room with people sitting around listening. You probably will not have too much success with the person you are arguing with, but you can suggest to the listeners that there is a viewpoint here that they have not heard before. An argument can function, in effect, like an advertisement or trailer for your ideas.

The second main thing that arguing can accomplish is internal. It is excellent practice for your own inner clarity. The more you try to answer objections—real objections, raised to you in person by real people who will not be satisfied with some facile retort—the more you will actually understand your own viewpoint. The more sheltered you are in this regard, the less you know the possible objections to your viewpoint, and the less you actually grasp its full logic and ramifications. In this regard, the Catholic Church is entirely correct in its use of the technique of the devil's advocate. Someone is not regarded as practiced and knowledgeable in his view until he can defend himself against someone else taking the position of the devil. It is a very effective technique, assuming the devil obeys some minimal rules of logic and order. In arguing, your opponent is happy to provide you with someone playing that part. As I said, you will find it helpful, and I quote one sentence from Ayn Rand in this regard. "If you keep an active mind, you will discover (assuming that you started with commonsense rationality) that every challenge you examine will strengthen your convictions, that the conscious, reasoned rejection of false theories will help you to clarify and amplify the true ones, that your ideological enemies will make you invulnerable by providing countless demonstrations of their own impotence."*

When (and When Not) to Argue

The first issue that I want to discuss is the topic of when to argue and when not—in other words, when to get into a full-fledged back-and-forth discussion, and when to refrain from it. There are many cases, as we will see, in which it is not appropriate. In such cases, if it is a moral or otherwise significant issue, you could make clear that you disapprove of the person's view, so that you do not leave yourself in the position that your silence or refusal to argue implies agreement. Nevertheless, there are

---

* "Philosophical Detection," *Philosophy: Who Needs It*, pp. 21–22.

many cases in which, given that disclaimer by you, it simply makes no sense to engage in argument. I would summarize it like this: Assuming you want to argue—and remembering that there is no moral duty to argue—you have to decide: Is it worth it? Is it worth the strain, or do you think you will do anything for your inner clarity, or toward conversion or suggestion of a viewpoint to other people?

Assuming that you are interested and do want to develop along these lines, I would say, in essence, argue when you believe that your opponent, however confused, is honest. He may disagree violently with you. But the question is, is he open to rational argument or not? If he is dishonest—which means that facts, arguments, and reasoning make no difference to him—then, of course, it is a waste of time. It is a waste of your breath, because you are giving arguments to someone who you believe holds that arguments are irrelevant. Moreover, if you argue with such a person, you are actually sanctioning his pretense. If he wants to engage in argument with you, that means he wants to pretend that he is a man of reason, that he has arguments for his view. If he does that while simultaneously denying reason, he is engaged in a real fraud, and your refusal to comply is much more dreadful to him than any amount of refutation by you.

I recall when I first discovered this many years ago. I was arguing with a religious person, and we exchanged a few comments back and forth, and he was eager to continue. So I asked him, at the outset of the discussion, "If I am able to give a case that you cannot answer, will you then abandon your belief in God?" He said no. He then said to me, "Would you become a believer if I could prove Him?" And I said, "Yes, I certainly would." Then he said to me, "Well, you cannot prove that there is no God." And I said, "Fine, I do not think that you can prove that there is one. But the question is hypothetical—*if* I can prove it, so that you have to say, 'I simply cannot refute this,' will you abandon it? I am prepared to say the same for the other side." And he said, "No, I would have to say that even if you can prove it, then I will revert to faith." At which point I said, "If so, what is the point of going through the pretense of arguing? You have already said that you are going to believe it on faith anyway, which means you *do* believe it on faith, not on the grounds of reason. So why pretend?" And we just sat there and looked at each other, and I would not argue. It was perfectly pleasant, and I could not quite figure out, at the time, why he was so devastated by that.

The question is, of course, how do you judge whether somebody is intellectually honest or not? You cannot judge that point by the sheer fact that he disagrees with you. Obviously, your ideas are not self-evident. They have to be learned; they are philosophy, which is a very complex subject; a vast number of honest errors are possible along the way, particularly in a confused, mixed-up world such as we live in at present. Nor can you decide that someone is dishonest simply because you are unable to convince him. Maybe you are being unclear; maybe you are not arguing very well; or maybe he is really badly confused, even though honest, so that your presentation is clear, but he just cannot get it because he is so mixed up. It is often very difficult to judge. In many cases, I would say, it is impossible to know, at least for me, and I generally follow the policy of giving the benefit of the doubt if I am not sure.

There are, however, certain guidelines that you can follow in judging whether somebody is honest. One pertains to the content of the person's views, and one pertains to his method or manner of approach. With regard to content, there are certain philosophic positions that are at the basis of all civilized relationships, and if these specific positions are explicitly denied, I would say that has to be dishonest. I stress that they have to be *explicitly* denied, not just by implication, because philosophy is one total system, and all the parts are interconnected. Any error on any one topic, if followed consistently, would imply the collapse of *every* valid viewpoint. Therefore, you could say that anybody who disagrees on any one key tenet is denying, by implication, every truth in every branch of philosophy. But I am speaking here not of denial by implication or one step removed, but open, explicit, self-conscious denial. For instance, I would say that a person who openly rejects reason—who says, as in the case I just cited, "I do not accept reason, period; I go by faith, even if my faith is irrational"; or who says, "I do not accept reason; I go by LSD," or whatever the secular latest equivalent is—cannot be honest, because "honesty" in this connection means the willingness to adhere to reason, and such a person has openly repudiated it.

It should be clear what I mean by "explicit" as opposed to "implicit." The sheer fact that a person believes in God does not per se mean that he is anti-reason. Philosophically, you could show that the advocacy of God, by implication, is an anti-reason view. But you have to show it. And as long as a person thinks that he can prove the existence of God, as Aquinas did, he can be completely honest, even though mistaken. Even a skeptic who says you can know nothing can be honest. If he says it as part of an obvious nihilistic attempt to destroy the mind, that is one thing; that would be dishonest, because it is then overtly anti-reason. But suppose he has gotten all mixed up by his philosophy classes, and he does not know what certainty is, and he has got three arguments that he thinks prove that you cannot know anything. Granted, he is being contradictory, because he claims knowledge that you cannot know anything, but maybe he does not *see* the contradiction. That is the difference between an explicit attack on reason and one by implication.

Take another example from the aspect of content. All civilized relationships depend on common values. Any viewpoint that explicitly advocates the destruction of values has to be dishonest—for instance, advocating the murder of innocent people. That would not be too common, but take a theory that perhaps is the closest to it today: egalitarianism, as advocated by John Rawls.* There, you have a view that states openly that if you are competent, by that very fact you should be cut down and made incapable of living; and if you are a loser, you are the standard of the good. It is an open assault on values as such, and I do not believe that it can be honest. You see how I would differentiate that, for instance, from the advocacy of welfare statism. A person can say, "We have to have a welfare state; otherwise what is going to happen to the poor?" He can

* John Rawls (1921–2002), American political philosopher. He is best known for his 1971 book *A Theory of Justice*.

be motivated, in such a case, by the question of helping human life, namely the poor or the weak. He can even say, "I believe each of us is his brother's keeper." He would be wrong in saying such a thing, but he would not necessarily be dishonest. The most I would be prepared to say is that he is intellectually passive, or at least conventional, and you would have to discuss the issue with him to see whether or not he is open to argument. If someone advocates the naked destruction of the able *because* they are able, though, that is a different proposition. In part, this is a contextual issue—how much knowledge is available at a given time, for example, advocacy of communism today as against in 1900. I would not hold a brief that most people even in 1900 were motivated honestly in advocating communism, but let us say that a character such as Andrei Taganov in *We the Living*, a kind of idealist who does not know what is involved by this doctrine, would be more conceivable at that period of history than today, when you would have to say that advocacy of communism in today's context amounts to murder.

Those are some examples just from the aspect of content. A viewpoint has to be an explicit assault on an essential of all civilized functioning before I would say it is per se dishonest.

The other criterion or guideline for judging honesty is the manner, or method of approach, of the other person. Does he come across as rational or not? Does he try to answer you if you make a point, or does he evade? Is he calm, or is he screaming? Does he change the subject so chronically that you can never make a point, until it gets to the stage that it is as though he is trying to stop you from speaking? Does he drop abuse, engage in personal attacks, vent hostility, spew insults, and so on? This, again, is not too easy to judge, because in arguments people get enthusiastic, not to say heated. A certain amount of chaos, of changing subjects, of agitation—even of antagonism and anger—is certainly understandable. So you can only use this as a kind of approximate criterion. When it becomes extreme, consistent, and blatant, the best thing to say is, "There is no use arguing under these conditions, and I will not take part on these terms." In my own experience, if I think the topic is out of bounds (such as attacks on reason), I simply state my view and say that I do not regard that as open to debate or discussion; or, if it is an issue of manner, I say, "I do not see how we can exchange views under these circumstances, so let us stop."

I would be happier if I could tell you that I could carry this out to the extent that I advocate. I do admit that it is very easy to get sucked into these things, because sometimes a person says something so provocative that you cannot resist a one-line put-down; and of course, the one-line put-down has no effect, and he immediately comes back, and then you give one more, and the next thing you know, it is out of hand altogether. I can merely say that, if you pick your spots so far as is possible, and refuse to get involved if you really believe the person is dishonest, you will save yourself grief—and ultimately do more for your own cause—by not sanctioning his dishonesty.

Do not judge too easily, though, that somebody is dishonest. I know people who do not want to argue on different grounds: They are actually afraid that they are going to be demolished in the argument. But instead of admitting to themselves that they do not know their own case too well, they take the way out of saying, "I am not going to sanction this person's dishonesty," as soon as he says it is a nice day outside. That is a rationalization to avoid. If you do not want to argue because you do not know the case, the best thing to do is to say in your own mind, "I really have not got the faintest idea what to say, so I will just keep quiet." That is much healthier than trying to figure out why the other person is really too vicious to be talked to. Then, presumably, you go home and figure out what the answer was, and the next time you can get your vengeance.

Let us suppose now that you do decide to argue a philosophical issue. Since we are talking about informal argumentation, by definition, there are no fixed rules. Obviously, there are the general rules of logic, and all the fallacies you should not commit, but those are broader; those apply to any form of communication, not simply arguing. There are also bromides, such as "know your subject," "remain calm," "be clear," "answer effectively," and so on, that are clearly of no use. What I want to do is cover a few more specific issues of strategy—how to manage or conduct the overall course of a philosophical argument.

Discover Your Opponent's Basic Premises

The first thing I would suggest is, try to discover your opponent's basic premises. This is what Ayn Rand calls "philosophical detection." The fact that somebody takes a position on some controversial issue of the day, which is where debates and arguments usually start, does not necessarily tell you from what premise he is speaking, what basic ideas he holds that lead him to this view. As a matter of fact, in most cases, he himself probably does not know, if he is not philosophical. In addition, he may be inconsistent; he may hold part of one philosophy and part of its opposite at the same time. But still, on the whole, there is usually some dominant philosophic tendency or angle or orientation in the person that underlies his concrete views on specific controversial questions. This basic approach is the crucial thing to try to discover, if possible.

Philosophy has a structure, and this is true whether anybody knows it or not. A political viewpoint rests, directly or indirectly, on an ethical viewpoint, and an ethical or moral viewpoint rests ultimately on metaphysics and epistemology. Typically, a person starts arguing some political question—wage and price controls, abortion, the draft, and so on—and you find, very quickly, that it is fruitless to resolve the debate on that level. But if you use the right method, you can push it one step further and elicit from the person the moral premises underlying his view on that question, and beyond that, his metaphysical or epistemological foundation. At that point, you reach the real issues in dispute.

In other words, the real issues are usually not the one that you happen to start with. You start with some daily controversy, which is really just the tip of the iceberg; your goal should be to dig out the entire berg and get an idea of what is separating you. Therefore, typically in an argument, you work backward through the various branches of philosophy until you reach the foundation. At that point you either see that the person is open, and that, in time, you can resolve the basic dispute between you, or you see that the person is closed, or that it would be a life's work to convince him—at which point you see that the original discussion is futile as well, because it rests on a philosophic chasm that you are simply not going to try to bridge.

Ayn Rand says many things on philosophical detection with regard to the meaning of various catchphrases, and I refer you to her article on the subject.* But how do you apply that in arguing with someone? The basic method is to keep asking, "Why?" to pursue your opponent deeper and deeper, and finally to let him tell you what he is ultimately relying on. You always keep your eye on the roots of his statements.

Let me indicate to you the pattern. It will not be as simple or straightforward or successful as this, because I am condensing the essence, but just to give you an idea: Suppose you are arguing on abortion, and someone says to you, "I am against abortion because it is murder. I believe every human being has a right to life, including the fetus." Let us suppose you decide to pursue it a bit, and you make two points. First, you point out the distinction between a potential human being and an actual human being, and you elaborate in what way a fetus has the *capacity* to become a human being, but is not yet a viable, self-sustaining entity, and therefore is merely a potentiality, and therefore no rights apply and abortion is not murder. Second, you make the point that if this person is concerned with the right to life, what about the mother's right to life? You explain to him the lifelong responsibility that he is imposing on her if she does not actually want the child, the sacrifice of her own life and happiness to an unchosen obligation, and if rights are his concern, it should be the rights of actual human beings, not the nonrights of mere potentials. You make some speech on that order. Here are some possible responses and how they would indicate different basic premises.

Ideally—and sometimes this happens, but I would not hold your

---

* "Philosophical Detection."

breath—the person will say, "I never thought of that." Of course, you will never win that easily, because the person will naturally have all sorts of follow-up questions, even if this is an intriguing view to him. He will want to know, for example, where you draw the line between the potential and the actual, and you have to know the answer to that. He will also say something like, "Are you saying that a woman should do anything she feels like, that she has no responsibility and can just live it up? Is that your idea of happiness?" You will get involved in a whole discussion. But those are obvious logical follow-ups to your original point, and it may indicate that the person is decent after all, that he merely was echoing what he was told with no special vested interest and no evil basic premise motivating him.

Now, though, imagine that you have made the same speech, the same two points, and the person tells you, "It is all a matter of semantics. You call it 'potential,' but call it whatever you want; I call the fetus 'human.'" That is a different kind of response. The first question that you have to find out is, when he says that it is all a matter of semantics, is this just a thoughtless catchphrase on his part, or does it indicate an actual philosophical viewpoint? If it is a thoughtless catchphrase, you can get rid of it right away and say, "Okay, that is out; now let us start again—what is your answer?" If it represents a basic viewpoint, though, then you are in business, in terms of philosophic detection.

How will you find out which it represents? Tell him something like, "Look, when you say, 'It is all a matter of semantics,' do you apply that everywhere? For instance, if I call this table an 'elephant,' is that a matter of semantics? Can I make it into an elephant? Is there a reality or not? Is it there or not?" A person for whom it is just a catchphrase will say, "Well, no, obviously a table is there; that is not a matter of semantics." Then he will be a little shaky and say, "Well, it is intangible things that are matters of semantics, not tangible ones," and then you just pursue him and show him that it is the same principle. In that case, he is not, to that extent, necessarily motivated by a bad fundamental. On the other hand, though, there are certainly types who will say, "Absolutely. If you call it an elephant, it is an elephant. You call it whatever you want; it is all a matter of language; we make the world whatever we want." In other words, it indicates a fundamental rejection of reality. If that is truly the case—and you pursue it a few times to make sure that he really knows what he is saying, and that that is his actual view, or at least the view he is taking for the argument—you have now traced his view on abortion, and you have shown that he is resting it on a certain basic assault on reality.

Similarly, with regard to epistemology, if you wanted to pursue that line, you could tell him, "Semantics pertains to how we use words, and words are concepts, and all human knowledge is in terms of concepts. If you say, then, that semantics is arbitrary, are you saying that all knowledge is arbitrary, that anyone's view on anything is as good as anyone else's, that there is no such thing as objective truth? Is that your view? Are you a complete skeptic?" Some people will have to pause, and others will say, "Absolutely; I always believed that. You cannot know anything; it is all a matter of opinion." Once you have elicited that, you see his basic epistemological view. You can then ask him, "Do you apply that everywhere? Are all definitions arbitrary?" He says yes. "All value judgments arbitrary?" Yes. "Can anybody know anything?" No. "In science?" No. "In ethics?" No. At a certain point, if he is holding to this view, you have begun to get, assuming this combination, that the guy is against reality; he is against knowledge; he is a kind of militant skeptic. Then, if that is the case, there is no use in pursuing the argument any further. On its own terms, there is no use—what is the use of arguing about abortion if he claims that there is no reality, that you cannot know anything, and that every view is as good as any other? On that kind of basis, you are never going to convert him to anything. There is no way even to deal with him, because he rejects the precondition of all communication.

On the other hand, he might say, "No, I do not go so far as to say that we cannot know anything." Then you simply have to, in an innocent, kind of Socratic way, say, "Where do you draw the line? Where is it a matter of semantics and where is it not?" He will say, "Well, I do not know." You say, "You said it is all a matter of semantics; are you now retracting that?" At some point he will say, if he is honest, "Well, I never thought of that; I will have to work on it further." You may stimulate him, you see, and indicate that he has problems. In either event, whether it turns out happily or not, the argument about abortion turns—and this will happen very quickly if you push it that way—into an argument on epistemology and metaphysics, and will be much more decisive whatever the ultimate outcome. If you could ever get this guy to grasp "reality" and "reason," by the time you did that, and then you came back to abortion—this would be in the next century—it would pass like this; there would be no problem, and you would at least be arguing on the issue that actually mattered.

Consider one possible further response, just to show you pushing it back. He might say, "When you say a woman has a right to pursue her own happiness, well, does a woman not have certain duties? You are not supposed to be selfish, after all." Again, you cannot pounce right away; you have to decide whether that is a catchphrase that he does not really understand, or whether he really does understand and mean it. You have to try to explore as a scientist, which is possible only if you do not feel threatened. If the minute he says that, you feel, "I have got to make a twenty-minute speech on ethics and answer everything," and particularly if you feel, "I do not know the answer," then you cannot be too scientific about your process. But the ideal thing to do, if you get an answer like this about selfishness, is to give yourself the assignment to explore what it actually comes from within him. He says you have duties, so you ask him, "Well, what duties would you say we have? Where do these duties come from, or who imposes them? Why should we obey them?" Just a few questions like that, not so much to go on a polemical attack as simply to grasp the actual structure of his view.

If that were the starting point, for instance, he might say, "Everybody knows our duties come from God. You are supposed to love your neighbor, including your fetus." In other words, he might indicate to you a religious viewpoint. If that is true, and he actually believes in God and faith and the teachings of the Bible and so on, it would be useless to say, "Let us set that aside and just argue about abortion," because whatever you say about potentiality or actuality or what have you, he will say, "I had a revelation from God that abortion is evil." Or you might say, "A woman has certain rights to her body," and he responds, "I have faith in the moral teachings of the Church." If you are going to continue, you have to turn the conversation away from abortion to the questions of God, revelation, and the like—in other words, metaphysics and epistemology. You have to decide either to explore and argue on this level, or to drop the discussion.

You will sometimes find that your opponent is very inconsistent. For instance, as proof that an embryo is really a human being, he will say that God has established that. As the source of man's duties, though, he will say society. Those are two different views, one pre-Kantian and one post-Kantian; he is not, so to speak, synchronized with one overall viewpoint. He is part religious, part subjectivist. As soon as you see that combination in a person, you see that he is more or less grabbing at random, and you have to tell him, in some polite way, that he is all mixed up, and try to organize his alternatives for him.

We will not pursue this example further, but the general point here is that in philosophy, controversial concretes rest on basic foundations, and the only real hope, in a serious argument, is to work back to the fundamentals, and then either argue those or decide that arguing is useless.

Do Not Concede Your Opponent's Premises

When you reach the fundamentals, and assuming that you decide to continue arguing, the next point to remember is: Do not concede your opponent's premises. In other words, do not grant them. Many people do this; they actually reach the basic premise, and then they concede it, either out of cowardice and appeasement, or in a shortsighted attempt to win the specific argument they started with. But this is a very grave error. Conceding basic premises is the attempt to show, on the other person's own terms, that he is wrong. In other words, you try to accept his basic ideas, and then show that he is being inconsistent even granted his own foundation. This should remind you of rationalist polemics. We saw this in the paper on certainty, where I conceded certain premises for the sake of argument and was completely lost. In general, this is a harmful, useless technique; in ninety-nine cases out of a hundred, you are doomed to lose.

Take the abortion example. Here is an example of conceding a premise once you reach it. Suppose you say to the opponent, "All right, I grant you that the mother has a duty to the unborn child; I grant you that the child is the standard of value, and everything else should be sacrificed to it. But on your own terms, even granted that nothing counts except the welfare of the baby, if the baby is unwanted it will not be happy—it is going to have a miserable life. The mother will not love it; she will resent it; she will not bring it up properly. So for the sake of the baby, on your own premise, the woman should have an abortion." I am sure you have heard this, because this is said repeatedly by liberals who try to combine altruist ethics and pro-choice politics.

That argument is hopeless. It completely concedes the basic premise, and the religious opponents of abortion wipe it out utterly. You have conceded the premise: "The fetus is a full human being with rights, but for its own happiness we can do away with it." The immediate comeback is then, "In that case, you are condoning murder. You are saying that whenever a victim would be unhappy, it is okay to commit murder." That is exactly what the people who use this argument are saying. They do not say that the fetus is not human; they concede that it is, and that it has rights and everything, only they are altruistically concerned for the baby's welfare. That is obviously ridiculous.

In addition, the opponents of abortion very often come back and say, "Look, if you grant that the child is the primary value and that sacrifice is the noblest virtue, the mother has no business resenting the child. She had jolly well better live to serve the baby, whether it makes her happy or not. After all, you concede that I am right, and that she owes the child a duty, so she had better come through. To hell with what it does to her life; it is just a sacrifice, and you grant that sacrifice is her duty." You see that there is no answer to that—except the liberals could come back and say,

"Instead of sacrificing to her unborn child, the mother will join the Peace Corps and sacrifice in Tanzania." That is obviously senseless; they have lost the argument. It is equivalent to the conservatives' attempt to defend capitalism by saying, "We agree that people should live to serve the public welfare, but people do not have any incentive under socialism. So we have to leave them free, because such is human nature." In other words, they concede the moral premise that the public interest comes first and that the individual is a sacrificial animal, but then they say, "As a means to your end, we need capitalism." The immediate answer is, "The capitalists had damn well better reform, and if they do not, we will have special schools or camps to reeducate them." There is no answer to that. There is no reason that that should not be done, if in fact they are serfs and simply do not recognize their moral duty.

The same type of collapse and defeat will happen if you concede an epistemological premise. Suppose, for instance, that in the abortion debate, you think you are going to be smart and get your opponent on his own terms with regard to semantics. You say, "If it is all a matter of semantics, then anybody's language is as good as anybody else's, and I am going to apply the label 'good' to abortion. So by your own statement, I can call abortion good." There again, you are trying to argue, and catch him, on his own terms. Of course, his immediate answer will be, "It is good for you, but not good for me; I do not apply the term, and there are more people in my camp than in yours." Now you cannot win. Once you say there is no truth, you have wiped out any viewpoint that you have.

If you have any questions on this topic of conceding premises, I will give you two horrible examples to remember, which do not even need to be elaborated, just named: the Republicans in relation to the Democrats, or President Carter in relation to the Russians. Intellectual appeasement leads to just as bad a result as does political or military appeasement. Therefore, I would sum up the principles so far by saying: Detect your opponent's foundation as well as you can, and if you disagree and intend to continue, challenge it boldly head-on—do not try for a polemical advantage by accepting his premise for even a moment.

Select the Essential Point to Answer

This next general point of strategy applies when you are on the receiving end, and you are being peppered by all kinds of points: Select the *essential* point to answer. Which, of course, presupposes that you know what it is.

This comes up as follows. Typically, your opponent in a discussion will hurl many different objections at you, all at the same time. Very often, in one sentence there will be three different objections. This may be honest on his part; perhaps he does not see that there are three different objections. After all, his whole viewpoint is not the same as yours, and what is important to you is not necessarily important to him. So he throws this torrent at you, and then he says, "What do you say?" Assuming you know the case, your desire will be to say patiently, "You made three different points; let us take them one at a time." In most cases, that is useless, because you get through two sentences on number one, and he right away raises four new objections to those first two sentences; you add one more sentence, thinking you will go back to point two, and he has got another one, and so on. The pressure builds and builds, and, of course, the crow epistemology sets in; you lose the whole thing, you do not know where you are and you do not care, and you cannot discuss it. This is enormously common. This is the form of the crow epistemology in argument.

If you are arguing philosophically, and you are aiming to go back to fundamentals, and you understand your own viewpoint, you will know what to do whenever you have such a barrage directed at you: Always choose one issue, the most essential one, and restrict yourself to that. Remember, this is an informal argument; you never signed a paper saying, "When I leave the room, everything I know about this subject will have been presented in the best possible order." Nor is this like a formal written statement, where you have time to think and edit. Therefore, if you omit to cover some point, you are not in any way implicitly left in the position of necessarily agreeing with the point you did not answer.

The best thing to do is to select the single most crucial point out of the whole barrage, as best as you can tell at the moment, and then just sweepingly deny all the rest. In other words, the pattern would be like this: "I do not agree with a single word that you just said, but I am going to confine myself to point X." If you do that, you leave yourself free. Then, either you start on X, get another barrage, and do the same thing again until you decide it is hopeless or you get somewhere; or you successfully deal with X, at which point your opponent, if he is honest, may say, "Why did you disagree with the rest of it?" Then, if you remember why you disagreed, you can go back. If you choose your X correctly, it will often cover the rest of what he says anyway, because if it is an essential, a great deal will rest on it. Therefore, do not let your opponent overload you, either inadvertently (as in most cases) or deliberately.

This is not that hard to do. If you are on the radio or on TV, though, it is murder, because then the pressure is really intense. As I know from some small experience in that field, you really have to concentrate, because the interviewer will ask some question, every word of which is a disaster. There are masses of people listening; you have to pick on the spot; the producer holds up the sign saying THIRTY SECONDS, and you have not even got time to say, "I disagree with it all"—what do you challenge and what do you let go by? In a living room, by contrast, there is much less pressure. You can always go back and say, "By the way, I never got to this point"; it is more informal, and so on. So it is not as hard, or as ominous, as it sounds. The point is still, however, that you *do* have to be selective. As a rule, there is more to answer than time permits, so you have to be content with restricting yourself to the essential. But you will be surprised how often it short-circuits an otherwise endless, meandering discussion, because it goes right away to the heart of the disagreement.

Suppose now that we change the example. You are arguing about the draft, and you are against it; you are in favor of a volunteer army. Let us suppose an opponent peppers you simultaneously with three objections, as follows: A volunteer army is too expensive, because it will contribute to inflation and taxes, and we cannot stand any more government spending; a volunteer army is unfair to the poor, because they are disproportionately represented in the army; and a volunteer army is unpatriotic, because it is un-American not to offer your service to your country when it is demanded. Of course, you could write an essay on every one of those three points. But if you had to choose one, choose the issue that a volunteer army is unpatriotic. That is the purely philosophical one, the one that focuses the moral issue.

The implication of saying that a volunteer army is unpatriotic is that the country has a mortgage on your life, that America is the land of self-sacrifice, duty, altruism. If you contest this, in one stroke you are able to establish, even if only briefly, your own basic view: that if man has a right to his own life, the draft is therefore anti-American; this was supposed to be a free country with limited government. If you get that in briefly, just enough to say, "You are crazy to say this is unpatriotic—I am the patriot; America was founded on the premise of individual rights and liberty," you will have laid the base for a quick answer to the other two objections. You can say, "No, a volunteer army is not too expensive; we just have to cut out all the useless welfare and government spending programs that are based on the premise that you started with, which is the opposite of the American viewpoint." In other words, you have already indicated that you do not accept altruism, so you have a quick answer to, "The draft is too expensive." The same goes for the claim that the draft is unfair to the poor. You can very quickly say, "Of course the poor cannot get jobs today—the whole economy is frozen, thanks to the government doing what you think it should be doing. If we had an American system, there would be ample employment, as there always was." In other words, by challenging the one essential, you lay down your base, and thereafter, most times, you can sweep aside all the lesser points in the process.

For this reason among others, then, it is very valuable to stick to the essentials. You will also find that this helps you in detecting what the other person's foundation is, because the essentials are the real issue. If the person advocates the draft, it really comes down to altruism and statism, as we have already discussed.* The other objections—that a volunteer army is too expensive, unfair to the poor, and so on—are just rationalizations of the moment. You see the difference between going to the essential point and arguing, out of the blue, that a volunteer army is not too expensive. Then you have to start haggling over how much we are spending, what we are spending, how much a volunteer army would cost, and so on; and then your opponent will tell you, "Well, in the latest study at the University of So-and-So, they said that a volunteer army would cost X, and then we have to have job training for all the corporals," and so on. Once you get into that desert, it is hopeless; you simply get nowhere.

I would therefore suggest this: As you listen to the other person speak, you should be reviewing, lightninglike, what things you can pick on. When I am arguing, I have a kind of monitor going as the other person is speaking, and either I put a certain point on hold ("That, I should remember"), or I let it go ("That is not important enough"), or I sift it out ("That, I will pass by"). Sometimes a red light will go off, and I will think, "That one I am going to answer, no matter what." That is the signal that it is an essential.

This is partly a matter of experience, of course. It is nice to have twenty years of standing before a class and getting peppered by five objections at every sentence, because after a while, by sheer accumulation, you get to know that there are only so many combinations, and you learn which to pick. Partly, too, it is a matter of how well you understand your own views, of whether you are clear on what is a philosophic essential and what is just a detail.

Countering Spurious "Facts"

To reduce the pressure of all these countless points to answer, but as a somewhat different topic, I want to say something about what to do when

---

* See above, pp. 58–60.

you are confronted with so-called "facts." In other words, not philosophic argument, but alleged hard evidence—itself dubious or blatantly senseless—purporting to be facts that supposedly refute your argument. This happens most commonly in politics. There are all the alleged facts of the evils of nineteenth-century capitalism, or all the alleged disasters that are going to come from nuclear power plants, pollution, and so on. But it is not by any means restricted only to politics. It is now very much in vogue, for example, to cite psychological studies in support of dubious "facts." For instance, you will be arguing on abortion, and you will talk about the mother's right to happiness, and then they will tell you that there has been a study at Purdue showing that mothers who were forced to have children against their will had a happiness quotient 3.8 times the norm, and therefore if it is the mother's happiness that is at stake, she should be forced to have a child.

How do you deal with this torrent, which is highly favored by many people who do not know philosophy and think they are on solid ground if they can simply sling "facts" at you? Let us be thorough. One option is to become omniscient—in other words, to learn the answer to every possible factual claim, true or false, that could ever be made. That would involve you in a study of werewolves, Indian rope climbing, stigmata, and a whole host of things. You would probably have to spend at least five years mastering the literature on Three Mile Island alone. This is obviously impractical, partly because it is impossible, and partly because it is useless. Even if you knew all of those issues, in the overwhelming majority of cases, these are not the issues that you and the other person disagree about, or are arguing about.

Let me clarify something here: I am not against facts as such; that would mean being against reality. Facts, including the facts of history, economics, and psychology, are certainly important. They are important even to philosophy, because philosophy does not float free in another dimension. We are here talking in the narrow, specific context of arguing with other people. In *that* context, the vast majority of alleged facts are an utter smoke screen, a cover-up, a rationalization. This is blatantly clear, for instance, in the environmental movement, whose members seize on anything with any plausibility and none, and then immediately switch to the next point as soon as that one is answered. Faster than you can read them and refute them, they are onto the next "fact," and they have allegedly reputable scientists in their stable.

Some technique or method is necessary to escape complete strangulation by this kind of data. In my experience, the single most effective thing you can do—not an infallible one by any means, because there are some people who are deaf to ideas and want only to give statistics—is to *learn to isolate the philosophic issue at stake from the dubious data*. In other words, switch the discussion from a debate about facts to one about philosophy.

Your opponent, in many cases, will be unable or unwilling to name his ideas—which is one reason that he gives you all these facts. But sometimes a person will state his ideas, if you ask him to (or are able to make him do so). I have sometimes had success with provoking a person into naming his ideas, as follows. Suppose you are arguing with an anti-nuclear type, and the claim is, "There is no safe method of disposing of nuclear waste, and therefore radiation will be roasting our great-grandchildren." You can argue about that, and tell him how many scientists have established that you could dispose of all nuclear waste, for I do not know how many centuries, in however many square yards or acres—but it will not make any difference, because the argument will just go on forever. A better thing to do is to say, "We disagree on this point, but I would like to know—are we discussing exclusively a question of safety? Is this simply a factual dispute over the disposal of nuclear waste? Because if so, that is pretty dull. I do not agree with you, and let us just stop. But let us see if that is all it is." If it is true that that is the dispute, then I would say something like this: "Assuming we were able to prove that nuclear reactors really are safe and that there is no problem of disposal, and that that issue is out of the way—would you then agree that we should expend every effort to develop nuclear power as fast as possible? Would you be a passionate advocate of nuclear power in such a case? Would you think it a magnificent example of the kind of innovation possible in a capitalist system? Would you admire heroic human creativity, man's triumph over nature, as manifest in the ingenuity of this kind of achievement?" If the person says, "Well, I guess I agree to all that," then you do not have any dispute with him, because there is nothing there to argue; he has just swallowed one stupid practical point, and you can tell him, "Look it up in the library; it is not worth discussing."

In the great majority of cases, though, that approach would raise a torrent of protest, more or less coherent, denouncing man, capitalism, machinery, progress, the Industrial Revolution, and so on. In other words, in the great majority of cases, the anti-nuclear protest is merely a tactic, not a viewpoint. If so, there is no use arguing forever over the safety of the reactors, because even if they were safe, this type of mentality would oppose them on some other grounds, or would simply switch to denouncing a new evil. The student protestors in the 1960s, for instance, would swarm on Columbia University and say, "We will not permit a gymnasium to be built in this building; it is an outrage, it is racism, it is evil against the poor, and so on," and the *day* that Columbia University said, "All right, we will not build a gymnasium," the protestors would lose all interest and switch immediately to, "We will not permit something else." That is, obviously, simply provocation as an end in itself. The same is applicable in the great majority of these cases. I therefore counsel, if you can do it, refusing to let a person conceal his real premises under the guise that it is only safety (or cleanliness, or whatever) that he cares for. In some way, provoke him into revealing, or ask him to identify, his actual premises. You can also do it for him; I have sometimes said, "Look, as I understand it, your alleged fact is meant to support the following view. If so, let us discuss that." And sometimes the person says yes.

Assuming that that does not work, or that you do have to deal with facts, there are a few lesser points I might make in conclusion. There are cases in which, on purely philosophic grounds, you can refute an alleged fact, by reference either to philosophy or to the inner logic of the viewpoint. This is *not* true, by any means, of all wrong "facts." You cannot, for instance, by *philosophic* means, show that nuclear power is safe, or that saccharine does not cause cancer, or the like. These are obviously subjects out of the special sciences, and philosophy per se cannot have a viewpoint on them. On some issues, though, you can call philosophy to your side and deny an alleged fact outright on philosophic grounds. Extrasensory perception would be an example. As that is put forth, it means awareness of reality acquired by no means, without any physical instrumentality, without senses. Since the senses are the physical means which connect man to reality, extrasensory perception would mean an effect without a cause, and is thus a naked attack on cause and effect. In politics, too, if somebody tells you, "Under capitalism, there was a history of ruthless, coercive monopolies," you do not need to know anything beyond the logic of the view to say: "How can they be coercive if competition is permitted? Capitalism means laissez-faire. How can people be forced to deal with these 'monopolies' if any competition is free to enter?" In a case like this, you can simply say, "I do not happen to know the history in the case you cite, but on its own terms, why would there have been no competition?" Very often the person will say, "I do not know, but that is what the facts are." And you say, "It does not make any sense, and I do not accept it." In other words, here you are rejecting something on philosophic grounds. If a Nazi started to hurl a whole set of accusations against Jews at you—not that you would argue with a Nazi, but assuming for the moment that you would talk to him—you would know that he is arguing from a racist premise, and you would reject it on those grounds. You would not start by saying, "There is no Zionist conspiracy in New York, and there is also none in Philadelphia." You would not deign to argue on that level. You would reject the whole thing on purely philosophic grounds.

The point here is not that facts are irrelevant; it is that you cannot take facts out of context. Philosophy gives you the basic integration of the kinds of facts that are available to anybody in any country at any age; it gives you the nature of man. That alone is then the foundation on which you can interpret somebody else's "facts" one way or the other. You can then see whether his claims integrate with what you know or clash with it, even if you yourself cannot validate them. That is why at a certain point you should say to the person, "Look, on the level of facts we can argue until doomsday. Every book that you cite one way, I will cite another way. We are not going to resolve anything this way, so there is no use. If we are going to have a discussion, let us define the principles involved. We cannot interpret what facts are reliable or not until we have some framework to know what the situation is." The shorthand way, if you get exasperated, is to say: "I reject that; I reject all of it. There is no use citing any more facts, because I reject your source, and this is my reason. Are we going to talk about ideas, or quit talking?" Then you discuss the philosophic issue. It is in that sense that I say you can dismiss out of hand a torrent of facts—by which I mean a torrent of facts poured at you without reference to philosophy, on an issue that is inherently philosophical. That you can dismiss, and you can defend your dismissal without having to be a scholar.

There is another thing you can do with regard to alleged facts if you are forced to deal with them, and that is to challenge their epistemological credentials, the method by which they are established or validated. Facts do not fall from heaven. They come from somewhere. In the typical case, they come from "authorities, studies, the latest research, all historians," and so on. That is what the person will rest them on. Now, science today is in a mess. In part it is due to political motivation—which, on the part of many scientists, is blatantly leftist. But more basically, methodology—epistemology—is in very bad shape. You can see this in the arbitrary assumptions that are passed off as science; the reliance on statistics without any check, as against cause and effect; a kind of blatant pragmatism that says, "We do not care about reality; we just want numbers that work." You see the results in the kind of studies that they put out about saccharine, or in whole subjects on the order of ecology. If you know this, you can always say about a supposed fact: "Today's epistemology is so dubious that where the thing is politically controversial and I have no firsthand knowledge, I do not accept any claim, period. I reject it. If you want to discuss a broader issue, fine. But if not, I simply deny it. I do not accept your authorities, your historians, your scientists, your data, your studies."

You might ask, "Why is it okay to deny somebody's claim? Do you not have to prove that he is wrong?" No, you do not. There is a very important logical principle, not even distinctive to Objectivism, called the onus of proof principle. It states that the onus of proof is on him who asserts the positive. In other words, if somebody tells you that such-and-such is the case, and he merely cites a dubious modern authority, that is the same as giving you no evidence, just an arbitrary declaration. According to a basic principle of logic, you are entitled, on the onus of proof principle, flatly to deny it. You cannot be asked to prove a negative, and it is impossible to do so. Therefore, you are entirely justified in saying, "I challenge your authority; I reject that fact. Either we have a philosophic issue, or we have nothing to discuss." I do this routinely, for instance, in regard to unidentified flying objects, environmentalist scare stories, the alleged virtues of Swedish socialism, and the like.

Finally, in any argument, it is always possible to find yourself stumped. You know your opponent is ultimately wrong, but do not know why and you cannot think of a response. That is a very painful situation, one in which I found myself many, many times in the process of learning philosophy and learning to argue. What I would certainly do is admit it, at least to yourself. The single most important thing in becoming clear in your own view and good at argument is to tell yourself when you do not know the answer. To your opponent, you might say, "I have never heard that one before, and I will have to think about it," or, "I do not know the answer to that, but I know that what you are trying to prove by it is wrong, and here is why." (If you do not want to give him the satisfaction of admitting he stumped you, you can simply say, "I do not care to continue this discussion.") But in your own mind, you should say, "I actually do not know the answer to that point." There is no methodology that will save you when you do not know the answer; you have to figure out the answer. You might try to get your opponent to take it in slow motion by saying to him, "Well, I do not know what is wrong with your argument. Take it again one step at a time. Where do you start?" He will give you his first premise, and you think on the spot, "Do I agree with that?" Then you ask, "Where do you go from there?" If he is willing to do it, in the process you may be able to see where he went wrong. Usually, however, you have to think about it at home, and there is no recourse but to admit it.

In conclusion, to become adept at argument, you need practice. Like writing, or like speaking in general, arguing is a skill, an art, and it cannot be learned just theoretically. You need practice in learning how to detect your opponent's fundamentals, practice in challenging fundamentals, practice in picking up essentials, practice in dealing with dubious facts, practice in judging your opponent and deciding whether it is worth continuing the argument. The only method that you can improve by, the only way to train yourself, as far as I know, is to do it. Plunge in and argue, where the circumstances are appropriate. Then, in your own mind, review your performance after each occurrence. After each argument, in the privacy of your own home, replay a kind of mental tape of the whole encounter, with you as simply an outside observer. Replay it from the perspective of, "What did I answer right, and what did I answer wrong? Where was I unclear? What would I say differently now if I had exactly the same situation again? What am I dissatisfied with? Was there some point that I really could not answer, and I was kind of floundering around, even if my opponent never actually caught me out or did not have the skill to trap me explicitly?" Very importantly, you should ask, "Was there a question I was afraid he would ask, even if he did not?" In other words, give yourself a critique of your own performance. I do this still, to this day, after every argument. I simply say, "The right answer to that point is this, and from now on, if the same point is raised, I will take this tack, not that." Then I promptly forget about it. You just stock your subconscious with right answers, so to speak, and you find that next time, or a couple of times later, they occur to you. That is the only way to improve.

Another, corollary method is to watch other people argue and try to identify their flaws and virtues. If someone is asked a philosophic question, particularly someone you have reason to respect, it is very helpful and instructive for you, in that split second between the time the question

is asked and the time the person answers, to say, "What would I answer
to that question?" and prepare your own answer. Then see what the person actually answered, and if it was someone who knows more than you,
ask, "What could I learn from that? How could I improve?"

These are the only methods that I know of for becoming adept at
argumentation. It takes time, but the results help in the clarity that they
engender in your own mind.

MOCK DEBATE

By way of illustrating some of the topics that we discussed, we are going
to have a brief mock debate. Dr. Harry Binswanger has generously agreed
to take the position of the devil's advocate in this brief exercise. We deliberately worked out notes to illustrate certain types of problems, so this
will not be a spontaneous argument. I will also keep interrupting to inject
methodological comments as we go on. This is going to be a debate about
free will and determinism, which, we will assume, started over some discussion of Senator Kennedy in regard to Chappaquiddick. It started, in
other words, on some daily political concrete, at which point my opponent picks up:

HB: Well, you have to understand that Teddy grew up in the Kennedy
family, where there is a lot of pressure on a person to become president. So no matter what happened in his personal life, he would
have had to defend himself and deny any responsibility for the
wrongdoing, and in short, I do not think he could have helped but
do what he did, given his upbringing.

At this point, I seize on the general deterministic implication in his statement and say:

LP: I disagree. I believe that he could help it. Human beings do have
choice; they have free will; they are responsible for what they do. I

do not accept such a thing as family pressure or conditioning as exonerating him.

In other words, I jump to the general philosophic issue right away.

HB: But if you believe in free will, then you endorse that whole religious mystical idea of a soul that is separate from this world and bound to a higher dimension, in which all kinds of irrational things occur. I think that with modern science today, we have come to understand that a person does not make choices in a vacuum, as you say, and the soul is something that we have to dispense with, due to the modern findings of science.

You see that you feel immediately that sense of being swamped. He has made three different objections in this case. He has equated free will with religion. He has dragged in modern science and claimed that free will is incompatible with science. Moreover, he has said that he does not believe in choosing in a vacuum, which implies a kind of warped view of choice as something arbitrary and indefensible. Naturally, I cannot begin to take on all three of those at one time. So in my mind, I have to think: "Religion, science, vacuum—he gave me three roads to follow; what should I choose?" In this case, I would choose the religious one first, simply because it is the religious view of cause and effect that has led to the view that science is an enemy of free will, and it is the religious view of free will that has led to the view that choice takes place in a vacuum. If I repudiate the religious view, then in one stroke I will go to the essential, clear away the ground, and get rid of one basic misconception of my view. That is my instantaneous mental reasoning, and therefore I say to him:

LP: You have me all wrong. I disagree with all of that, but the main point is, I do not have anything to do with religion. When I talk about free will, I do not accept the soul; I mean only man's consciousness, which I regard as a completely natural, this-worldly faculty.

HB: Well, wait a minute—what do you mean by consciousness?

That is a perfectly legitimate question on his part, and I do not want to go into a dissertation on definitions, because that will get us off the track. So I answer, in a commonsense way:

LP: By "consciousness" I mean simply the faculty of awareness, the faculty of perception, the thing in us that thinks. And all I say is that man has the power to think or not. And this is directly perceivable. Right now, for instance, you can listen to what I say, you can direct your mind to it, or you can simply go out of focus and drift in a daze. That's perceptible to you, and I say everyone has that power, and that's free will.

HB: But if that were true, if there were free will to that extent, then that would just make hash out of psychology. You could not explain or predict human behavior. We'd have to throw out Freud and Skinner and all the findings of modern psychology. Human action would be mysterious.

One thing is obvious—he has now switched from the question of what free will is to whether it is compatible with prediction. So I might, if I want to keep order in the discussion, say to him:

LP: Well, look, you are changing the topic on me. First of all, do you agree that it does not have anything to do with religion?

But suppose we let him go, and I do not try to change the topic. What one point would I have to make to cover this idea that free will makes psychology impossible? I have to distinguish the basic choice, which I regard as free, from its results. I have to say that I certainly believe that human actions are explicable by a science of psychology, and predictable within the limits of the basic choice. Given that a person chooses to think, that leads to certain kinds of ideas, value judgments, emotions, actions. There certainly can be a science of psychology. Then, as the final idea to throw away as I am leaving, I say, "There certainly can be a science of psychology, although of course it would not be the junk that Freud puts forth." In that way I have dissociated myself from the wrong side.

HB: Then you say that the fundamental is the choice to think.

LP: Correct.

HB: Then what I want to know is, what makes a person choose to think? It cannot be just an accident; there has to be some cause. Why are some people better thinkers than others?

Here again, you see that it is much harder to defend than to attack, because—and this is true in all these debates—he does not need any context; he can just throw anything at you, and you have to dig out of a whole mass of stuff and figure how you are going to lay your foundations. You thus have a much harder approach. He says, "What makes a person think, and what makes some people better thinkers than others?" What makes a person a better thinker is already a different question. So you have to say:

LP: We are not talking about better thinkers. There are reasons why some people think better and worse that pertain to their education and their ideas and so on. We are talking about the basic choice to think or not, regardless of how well the process is carried out.

And then you have to say:

LP: What makes a person think? Well, you imply something has to make him. And the whole point of free will is that nothing makes him; he chooses.

HB: But if he chooses, there must be a cause as to why he chose what he chose. Are you saying that this is an exception to causality, that there's just an explicable causeless event that occurs, which is focusing?

Now he is stating explicitly what he was hinting at earlier, when he said you have to choose in a vacuum. He is stating openly what that view is: namely, that choice is completely causeless. You would have to give him a brief thumbnail description. In effect, you would have to say:

LP: Oh, no, I believe causality and free will are completely compatible. They are in no way at war with each other, if you have the right view of cause and effect. Man's nature is the cause; the effect is the capacity to choose. You are, I would say, accepting the billiard-ball view of cause and effect—that if there's cause and effect, it can only be like one billiard ball from the outside striking another and making it react. Of course, on that model, there can be no free will. But causality is not restricted to that viewpoint.

HB: Well, that's interesting; I never heard that. I was assuming that the only cause and effect there could be would be a billiard ball. But you are saying besides that sort of billiard-ball causality, there's a different kind. I have to think about that.

If you get that response—which is very uncommon—obviously that is a very good sign, and that should certainly whet your appetite to pursue this conversation further. But now let us tune in a little later in the conversation to get another aspect:

HB: Do not the facts indicate that there is environmental control over a person's development? For example, we know that a child gets his values, in the socialization process, from his parents. In fact, they did a study recently at Cornell, I think it was Professor Farnheiger, yes, in the laboratory for primate behavior, who did a very interesting study on identical twins, which found that twins raised in different environments came out with different values and different personalities, whereas twins raised in the same environment had very much the same values and personalities, indicating the genetic factor is not nearly as important as we thought. And also, if you are going to say that children are not controlled by their environment, then you are going to say that if a child is brought up with maniacal parents who, say, feed it LSD from age one through adolescence and bring it up in some sort of crazy religious cult, that that child's going to be the same as a person brought up in a rational environment. I just cannot accept that. And if you just look at the facts, furthermore—I mean, really, we have to be empirical—if you look at the facts, people do tend to have the same values as those in the environment around them. And does not that show that the environment is the determining influence?

Now you have to answer that, and you can barely even retain the number of different points in there. He has thrown factual studies, misinterpretations, and everything else at you. You have to decide, running through all that, what is the *essential* misinterpretation of the proper view of free will that is causing him to come to all those different points. This is difficult. What type of point essentially unites all of these random environmental observations? He is giving a lot of alleged evidence showing, in effect, that children follow their parents and so on; therefore, he believes the environment does produce effects on the children, so you cannot say that they are free. In other words, he is pointing to the fact that a lot of people conform to their environment, and saying that this shows that they do not have choice.

One way to understand this is to say that he is failing to make a basic distinction between influence and determination. In other words, the environment can influence you without determining you. But if you put it that way, he will immediately want to ask the question, "Can it influence you against your will or not? Can it make you into something that you do not choose to be?" So what you would really have to say is, "You do not understand what I mean when I say the choice to think or not. You do not really grasp that. You are assuming that everybody chooses to think—but that does not follow. All I say is that people have the choice, one way or the other. In other words, they are capable of being intellectually independent, but that does not mean that they are *going* to be. The very fact of free will leaves open whether they develop their faculties or not. It leaves open *what* they choose." Then, of course, if he asks, "Then *why* are so many unthinking on philosophic questions?" you can answer simply enough: "Philosophy is very complex; it takes a great capacity for innovation, and most people are simply passive—but that does not prove they do not have the capacity to think on anything, nor that they do not have free will."

As to his other point, you would have to say something about the LSD parent, because otherwise you will have left open the implication that you believe a child given LSD from the age of one nevertheless has free will—which, of course, is impossible. The error there is the same type of error: namely not understanding the nature of free will, albeit somewhat differently in this case. "Free will" does not mean unlimited omniscience or omnipotence. Certainly, you can destroy a child's brain, and thereby destroy all his rational capacities, before he is able to get off the ground. That is not the same thing as saying that if he *has* a healthy brain, he has no capacity to think. You would have to make those points, although not in this simple a way, because you would get halfway through one point and he would have two more. Such as:

HB: Well, I agree with you that philosophy is the determining factor here, and it's very complex. The problem is that a young child is not a philosopher, and is not able to think logically about these issues. He absorbs them long before he's old enough to weigh them critically.

This is a very common point, one you can just answer straight:

LP: If he is able to understand what they are saying, he is able, on his terms, to judge it. If he cannot understand it, by that fact it is gibberish to him, and he will not be influenced by it. So either way, it is not a problem.

HB: It seems to me from what you have presented that you are talking about something that is not really free will. You have a different conception of free will than what we traditionally understand as free will. Free will is a causeless, mysterious, mystical idea of something that just happens in the person, and you are talking about control over a person's mind. It's something very different; it's not free will at all.

Here, he is indicating, in so many words, a rejection of the basic view that I put forth. I would have to say:

LP: I made it very clear that I do not accept the religious view, which is what you are here assuming. You are assuming that free will has to be something mysterious, unscientific, noncausal, and you are just reiterating that. Your basic approach is coming back to the surface again, but I have already repudiated that. I simply point to the facts of nature, without any reference to religion or mysticism, and say, look, we have minds, and you yourself can see that you can use your mind or not at any moment, including this moment. So it is a factual question with nothing to do with mystery or religion.

HB: Wait a minute—where did you do your graduate work?

Right away you are suspicious of that.

LP: New York University.

HB: Oh, well, no wonder—you studied under William Barrett, no doubt. The views that you hold are reflecting his existentialist kind of commitment to free will. Now I know where you are coming from.

It is very convenient for him, in terms of argumentation, to say this. He is immediately ascribing my views to my background. He is saying, "You have no choice; you are just a puppet mouthing what you have been taught"—as, of course, as a determinist he would have to. Then you merely say:

LP: That must be true of you; it must be true of everybody; it must be true of determinists. Determinists, too, have no way of knowing whether their ideas are true; they are simply puppets pulled by strings that they cannot control, and therefore, nobody can know anything on your view, even the truth of determinism. So your view is self-refuting—it leads to complete and utter skepticism, even about itself.

HB: Well, maybe we *do* know nothing; we only *think* that we know something, but actually, we do not know anything.

LP: Are you serious about this?

HB: I'm serious in the sense that one is serious in discussing philosophy.

At that point, I would have one or two exchanges to elicit whether he regards philosophy as just a game, and then I would end the discussion, because he does not take it seriously. Or, as a different ending, if I decided he did not really feel that way, and I wanted now to pursue what his fundamental premise could be, I would actually be puzzled for a moment. I would, in effect, think aloud and say:

LP: Well, look, here you are talking skepticism and how nobody can know anything, and when you started, you were this big champion of science, explanation, prediction, and I was the mystic who could not have any rational scientific knowledge.

Now, that would not be just polemics. I am trying to probe how in the world he is going to combine being for science and against knowledge.

HB: I'm glad you asked me that question. Science deals with observables. Science does not deal with the ultimate truth, science does not give you Truth with a capital "T," but it just gives you the regularities that we can observe relating the phenomena. What you were talking about is real knowledge, knowledge of some ultimate reality beyond logic.

There you have the final revelation. He is giving you one overall integrating view, and you know all of his essentials, assuming he is philosophically self-conscious. The viewpoint that he is there articulating, which now connects everything he has been saying throughout, is mysticism—specifically, two worlds: one a superficial world knowable by science but ruled by determinism, and the other a world beyond, which is ultimate reality, but not knowable by reason. That is pure Kant. At that point, you have completed your detection. You have also completed the argument effectively, because you now know exactly where he stands, and it is no longer a debate about free will. You can now decide either to pursue it, or to say, "I know you; that is enough."

CHAPTER 11

ANALYSIS OF STUDENT ARGUMENTS

Argument: Capitalism

FIRST WE ARE going to look at a brief debate on the subject of capitalism by two volunteers, one pro-capitalist ("A") and the other anti-capitalist ("B"). The conversation presumably began when one of them made some remark indicating that he is for capitalism—and then it picks up.

A: I'm a strong advocate of capitalism, because I believe it is the only moral society, because it recognizes individual rights.

B: Well, what about other people? I mean, individual rights—you are talking here about what can happen in monopolies. I mean, when someone owns a business they can just buy up other businesses and raise prices, and then where are we?

A: Well, in a free society, you are talking about someone acquiring or earning property or earning whatever it is that they have, and if they continue to prosper, they are prospering in a society that recognizes free trade, so they are therefore earning what they get, and if they earn it with their own labor, then they deserve what it is they have earned. It has not been stolen, because it's a free society.

B: What about the people working for them? If it wasn't for those people working for them, then they would not be able to make any money. So, you know, they can just give the wage that they want to those people, and those people have to accept it.

A: When you have an employer and an employee, they are both trading. A man needs work done for him, he has an idea, and he either has capital or he has entered into an agreement where people will invest in his idea; then he will need labor to put it into practice. Now, in a capitalist, free society, you do not go out and conscript your labor with a gun. You go out and you offer people in exchange—

B: But look at unemployment right now. People just have to take jobs wherever they can get them. I mean, it's so hard to find jobs.

A: Oh, no, you do not *have* to do anything in a free society except not initiate force. So you can choose to work for anyone who has work available. You do not have a right; you cannot force someone to pay you wages for doing something, but you have the right to work for anyone who will offer you a job.

B: Well, where else are you going to get money; where else are you going to work? They really are putting a gun to your head there, I think.

A: They are not putting a gun to your head, and that's the idea; finding a place to work is a very strong benefit of a capitalist society, because there would be many companies trying to produce goods for the people in society.

B: Ah, but that's what leads to depressions, because—

A: What, producing goods?

B: Yes, because—

A: This is a revelation.

B: —because there becomes an overabundance of goods, you see, and then there's not enough money for people to buy the goods, so there's depressions. That's what happens when there's too much business, namely depressions, and big business is the cause of depressions.

A: I thought we were just talking about unemployment; now you are telling me that there are too many goods.

B: Well, that's what happens when people are free to produce as much as they want. You see, government control is what we need. Because we have government control, then we know exactly how much can be produced by any one person, which will not lead to a depression, or a recession which will lead to depression.

A: Okay, it's hard for me to come at those one at a time. Now, on the one hand you are telling me that there's unemployment; on the other hand you are telling me that there are too many goods, that the standard of living in a free society would be too high and people would stop wanting new, better, or additional goods. Now, I have never in my life met someone who said, "I no longer want anything; I do not want a better stereo; I do not want a yacht," if he happens to have a rowboat, "I do not want three planes," if he happens to have one. It's like talking about some kind of utopia where all the goods that could ever be wanted by anyone are produced, and now there's unemployment. Well, it just does not happen; I do not understand where you are coming from.

B: No, no, no, I think you misunderstood me. What I'm saying here is that if everybody produces as much as they want, if I own a business and I produce as much as I want, and a lot of other people are producing as much as they want also, there just gets to be too much of one product, which causes a crisis of overproduction and capacity exceeding demand, so what ends up happening is we have a depression. And the only way to solve that is that we have government control.

A: Okay, the nice thing about a capitalist system is that there is a market where, if you produce something and people want it, they will pay you for it. If you produce things and they do not want it, they will not pay you for it—

B: Ah, what about oil? They tell us what we have to pay. We have to have gas in order to run a car. So the big companies, they decide what they want to charge for oil, and we have to buy it. So I do not understand what you are saying here.

A: So now you are saying the country in fact needs oil, needs it desperately. Just a moment ago you were telling me that there's such a problem in capitalism because they produce too much. Now, to the degree that these oil companies are left free to produce, they will continue to produce and bring new oil online if it is profitable and at a price.

B: Why did they tell us there was no oil? They told us there was no oil at one point, and then they come back and they raise prices?

A: *They* told us that there was no oil?

B: Yeah, the oil companies said there were no more oil reserves.

A: The oil companies have never said that there is no more oil in the ground. There is plenty of oil, and it can be extracted at various prices depending on the quantity of oil that's needed and how fast it is needed.

B: So we suffer because they decide that they are not going to drill for oil.

A: Well, you have a right to do what you want to do. If they choose to produce oil, they will produce oil; if they choose not to, they have the right not to. Other people would jump in. If there's a profit, then there will always be people who, in their own self-interest, will devote their labor, their capital, and their management skills to drill for oil.

B: But do I have a choice there? How many people can open up their own oil company? It takes an awful lot of money to be able to do that. I mean, the industry is controlled by only a few people, you know, the few people that are manipulating prices and buying up all these concerns. How could I compete with someone like that?

A: You could not, which is the reason you are not producing oil. It takes a massive amount of knowledge, a great deal of accumulation of wealth, and the people who have been producing it over a long period of time have built up the expertise, the capital—

B: Ah, but what if it was passed down to them by their parents? I mean, then I do not have a chance to even compete with them because they are given this money by their parents—that's unfair advantage to another person.

A: I see; now you are not talking about monopolies; you are talking about should there be inheritance.

B: Yes.

A: Well, you see, in capitalism, you have the right to your life, to the products of your life, and to dispose of them or not dispose of them in any way you see fit. If you wish to give them to your children, or to your friend, then you have the right to do it, because you produced it; it is yours by right; you have earned it. As long as we do not have a totalitarian state, you can do anything you want with what you have earned as long as you do not interfere with someone else. If you want to pass it on to the children, it is your right to do so, because it's yours. No one can tell you that they think you should give it to person X when you want to give it to person Y. It's your life, and you are free to do that.

B: Okay, well, I can go along with that a little bit.

COMMENTARY

Let me preface the discussion of this by saying that there is no doubt that the defense of the positive is much, much harder in this type of format, because the attacker can have sublime, blissful irresponsibility. She can simply hurl any accusation she has ever heard from any left-wing newspaper or history book, without any basis, and he has to try to dig out the whole thing, and he just gets halfway through and she hits him with another one. That, of course, is true whenever you are taking a view that is widely unknown and undefended; you cannot count on a context, and you have to give a whole lecture on every point. Therefore, I could hear the pro-capitalist sigh each time, as though his mind were saying, "Oh, that one, too?" The anti-capitalist did an excellent job. She not only took all the kinds of things that you would hear, but she got them in appropriately. Every time her opponent got into midflight, she would cut him down with the next one, and then he'd just pick himself up and she would zing right in again. That was really very effectively done. You see how easy the other side has it—they do not have to defend anything; they just toss points out.

We have to focus the critique on the pro-capitalist speaker, because he is the one who had the ball to carry. I would say he did a mixed job, with one or two definite problems that ran throughout. He did a lot very well, by the way; I should preface the criticism by saying that on many individual points, he did as well as he could within the time and under the circumstances. That is, he started to re-create his context until his opponent attacked it again. But the point is, the approach that the pro-capitalist speaker was trying had a fatal flaw: He entirely let his opponent set the terms. The way the debate was structured, she had carte blanche to say anything. She could say, "Capitalism has exploitation, monopolies, unemployment, depressions, oil, et cetera," and whichever she brought up, he, in effect, yielded. He gave himself as his assignment, "Now I have got to answer that one." That is inherently hopeless as a method of argument.

To a limited extent, you do have to do that; this is not a lecture by you. If your opponent raises an objection, you cannot say, "That is irrelevant, next point," because she will not acknowledge that it is irrelevant. But as far as possible, you have to try to steer the direction of the debate, rather than let her do so. If you let her do so, what happens? She is completely disorganized; she has no overall view, and she will just jump from point to point and hit you on the head time after time. You never get a chance to develop any one point; you never establish your premise, nor ever find out what her premises are. Therefore, it goes on and on, and the net effect is that you feel demoralized, because you never really made anything clear, and she feels, "This guy has got nothing to say; there are thousands of objections to capitalism, and he has no real answers." So you do not accomplish anything.

What could the pro-capitalist speaker have done differently, short of giving a lecture? Suppose he had taken her first objection to capitalism, which was the existence of monopolies, and shown that government controls require the use of force. Then she would say, "Yes, but it is force in a good cause, because we have to prevent these evil monopolists from harming the people." He would be hard-pressed if he started on monopolies (although she is well-advised to start there, because their existence is taken for granted).

That capitalism leads to monopolies is not a philosophic issue; it is economics. It therefore comes under the heading of facts. The anticapitalist's method was to drown her opponent in alleged facts—monopolies, unemployment, oil crises, and so on. She stuck to journalistic things, and she did not say much about philosophy, except that every once in a while she would inject a comment about unfairness, exploitation, and the like. As soon as you see that it is this type of argument, if you want to establish your terms and not just be bombarded by one "fact" after the other forever, what do you have to do? You might want to get it over to some point within politics, such as individual rights versus society. But that in itself is not going to be enough, because she will say, "Individual rights are all very fine, but what about monopolies and unemployment?" She will have that whole arsenal, which you have to hit on the head. There are two ways of hitting it on the head. One is to reply to each objection one at a time, as this speaker did—but then she goes on forever, because by the time you get to her last one, she has got research assistants coming in with more. So you cannot do it that way.

You do want to get the argument into philosophy, but you cannot just say, "Let us discuss rights." You have to have some way of undercutting her in this assault. One crucial thing is to separate the system you want to defend from today's state of affairs. That is not the broad point, but that is one thing the pro-capitalist did not do, and is very important in arguing any political or practical topic. Everybody thinks that by "capitalism" you mean what goes on today. Therefore, they are filled with the idea, "Every problem of today's society is a problem of capitalism." They thus feel entirely free to toss every problem of the mixed economy at you and say, "What about unemployment, what about inherited wealth, what about the oil crisis?" Without anything further, if all you do is say, "We really do create jobs, and we really do produce oil," and so on, she comes right back with, "But look at the unemployment figures, and look at the oil crisis," and so on. You have to take the approach of saying: "Everything you are saying is irrelevant. There is no use arguing on that level, because you are not talking about capitalism. None of your objections have anything to do with capitalism."

Normally, she then says, "What do you mean?" Then you say, "By 'capitalism' I mean the complete separation of state and economics—no government control over roads and post offices, no antitrust regulations, no welfare," and so on. When she hears that, you have already changed the nature of the debate. You are telling her, "Think before you raise an objection; be sure it pertains to capitalism, and not to a system that I repudiate." That in itself puts her in a hard spot, because after even that much, she has to think to herself, "I cannot just trot out anything. He has put a certain distinction here. Some things apparently do not apply to capitalism." In other words, she has got to be much more cautious now. She cannot ask about today's oil situation, for instance, because you will say, "We never had an oil crisis when the economy was freer; we did not have unemployment, and so on. Therefore, all the things you are pointing out are irrelevant." You would thus use the wholesale approach to undercut a whole bunch of objections. It would not undercut all of them, but it would get rid of a certain amount.

Assuming you wanted to make it philosophical, what would you do to force such a militantly unphilosophical opponent, filled with all these disconnected facts, onto a philosophic point? The best way I know is that when she throws out the first alleged evil of capitalism, you could simply say, "There are no monopolies under capitalism. So whatever you are talking about is not capitalism." When she gets to the next one, about there not being enough jobs or whatever, you already have two examples, enough to draw an abstraction, and that is the point at which I would say: "Look, we have a basic disagreement here, so we may as well not argue about the details of it. None of the things that you have mentioned, and ten thousand others like them, ever happened under capitalism. All of it is completely wrong." She has just said monopolies and unemployment, so you say, "Capitalism never led to monopolies, never led to unemployment, never led to starving widows and orphans," and you list about eight possible objections in advance of her saying them, so she knows you know the whole thing. Then you say, "Now, if you are going to argue on this kind of factual point, that is a historical question, and we will have to go to the history books. What history do you know, how do you know it, and what makes you think all these things happened? I say not one of them happened, and you have not got a leg to stand on." You simply make a flat denial, and that puts her on the spot—why does she think capitalism causes unemployment, in which year, in which industry, how many people, what were the conditions, what were the wages, and so on? She obviously does not know any of that.

Now you say, "Let us discuss this question seriously. Capitalism is simply a system in which people are left free to use their minds, produce, and trade. You tell me why anything inherent in that would lead to all these catastrophes. Tell me, what would? Then, if you like, we will discuss the alternative you propose, and I will tell you why all those catastrophes *are* inherent in *your* definition. If you can make it clear, you are free to argue. But show me why it follows from the essence of the system, because I say it does not. There is no use in arguing facts; if it follows logically, you can show it." As soon as she tries, you can immediately go on to philosophy. She says, for instance, "Monopolies follow because of greed." You reply, "What is greed?" She is already on the defensive; she has to define a term (and it is relevant—you are not being dishonest in demanding it). She says, "Well, greed is getting what you want by hurting other people." You reply, "You think production is possible only by hurting other people? Let me explain otherwise." Little by little, you would have to indicate your case. How successfully you could do it is a different question; it depends on your own knowledge, her honesty and interest, and the length of time available to you.

The main thing you have to do, though, which this speaker did not do, is switch over from arguing facts to arguing philosophy. He did not give himself the assignment, "Put an end to this level of discussion, turn it to philosophy, and get my basic premises on the table." You have to get your cards on the table. You have to get out as soon as possible, "I stand for complete laissez-faire. It is based on man's rights, it means the freedom of the mind, and anything else is death and destruction." That much is all. Once you have that, then the other person has to worry what to do in the face of that. But this speaker never got his premises out, nor hers. This debate was, then, an instance in which the debater could have benefited from trying more deliberately to go into philosophic discussion and philosophic detection, rather than remaining on the defensive. The thing was drowning in facts, and my instinct would have been to make it as abstract as possible right away, in order to assert my terms and make it philosophical.

Argument: the Existence of God

This next argument is on the topic of God, or religion, and it features an atheist ("B") against someone ("A") who is going to be defending a religious viewpoint.

A:　I understand that you do not believe in anything called "God," and I do, and I'd just like to say what I think God is. To me, God is a superior living entity, superior to any other living entity, regardless of what that other living entity is or where it lives. And that's what I mean when I say "God."

B:　So you say that that's your definition of "God." Are you saying at the same time that you believe that God exists, or that you accept the existence of a God?

A:　Well, I believe God is an entity that's extremely powerful, extremely creative, extremely intelligent, and responsible for my existence and the existence of everything in reality. That's what I believe.

B: Yes, but you used the word "believe," and I'm familiar with that word, and I think that it means according to the dictionary that you are placing your faith in something for which no logical proof exists. And if you use the word "believe," then you are saying in essence that you are placing your faith in something for which no logical proof exists.

A: Well, I do not know exactly what you mean by "faith," but I'm convinced of what I'm saying. For example, I would not maintain that God built the Statler Hilton Hotel. That's silly; individuals did that. What I say is, God created the means. For example, science. And in science, there's a principle which states nothing can be created or destroyed, only changed in form. Which means everything that is, was; everything that is, always will be. And my Baltimore catechism told me God was and always will be, and that's what God is. And therefore, I'm convinced God is, because there is something in reality and always was and always will be, and that's what they told me God was, and that's what I'm convinced of.

B: So in other words, you are saying *they* told you, and you have accepted what they have told you, without proving it to yourself or anybody else?

A: Not exactly. For example, I know that everything in the universe always was. Its form was different, but it always was. It is now, and it always will be. And to me, that's God, and that's what I have to hold. What I do not know completely is that it's an actual living physical being, but it's something that's superior to me and superior to any other living entity, and is responsible for my existence, my life, my mind, my everything.

B: If, for the sake of argument, what you say or what you believe happens to be true, how do you place something for which no proof exists above what your senses tell you, what your mind tells you?

A: I try not to. I will agree with you that there does not seem to be too much evidence for God. But what I would say is—see, I would never argue, like some people would, that God is unknowable, because then you are arguing about nothing. I would say that more likely, to me, God is unknown. That is, there is enough evidence out there, if I'm willing to check it out—the Bible, the Dead Sea Scrolls, some historical writings, different things—that I could prove the existence of God to myself if I wished to. So I say God is unknown. But that does not mean he does not exist.

B: But you are saying that something exists. If I say that I do not accept the existence of your God, then you have to prove that to me.

A: Yeah, and I would first refer you to the Bible; then I would refer you to the Dead Sea Scrolls, and—

B: Okay, okay, but if you refer me to the Bible, you could probably refer me to the story of Moses, for instance, who, the Bible says, raised his arms and the sea opened up and everybody walked through the middle of the sea. Now, do you accept that?

A: What I accept is, it's been shown historically that when people from Israel went to the Dead Sea, it was at low tide, and later, when the soldiers came, it was high tide. What I'm saying is the Bible made it dramatic, and that God is the one who caused it to be at low tide when they came and caused it to be at high tide when the soldiers came.

B: I really do not know what to say to that, except I have never seen it happen, and I have really never met anyone who can seriously say—

A: Well, let me tell you something that happened to me Sunday night. I was standing on the platform of the subway at 34th Street and Sixth Avenue and a young boy, when a train was coming in, pushed me, and I nearly fell into the tracks and I was nearly crushed to death. Fortunately, my body went backward and the train missed me. If I say the hand of God pulled me back, who are you to say it wasn't?

B: Um, what did the hand look like?

A: I didn't see it, but I felt it, and it saved my life.

B: Well, I feel a lot of things, but that does not necessarily mean that they exist in reality.

A: That's true, but do you believe in Thomas Jefferson?

B: I accept the existence of a person named Thomas Jefferson—

A: Thomas Jefferson was a myth and he was invented by the Founding Fathers and you could not prove to me otherwise.

B: But there are pictures that have been painted—

A: I have paintings of God.

B: If you have a painting of God, please show it to me; I have never seen one. I have seen paintings of a man who was called Jesus Christ; I have never seen a painting of God, but that is not what we are talking about. Somebody could imagine that a god exists, and they could paint what they imagined, but that does not prove the point—

A: Well, someone could have imagined that Thomas Jefferson exists and painted a picture of Jefferson.

B: No, there is historical evidence for the existence of—

A: Such as?

B: He wrote the Declaration of Independence.

A: There is some evidence to indicate that he did not physically write the document, that Benjamin Franklin did.

B: Okay, let us say there is evidence that— We are getting off the subject.

A: No, I want to know—

B: We are talking about God; we are not talking about Thomas Jefferson.

A: We are talking about evidence.

B: Okay, and there is no logical proof that your God, as you define him, exists. Even Thomas Aquinas—

A: Have you read the Bible?

B: I have read parts of the Bible, but the Bible can be—

A: Have you read the Dead Sea Scrolls?

B: I have not read the Dead Sea Scrolls.

A: Okay, have you read the historical writings? Have you read a book called *The Incredible Christians*?

B: No, I have not.

A: Have you read Antony Flew's *God and Philosophy*?

B: No, I have not.

A: How about George Smith's *Atheism: The Case Against God*?

B: No, but the point is, just because somebody wrote these books does not prove that your God exists. There was a philosopher, I forget his name, who said that if a tree falls in the woods and you are not there that the tree did not fall. But the tree *did* fall, and all you would have to do to prove it is go to that point and see the tree lying on the ground.

A: I'm not positive, but I think the same philosopher—no, it was Bishop Berkeley who said if God perceives the tree falling, then in fact it did fall.

B: I think we could go on for hours, and I think it's about ten minutes right now.

A: It's eight minutes and twenty-eight seconds. The thing is this—I have read *Atheism: The Case Against God*, I have read *God and Philosophy*, I have read John Galt's speech against God, and I know all the arguments for atheism. Apparently you have *not* read the Bible; you have *not* read the Dead Sea Scrolls; you have *not* been inside a church; you have *not* examined the life of Jesus. I think I got a better case.

B: Well, I have done a few of those things, and I still have not found any logical proof that your so-called God exists.

COMMENTARY

This was obviously a brief snippet out of what would be a much longer argument, and it is very good for illustrating certain things. The pro-God side had a more forceful presentation. He knew exactly what analogies he wanted to use, what authorities he was going to quote, what type of experiences he was going to cite; he was ready, and he was obviously trained in argumentation. As soon as something was said, it was like a certain button was pressed and he gave us the response. So in that sense, the atheist was at a certain disadvantage, since he obviously did not have the experience that his opponent had.

The atheist did try to bring out that belief in God is an act of faith, a belief for which his opponent has no evidence. He tried that point several times, only he never really made it convincing. In other words, he was trying an epistemological tack; rather than directly attacking God, he was saying, "You have no way of knowing this." But instead of his opponent saying, "I guess I have no proof, so I am refuted," which the atheist had more or less hoped or expected, his opponent jumped in and said various things that were very realistic for a trained debater. It is very infrequent that a person will say, "Yes, my belief is absolutely arbitrary; I have got nothing to go on at all," and then throw himself at your feet. In a real-life case, it is a mixture of faith and nonfaith. In other words, it is faith, and then when you say that faith is arbitrary, he will throw in an analogy or an alleged historical parallel or some experience he had, and say, "Is that not evidence?"

Attacking faith is an essential point in debating religion. In order to bring that strategy to fruition in an argument, in order to make it successful, you have to pin your opponent down by getting him to agree on the method he is going to use. One thing you can do is get him in advance to stake his argument on what he is calling "evidence." In this case, the religious side was very adroit in moving from, "There is evidence," to, "There is no evidence," because part of the time he was giving evidence, and the other part of the time he was saying it is unknown—not "unknowable," he said, but "unknown." But if it is unknown, an obvious comeback is, "How do you know it then? On what basis?" Then, when he gives his historical data, like the parallel to Jefferson or the Dead Sea Scrolls or whatever, before you argue with that, the first thing you have to do is determine if he is going to rely on this, or on a hit-and-run approach. In other words, before even going into it, I would say: "Look, before we discuss the Thomas Jefferson parallel, I need to find out if you are really going to rest the case for God on that parallel. I need to know that you really think that the two are similar, and that if I can show you that there is an essential difference between those two, you will withdraw your argument for God and become an atheist. In other words, is this just a debating gimmick, and as soon as I hit it, you are going to vanish and show up somewhere else, or do you really believe this? Because then we will have to take it slowly and see." That would give him pause, because then he realizes that he is sticking all of his eggs in one basket, whereas one of the things that this speaker was able to do—which is exactly what is done in real life—is to have an egg in each of twelve different baskets, and each time you break one, he just brings out another basket, and by the time you get to the twelfth one, he has got a whole new supply, and it just goes on forever.

What, then, should be your answer once he says, for instance, that he is relying on the parallel to Thomas Jefferson? After all, the religious argument goes, you have not directly perceived Thomas Jefferson, and you have not directly perceived God. In both cases, then, you are accepting the existence of an entity on something other than firsthand evidence. In each case, you have a document written by the unperceived entity in question (the Declaration of Independence and the Bible, respectively), so what is the difference? Put more generally, the idea is that any inference to an unperceived entity is in the same category, and if we can do it with one, we can do it with all. The question, then, is: Is that true, or is there some *essential* difference between our present-day inference to Thomas Jefferson and the inference to God? The atheist tried to say he has never seen a picture of God. That would be relevant if it were pressed a little further. But he did not press it, because the answer was, "There *are* pictures"; there are symbolic representations of God on the Sistine ceiling and elsewhere. That in itself, then, was not an unanswerable statement.

The question to ask is whether there can be evidence for God. If you know clearly in advance the answer to that, then you can wipe out all attempts to base belief in God on the Dead Sea Scrolls, Thomas Jefferson parallels, subway experiences, or whatever. Evidence for God is, as such, an impossibility. If you know that, you do not have to argue ten different varieties of alleged evidence, because you know the whole thing is out—*if* you make a certain point at the outset. The atheist in this argument could have done one thing that would have laid the base to show that there is no evidence for God, that there *can be* no evidence for God. Suppose you heard this argument between two people:

A: There is a gloop in the lobby of this hotel.

B: No, there is not.

A: It is just like Thomas Jefferson.

B: No, it is not.

A: Have you read *The Theory and Practice of Gloop* by Professor Schmohawk?

B: No.

The obvious question that would be insistent in the forefront of your mind before you could resolve this is: What is a gloop? You would want a definition. Now, in some arguments a definition is not necessary. In the case of God, though, it is essential, because the essence of the argument revolves around the type of entity that the religious person is trying to establish.

The pro-God side here was very cagey about that, because he gave an abundance of definitions, which switched all the time, and none of which were God. The essential thing you would have to do is point that out. When he gives a definition, you should not think, "That is just a preliminary; now we are going to get on to how he proves it." You have to stop right there and say, "What type of entity is this? Are we sure we know what we are talking about?" If you analyze what he said, in fact, you will see that part of the time he was talking about God, and part of the time he was not, and the plausibility he got is by the oscillation.

He began with, "God is a superior living entity," without further definition. His atheist opponent did not ask for any elaboration of that. Per se, of course, a superior living entity is hardly an impossibility. "Superior" is undefined in that statement, so it could mean stronger, more intelligent, more cunning, or who knows what. There are many realistic possibilities under "superior living entity." Therefore, if that is the definition of what God is, the appropriate comeback in such a case would be, "If that is all you mean, you are talking about a question of science. You are asking, in effect, whether Mars is populated by a living entity that has powers that we do not. I do not know; that is a scientific question, and we would not argue that philosophically. Is that what you worship when you go to church? Is that what you pray to?" You would have to ask him a few things like that, and immediately, if you pressed that definition, he would have to say, "No, I do not mean just like human beings but with more muscles, or with a higher IQ. When I say 'superior,' I mean . . ." Now, he will not tell you right away; if he did, the whole thing would be over—but he will say something like "responsible for the important things in the universe."

You have to acquire the ability to take these things literally and then play them back to the person: "If that is what you mean, is it this?" Then he says, "No," and you have to drive him until he finally admits what he is saying. Suppose a person says, "God is that which is responsible for the important things in the universe." The first question is then, "What are the important things that he is responsible for? War? Sex? What?" Suppose he then says, "For existence as a whole." Then, of course, you have got a definition that does capture the essence of God ("God is that which is responsible for existence as a whole"), so you have accomplished stage one. That is very different, however, from "a superior living being." It is also much easier to argue about, because then you have said that God is outside the universe. Or put another way, then you have said, "God is outside nature; he is supernatural; he is part of a dimension that completely transcends perception, argument, logic, reason, science, law, and so on." If you establish that, any claim for evidence for God is out.

The main thing you have to do in an argument of this type is to show the person that you cannot argue for God. God and argument are two opposites, because argument takes place within the universe on the basis of sensory experience, and can lead only to something that can be established on the basis of experience. God, however, by his nature, is a supernatural being. He is not just another thing in the universe; he is something in another dimension, a dimension completely opposite to the one in which we live. Therefore, as educated religious people themselves concede, he is something outside the capacity to argue. But if you go with "superior living entity," that sounds like a thing in the universe that you can argue about. If you then simply jump from that to "responsible for all of existence," but keep the connotation of "something in this world, natural and intelligible," then you have your God and eat him, too. You can then win any argument, because you can make arbitrary claims on the basis of your supernatural definition, and as soon as the person says, "How do you prove that?" you switch back to your natural definition.

Here is another instance. This is common in the religious camp, and it is a good example of the role of definitions. The theist says, "Nothing can be created nor destroyed; therefore, something must always have existed, and I call 'God' that which always is and will be." It is certainly true that nothing can be created or destroyed, and that all that can exist is change of form, and that there must therefore be something that always is and will be. That much is unquestionable (it was, in fact, Aquinas's third argument for the existence for God), so the argument is certainly true up to that point.

The only problem with that as a definition or an argument for God is that that which always is and will be is the universe. You would then say to the theist, "Do you make a distinction between the sheer physical stuff and an alleged supernatural creator of it? When you simply say, 'Something is and always will be,' that leaves wide-open whether that something is a supernatural thing or not. You have not given any evidence. I say it is the stuff we see around us, physical matter in different forms. If you say it is something beyond that, transcendent and supernatural, then you have to tell me what." In the argument here, the atheist let that pass by. The reason the audience had the net impression that the religious side won is that the theist kept giving definition after definition, and it seemed like he could give a radio program on God's nature—he knew more about God than anybody for many years, and he just kept bringing it out each time, and the atheist let him get away with it. What you have to do is to decide when these characterizations come forth, "Is this God or not?" If it is something natural, finite, part of this physical world, then you cannot call it by the term "God." Therefore, you can believe in it, but it is not relevant to establishing God. If it is relevant to establishing God, it is something supernatural, infinite, indefinable, beyond all argument—and then there is no use giving evidence for it.

In short, the essential strategy of the religious side is to use a natural definition to justify using evidence to come to a supernatural conclusion. If you are aware that that strategy is being employed, you can puncture it at the very outset by insisting on a definition, isolating its supernatural character, and then repudiating appeals to evidence as such. That, in essence, is the strategy that I would suggest in that type of argument.

More broadly, what the atheist did not do, in terms of method of argument, was similar to the problem with the pro-capitalist side in the previous debate. That is, the atheist had a tendency, in this argument, to let the other side come on strong; he just kind of reeled as each new attack hit him, and he gulped and picked up and started again from scratch. We thus have two examples from which to learn a general principle valuable in any topic: *Establish* *your* own *fundamentals*. Decide, "What are the

essentials of my case, the hard-core foundation, without which I am lost?"
If I am arguing in favor of capitalism, for example, I know I have to get
in early that it is the system based on rights, and that I believe in selfishness and reason. That is my foundation, and from there I can go wherever
the argument takes me. If I am trying to argue against religion, the first
thing I know I have to do is to establish the difference between God and
reason, to make it clear that I do not regard the claims of religion as
natural, but as supernatural, and that reason and evidence are therefore
out. That is a kind of insistent order from the beginning. Even if my opponent overwhelms me in the first couple of exchanges, the order will be
constantly saying, "Say that God is supernatural and force him to grant
that." As long as you have that in your mind, at some point you will have
a chance to come out with it. If you know the point, and if you have had
enough experience, you will be able to say it forcefully enough and turn
the argument against him.

In general, though, the advice I would give is: Do not try to answer
the person on the terms that he puts forth. You cannot just evade what he
says, obviously. But what you *can* do is say, "I cannot discuss it on those
terms because"—and by the sheer fact of saying that, you disarm him,
and then you try to get in your principle. That is the important point.

This would also apply to the point in this argument at which the religious side made a completely irrelevant speech that was very effective
nonetheless: "Have you read the Bible? Have you read so-and-so? Did you
study this, and this?" He gave a whole bunch of imposing titles, and it
suggested that he has erudition, he has wisdom, he knows this inside out,
and the poor atheist, in effect, is an ignoramus and has no business living
if that is the state of his knowledge.

The theist was obviously trying to intimidate his opponent in a certain way, because he was not citing the alleged evidence from these particular books, but peppering the atheist with titles. He wanted to undercut
his opponent by making him feel, "My God, I do not know what I am
talking about." You have to have an instinct in argument: If someone is
doing that to you, you have to come on strong in return and show that

you are not intimidated. Here, the atheist said, "I have read part of it," implicitly suggesting, "It would be nice if I had read all that, but I never got around to it." There is a more effective response. A good example of taking the offensive would be to say, "Now I see why you are so misguided, if you are filled with all that stuff." That verges on ad hominem, but it is not inappropriate, because you are on the receiving side of an attempt at intimidation. If you have not read the works your opponent is citing, you might want to say, "Tell me what I missed," which puts your opponent in the position of having to defend that this is relevant. You might also be tempted to recite your own barrage, to show that you are educated in your own literature. But that still concedes the point that in a philosophic argument on this kind of topic, the amount you have read is relevant. In fact, it is not relevant.

To discuss the existence of God, it is entirely irrelevant to know the Bible, the works of Antony Flew, sundry pamphlets, and so on. It is completely unnecessary and useless, because you are discussing a purely philosophic question. Therefore, in this argument, I would have said something like, "I have not read any of it," even if I had. I might tell him later that I had, but my instinct would be to say: "I have never read any of it, proudly, because I do not read complete garbage. On this issue there is no need to do any reading. It is clear-cut. I do not spend my time studying werewolves and all the rest of it, and for the same reason I do not read all the maunderings on this subject. If you want to discuss the subject, let us hear what you know, not these alleged authorities." Note, however, that if it is the type of subject on which you *should* have read and you did not, then that is not an appropriate response; then that becomes a counsel of desperation. Normally, though, in a philosophic issue, all of this type of reading is irrelevant.

In conclusion, let me say something about the etiquette or morality of allowing somebody to interrupt you, yell over you, and so on. It is virtually impossible to avoid that in an argument, because there is no structure and no organization; passions run high, neither side knows the other's view, and therefore neither side listens to the other. Each is preparing his next statement as the other is talking, and as soon as you stop for breath, he rushes in because he is afraid too many points are going to come out. So it is almost impossible to have a decorous, polite, "After you, Alfonse" argument. However, if someone is interrupting as intimidation, to prevent you from speaking, to swamp you in sheer sound and brazenness, then you have to say, "I am sorry, you are not giving me a chance to speak; I will not talk under these conditions." I do not think that either did that in this debate. The religious side was coming on a bit strong, but not beyond the bounds of what would be normal in an argument. He was trying to overwhelm his atheist opponent with so much verbiage that the atheist would not have a chance to figure out what to say, which is partly what came about. In that case, you have to then draw a line. If you find you are being rushed to the point where you simply cannot get your wits, and you are losing point after point, and you know you have answers but it is all going by too fast, you have to say, "Stop; I cannot argue this way. We either have to slow down and do it one point at a time, or I am out."

Mock Argument: Objectivity

This is one final sample argument to conclude our discussion of arguing. The subject of this one is objectivity—is objective knowledge possible or not? A volunteer is taking the pro-objectivity side ("PO"), and I am taking the other side. But as I told her, it would not be right to do this in an attempt to overwhelm her with a whole bunch of jargon or anything, and I am not going to do that. I am going to be, I think, much more polite than the opponents of objectivity would normally be, but actually I have made a list of what I think are the main kinds of arguments you would get against the possibility of objectivity, and at one point or another I am just going to deliver them quietly, I hope, and see how our volunteer does with regard to them.

PO: Not only is objective knowledge possible, but it is the only type of knowledge possible. If something is to be called knowledge, it must by necessity be objective. That is, it must be based on the facts of reality, or it must be in accordance with the facts of reality.

LP: You say there has to be objectivity if there's to be knowledge. Well, maybe that's true, but then is there knowledge? The thing that strikes me is there's so much disagreement among people. If you say something, you think it's obvious, and other people disagree with it, so how can you say when you know?

PO: The fact that you ask is there knowledge is a contradiction. The question "Is there knowledge?" is a contradiction, because for you to ask that question, you must have acquired knowledge before.

LP: What knowledge would I have to have acquired?

PO: Knowledge of the concept "knowledge," to begin with.

LP: Well, I have to know the word; that's true. I mean, I grant this much—I have to know certain words in order to speak. Or to be more exact, I have to have learned how people use the words. Would you call that knowledge? That's a linguistic skill I'd have to acquire.

PO: Are all words then empty, no meaning?

LP: Well, people use words, so I guess they mean something, sure.

PO: Don't they have a referent in reality?

LP: Well, I don't know where the referents are. I mean, they stand for something, but they stand in effect for what people mean by them, whatever people say they mean. Something like "book" could mean anything; people just arbitrarily decide what it's going to be used for.

PO: The sound, yes, the sound of the concept may be arbitrarily chosen. But the concept "book" is not arbitrary.

LP: What distinction do you make between the word and the concept?

PO: Well, the word stands for the concept.

LP: What is the concept as apart from the book?

PO: The concept is an abstraction that stands for things in reality.

LP: Like "gremlin"?

PO: "Gremlin" is not a concept. I do not know what it is.

LP: It's a little green—

PO: A little green what?

LP: Why do I have to acquire knowledge, objective knowledge, to have these concepts again? Tell me that. I do not see that.

PO: There is no such thing as nonobjective knowledge. "Nonobjective knowledge" is a contradiction in terms. Because when you say that you have knowledge, you have to be conscious of something.

LP: Okay. But what if people are conscious of different things, though? You know, so I, for instance, think that—

PO: You have different knowledge.

LP: But then, how can we say it's objective if everybody disagrees? That's where I start.

PO: Because, precisely, it has to be based on reality to be an objective concept or to have objective knowledge.

LP: So if people disagree, then one of them is not based on reality?

PO: Yes, if there is a disagreement, not both can be true at the same time.

LP: So for instance, I like cherry pie and Mr. X does not, so we disagree and therefore, one of us is wrong?

PO: Those matters are matters of taste.

LP: So is that subjective, just that one part?

PO: Yes, I think so.

LP: So then whether we like cherry pie or not, I win on that point then.

PO: Yes, but that's your evaluation.

LP: So could we say then that evaluations are subjective, whereas facts are objective?

PO: On matters of taste, like eating cake or not, yes.

LP: But what about basic moral principles, like you should tell the truth?

PO: That's objective.

LP: So in other words, there are values that are objective and values that are subjective?

PO: No, matters of taste, like liking cake or pie—

LP: Well, what is the difference between them and the others?

PO: Because when you evaluate a moral action, there is an objective standard, but if you happen to like cake, there is no objective standard.

LP: Okay, then, according to you, we need an objective standard to have objective knowledge, and the objective standard, if I understand you, has to be reality, right? Well, what is reality?

PO: I cannot define that. Reality is the same as existence—

LP: So then objective knowledge has to be knowledge based on—

PO: —on existence.

LP: Well, what is existence?

PO: I cannot define that.

LP: Do you have any contact with it?

PO: Yes.

LP: In what way?

PO: When you ask me to define "existence," I'd like to quote Ayn Rand. She says, "To define 'existence,' one would have to sweep one's arms around and say, 'I mean this.'" There is only an ostensive type of definition.

LP: And by "ostensive," you mean you'd point to it; you'd say, "Everything out there"?

PO: Correct.

LP: All right, let us say I do not challenge that much. There's something out there. But now, according to you, knowledge is based on what's out there. But how do we get this objective knowledge, since people disagree about so many things? We all are in contact with what's out there, aren't we? Or not?

PO: Yes, but you are not guaranteed to know; you cannot guarantee a correct knowledge of reality.

LP: Does that mean that any given piece of knowledge might be wrong?

PO: Correct, yes.

LP: Well, then, we can never say about any claim, "This is the objective truth," because it might be wrong.

PO: No, because there are methods to validate your knowledge.

LP: What are the methods?

PO: Logic is *the* method.

LP: Then any logical argument, the conclusion is accepted?

PO: Any logical argument, if you check the premises also and they are true.

LP: And how do you establish that?

PO: You compare it to reality; you see if it—

LP: That's how we started originally, and you said I could only compare by the use of logic.

PO: By the use of reason.

LP: Are reason and logic the same thing?

PO: No, they are not. Reason is your faculty of perceiving reality, and logic's the method you use—

LP: All right, let us be specific. The Mideast is reality.

PO: Correct.

LP: Now, some people say that the Shah should have been given haven in the United States, and other people say he should not.

PO: Uh-huh.

LP: Now, they both perceive the Shah, or pictures of him on TV, and they perceive the newscasts and so on. How would you resolve this? If knowledge is objective, presumably there is a right and a wrong here?

PO: Uh-huh.

LP: How would you go about resolving it? Or is that like cherry pie?

PO: No, it's not.

LP: All right. So how would you decide?

PO: Well, you would have to first of all check all the facts why the people believe that he should not have come here.

LP: Some of them say he should not have come here because you risk the chance of reprisal against the United States. Well, that was true; there *were* reprisals—there were hostages taken. So does that make their viewpoint objective?

PO: No. You have to first of all check the reasons why they let the Shah in.

LP: According to what I read in the *Times*, it's because Kissinger and a few other people phoned the White House.

PO: But what is correct?

LP: You ask me was it correct, but that's the whole question. I'm trying to say that people who question objectivity would say they could study all the facts, and one thinks one thing and one thinks the opposite, and there's no way to resolve it. So how can we say there's an objective answer?

PO: But there is an objective answer.

LP: What's the objective answer?

PO: I cannot tell you; I'd have to check all the facts.

LP: But you do not yourself know what it is?

PO: No.

LP: Well, give me an objective fact that you yourself actually know.

PO: This table exists.

LP: How do you know?

PO: Because I perceive it; I see it; I can touch it; I can feel it.

LP: But you know that people's sensory experience varies enormously, right? I mean, some people see one color; some see another; some people are color-blind; some people are completely blind. You know the thing about if you put your hand in water when it's hot, and it feels cool, and when it's cold it feels warm, and the same thing feels different to different people, and dogs and cats see in black and white, et cetera, et cetera, and therefore, how do you know any of these if the senses are our basic tie to reality?

PO: But your senses cannot go wrong; they have no choice.

LP: But maybe my senses have no choice but to tell me fact A and yours have no choice but to tell you fact non-A, so we have a contradiction.

PO: No, because your senses perceive that which exists, and existence is absolute.

LP: Well, okay, if I look at this tablecloth and see it's yellow, and a color-blind person looks and sees it's gray, are we disagreeing? He says it's gray and I say it's yellow.

PO: Yes, both are correct in that case. Because the color-blind person, it's true that he sees this tablecloth as gray, but—

LP: But what is it really?

PO: It's really yellow, but the guy, the guy—

LP: If his senses can give it to him wrong—

PO: Okay, but his senses are not normal to begin with.

LP: But how do we decide what's normal?

PO: Because he's color-blind; you are already calling him blind, not normal.

LP: That's right, he definitely has a different form of experience in that area, but is there anything against him besides the fact that he's in the minority?

PO: That he's not normal, that's it.

LP: Well, if we can do that, why cannot we do the same thing on the level of abstract ideas? For instance, say, well, most people believe so and so about the Shah, so if you do not, you are not normal.

PO: Not normal, no, but wrong, yes.

LP: Well, why do we make that distinction with regard to the senses, and not with regard to ideas?

PO: You see, in the case of the color-blind person, he is not actually seeing; he is not—

LP: Are his senses actually wrong in that way?

PO: Yeah, his senses are not normal; they are incapable of perceiving the tablecloth as yellow.

LP: Okay. (I will just indicate on the side here that if you take that line, you are going to be in hard shape to defend objectivity, but we will elaborate that further.) Let us just go on to one other point here. What do you say about this point, which I commonly hear. You say we have to go by the facts of reality to get objective knowledge. But after all, reality is enormously complicated; there's millions of facts, so we cannot possibly go through everything. Therefore, we have to select what facts we are going to take as the decisive facts in any given situation. For instance, we could just write a biography of the Shah and it could go on a hundred pages, a thousand pages, so we have to decide what are the essentials and what aren't. And since everybody selects differently, and you have to have some means of selection, and it cannot be a fact that tells you how to select, because that's what's helping you to figure out what the facts are, therefore you have to choose subjectively. And therefore, all knowledge is subjective, because the facts that you use are chosen by a subjective process. I hear that all the time.

PO: No, they are not. When you arrive at a conclusion, you have to check all the facts relevant to that conclusion, all the facts that you know, and if you have checked all the facts that you know and it leads you to that conclusion, then it's objective.

LP: But you have to decide which facts are essential, right? How do you do that? Isn't that subjective?

PO: No. Why do you say that?

LP: Well, I mean, if all the facts are all just there, and yet we are saying this particular fact is really crucial and this one is not so important, why do we discriminate?

PO: You discriminate in relation to the other facts. You cannot just take one fact and say that this is the most fundamental fact and forget about the others.

LP: How? Explain to me how in relation to the other facts.

PO: For example, you say, "Okay, I will take man's most fundamental characteristic." And let us say he walks on two legs, he has two eyes, he has a nose, and he's rational. And he builds skyscrapers and he speaks—

LP: All right, so we have a whole catalog, right, yes.

PO: Correct. So you select the fact that is most fundamental, that implies the most of the rest, that makes the other ones possible, and that is rationality.

LP: So you are saying that the same pattern that would be used with regard to choosing essentials in a definition would be applicable more broadly in any type of discussion?

PO: Yeah, I think so.

LP: So let me see if I can summarize this. You say that objective knowledge is possible based on facts, that we have access to the facts by the senses, but that in some cases the senses are wrong but that's a minority that is abnormal, but the rest is okay, and that you would get to the level of concepts, we can be objective if we use reason or logic—

PO: Both, because logic is the method of reason.

LP: All right, so whenever you are using logic, you are using reason. But we have to do it in terms of essentials. And if we do, we will find that all the conclusions that we come to, except certain things, which are a matter of taste—

PO: Yes.

LP: Okay. All right, I will let you go. Thank you.

COMMENTARY

My main concern in this argument, which the volunteer helped very much to illustrate, was simply to demonstrate that if you want to defend such a thing as the objectivity of knowledge, you ultimately have to be able to cover the essentials of metaphysics, epistemology, and ethics. It is an enormously philosophical topic. The reason Objectivism is called "Objectivism" is that that concept—objectivity—is central in every branch of philosophy. In metaphysics, it stands for the idea that there is a reality that exists independent of us. In epistemology, it stands for the fact that we can acquire knowledge of things as they are, not influenced by our arbitrary feelings. And in ethics, it stands for the idea that objective value judgments are possible. Since the concept has roots in all these areas of philosophy, as soon as you defend the objectivity of knowledge, you open up everything—the means of knowledge (which are the senses, and logic, and reason, and concepts), the object of knowledge (which is reality), and the various applications of knowledge (including value judgments and political and even gastronomic examples). Consequently, I chose it deliberately to show a completely non-self-contained issue. God is much easier to argue, because that is one specific thing; even capitalism is much easier. But here you are in a highly proliferating question that pervades everything. You therefore have to be up on everything, because the subject will change at any moment—and they are essentials; they are not just arbitrary.

I brought up an argument used very commonly by newspeople: that objectivity is impossible because there are so many facts, and you have to choose which ones you choose. The answer, of course, has to be that you choose in terms of essentials—but then you have to be able to say what essentials are. It is not a full answer simply to say what essentials are in terms of definitions. That would be the beginning; then you would have to show how that applies to selecting essentials in the context of news gathering, passing value judgments, and so on. I obviously did not pursue that, because that would be a whole evening's discussion. But what my opponent did would be a good beginning. Normally, it is a very abstract and lengthy discussion to present what an essential is, since, for example, the other person will interrupt to say, "What is rationality, and why is that more important than building a building?" and you have to go off on that tangent. I let her go on that, but she did have the general idea. Whereas if you did not know the Objectivist theory of definition, you would be completely stopped on that point.

It would have made a big difference if my opponent had said a bit more about repudiating disagreement as a criterion. If you see that your opponent is very hot on one point on which you disagree, it is always helpful to state openly, "This is a big point of dispute between us, and I reject it." That is better than just answering, because sometimes your opponent does not grasp from your answer that you actually reject this whole approach, so he keeps pressing and pressing. The main thing that unphilosophical people say is, "If everybody agreed, there would be no problem, but since people disagree, how can you say this person has the truth and that one does not?" When I repeated this idea several times, my opponent said, "If people disagree, one is wrong." It would have been better to say, "Look, agreement and disagreement are an entirely different question. That may be relevant to taking public polls, but we are not taking polls; we are talking about knowledge. Even if everybody agreed, I would not accept that as evidence that the idea in question is objective, because maybe they agree on a falsehood. So let us throw out the question of whether people agree or disagree, and talk instead about the question of whether they are attuned to the facts or not. I regard it as irrelevant that they disagree." If you make a point of repudiating that firmly, even more briefly than that, then it stops your opponent; he loses that string to his bow, so to speak, and he cannot keep coming back. The way my opponent in this argument did it, though, was to say, "If people disagree, one is wrong," but without stressing enough that she completely repudiates that approach. She did repudiate it, but not emphatically enough to scare me off from coming back to it over and again. It is an issue just of a little more emphasis. It is also another example of the importance of asserting your own terms in an argument, of feeling free to get your terms in and not just going directly on the defensive.

The issue of the validity of the senses came up. My opponent said, or implied, that a color-blind person sensing a yellow tablecloth as gray would be committing an error, that this is abnormal. It is, of course, abnormal, but she implied that that would make it mistaken. As soon as you accept that, you are in very bad shape, because you are then establishing the principle that it is possible for sensory data to be wrong under certain conditions. If the data that you get from the senses can be wrong, you are wide-open to the objection, "Who is to say when the senses are telling the truth and when they are not? We have no choice about them, and yet in certain cases they can go wrong and deceive us." It is not sufficient to say that it is abnormal for the senses to err, because then the issue becomes the criterion of abnormality, which cannot be simply numerical. Suppose another species is discovered on another planet or somewhere, and its members all see shades of gray where we see yellow, and there are many more of them than us; is their perception then "normal"? It cannot be a quantitative issue.

You have to draw a sharp line, in defending cognitive questions, between what the senses contribute and what the conceptual level does. You have to hold out firmly for the idea that the senses per se cannot be wrong, not even the color-blind man's perceptions. In a word, it is not wrong to see a yellow tablecloth as dark gray, say, because all that is changing is the form of the perception. The basic Objectivist point—and on this point we actually disagree with Aristotle—is that all sensation has to be in some form, and the nature of that form depends in part on your sensory apparatus. Thus, if your apparatus (in this case, the rods and the cones in the eye) changes in some way, your sensory experience will change. But that does not disqualify any experience. You always perceive somehow, but that experience is the raw data that we then conceptualize. In this case, if we do not see color differences, we simply do not directly get certain kinds of distinctions that we have to reach by inference from the senses that we *do* have. Color-blind people still end up with the same physics, the same understanding of reality, that ordinarily sighted people have; it is simply a difference in the amount of information that they are given directly by the eyes, and in the form of that information. You therefore want to avoid ever suggesting that the senses can go wrong, even in cases of so-called abnormal perception. If it is actually perception, that is it—that is it as perceived by human consciousness, by the consciousness possessed of those particular organs. The question then becomes how to interpret perception, how to explain it, and so on, and then it becomes a conceptual question.

Another point at which my opponent could have tightened up her argument was in discussing options. Most people arguing for subjectivity take the idea that if any two people have any difference between them, and everything is objective, then one of them must be wrong. That entirely ignores the legitimate role of options, a distinction that it would be important for you to master and be able to explain. There are areas where there are many different legitimate choices within the same objective principle. For instance, a productive career is an objective need of human life, and you can prove that. But it is optional whether you become a pharmacist or a doctor or a lawyer or an architect, or whatever particular form your career takes. You could not say that any one of those is objectively superior to any other. Nor does the fact that there is no reason to prefer one to the other mean that the choice is subjective. You would say that it is a legitimate optional choice within the framework of an objective principle, and therefore that the choice is objective, whichever one of the various possibilities it is. It becomes subjective when you include bank robbery as one of your options, because that violates the actual principle that man needs a *productive* career.

In a debate, you would have to be able to cover this type of point and know what you would take as optional and what not. Otherwise, the advocate of subjectivity will typically seize on some optional preference, like cherry pie or whatever, which is not a philosophic issue and does not prove anything; he will then force you into, "Well, if that is the case, then you are saying that only some things are objective, and where do you draw the line?"

To establish objectivity, then, you have to show your opponent that the senses are reliable, and you have to be prepared to separate out what is optional from what you really want to defend. But the whole debate is really about the conceptual level. The real problem is that people do not grasp the objectivity of concepts; they do not even grasp the terms of that problem. They just think, "Oh, well, it is all semantics," or "It is all just words," and therefore, the whole issue just floats. At the very beginning, when my opponent was trying to tell me that there cannot be knowledge if it is not objective, I said, "Well, that is simply our use of words." The issue that I was trying to get at there is the issue on which the objectivity of knowledge depends. People feel in advance that it is hopeless: "However much we analyze," they think, "we are all going to disagree anyway, and therefore it is all just a matter of opinion." The actual idea, which most people likely could not articulate, the view they have absorbed that makes them feel that it is hopeless and all a matter of opinion, is the issue of concepts—whether concepts are objective. But the way most people would experience it, it is not concepts, but *words* that are the problem.

The main thing you have to do, if you are discussing objectivity, is to get across to your opponent that how you use words is not arbitrary. You take the view that every word has to be formed by a definite method; it has to be based on a certain definite kind of fact; it has to be used and defined a certain way—and therefore, before you can discuss any other questions, you have to agree on how you are going to use words, which means concepts. If you know that area and how to argue that point, and if the person is at all decent, he will get a glimmer that there is something more basic than all these superficial disagreements. He will see that he is simply assuming that anybody can put words together and use them in any way he wants, and therefore anybody can say anything. In actuality, however, the debate is much more fundamental: Are there some rules by which language has to be formed and used, or not?

If you are defending objectivity, you have to ask the person, in effect:

"Do you or do you not recognize some terms that have to be adhered to in the use of language?" Ultimately, he is going to say yes or no. If he says, "No, there is no method of using language, period, and anybody can say anything," then that obviously wipes out any discussion. You can just say, "Ish da triddle de gloop," and he says, "What is that?" and you say, "That is the definitive refutation of your position, and that is the way I am using words." You just cannot go any further. But if he is an honest person, he may be intrigued enough, especially if he does not know philosophy, to say, "Well, what would be a rule for using words? I do not have any idea." Then you have to tell him, "Words are concepts, and you should read this book," and go from there. It really comes down to an issue of concepts, and if you can get the person to grasp that much, that will be the revelation that will, in time, enable you to get somewhere with him. I do not hold out a great hope for that in a drawing room discussion. But if you are serious about trying to convince someone of the possibility of objectivity, nothing less will do.

At one point my opponent said, "What is a gremlin?" and I said, "A little green—" and stopped, and she did not make me continue. In a sense, I contradicted myself, because I said the use of words did not imply any knowledge, and then I said what I knew. If she had pressed that point further (which she started to do, but I derailed her), she could have come to the idea that words involve knowledge, and therefore certain methods of usage. Therefore, as soon as I said "gremlin," that would be the point at which to say, "Look, that is exactly what the whole issue relies on. You think you can just take a word and utter it without any basis at all, and that is exactly what our whole debate is over." If she had done that to me, as an advocate of subjectivity, I would have begun to feel uncomfortable; I would have felt, "I am doing something arbitrary and she will not let me do it." Of course, there would still be a lot of stuff to cover; this is a long, long argument, because it involves a whole philosophy. But that would have been one way to get into it, and I wriggled out of it. (One of the techniques of argument is to know when not to let the other person wriggle out.)

Most people who argue against objectivity are skeptics on principle; they simply want to force you to admit that nobody can really know anything and anybody can say anything he wants. If you get into an argument with that type, there is really no use going on past a certain point, because it quickly degenerates into "Says you" and "Says me." But if a person is doing it for other than nihilistic reasons—that is, a desire just to tear down the possibility of knowledge—then you could say, "What makes you think objective knowledge is impossible? After all, we have a civilization; it seems that we know *something.* So what makes you doubt it?" That would put the skeptic more on the defensive. He might then say something like, "People disagree," and then you would immediately say, "That is irrelevant." Then you would use the word "reality," and he would say, "What is that?" and you would sweep your hand around and say, "It is all this." By that point he is already trying to remember, "What did I learn in philosophy class as to why objectivity is impossible?" And if you can get your opponent to that point, you are in business.

CHAPTER 12

CONCLUDING REMARKS

IN PRINCIPLE, PHILOSOPHICAL communication is the same as any skill whatsoever. In principle, it is like typing, or learning French, or what have you. But philosophy is difficult, and it is completely natural to find at the beginning that there are an awful lot of things you had never thought about. In *any* field, when you first hear the principles, you have the experience of feeling, "Oh, there is so much here." It is just a mass of stuff thrown at you, and you have not digested it, and there is a certain momentary discouragement of thinking that it is just too much to cope with. What you have to do is decide that you are going to just do it a little at a time, as much as you can digest, and you will apply it until something is clear, and then you will take a bit more, and so on. That applies just as well to philosophy. So I want to avoid this course having a paralyzing effect in that before you go to do anything, you feel that there are twelve major things you have to keep in mind and follow. You simply will not be able to get a word out, either on paper or orally.

The best advice that I could give to you would be this: In action, when you actually sit down to write, or stand up to speak, or engage in argument, you should thoroughly forget this course. I mean this not just as therapy, but as truth, because of the crow epistemology. You cannot undertake the impossible. You have to work with what you have, and when you are in action, speaking or writing or arguing, is not the time to retrain yourself. When you are speaking or writing or arguing, it is like you are in midstream—you have to go with what you have got. In that case, you have to take the attitude, "I am omniscient; I am infallible; I am the master of this subject. There is no one in history who has ever equaled me; the hell with Peikoff or anybody else." Then, when it is over, you can objectively decide whether there is a way you could improve what you have done, whether there is something you learned that you could apply now, in retrospect, and do differently the next time. But you have to keep the performance and the evaluation separate; otherwise, you will be paralyzed.

I would like the net effect of this course to be that you feel that communicating philosophically can be an enjoyable experience. Above all, I would like you to feel that it can be an experience in self-assertion, not in dutifully following dozens of impossible principles. With that qualification, I am happy to have given the course, and I particularly want to thank the people who contributed, subjecting themselves to this trauma in any one of its various forms, for helping to make it a success.

APPENDICES

APPENDIX A:

"Philosophy: Who Needs It"

Since I am a fiction writer, let us start with a short short story. Suppose that you are an astronaut whose spaceship gets out of control and crashes on an unknown planet. When you regain consciousness and find that you are not hurt badly, the first three questions in your mind would be: Where am I? How can I discover it? What should I do?

You see unfamiliar vegetation outside, and there is air to breathe; the sunlight seems paler than you remember it, and colder. You turn to look at the sky, but stop. You are struck by a sudden feeling: If you don't look, you won't have to know that you are, perhaps, too far from the earth and no return is possible; so long as you don't know it, you are free to believe what you wish—and you experience a foggy, pleasant, but somehow guilty, kind of hope.

You turn to your instruments: they may be damaged, you don't know how seriously. But you stop, struck by a sudden fear: how can you trust these instruments? How can you be sure that they won't mislead you? How can you know whether they will work in a different world? You turn away from the instruments.

Now you begin to wonder why you have no desire to do anything. It seems so much safer just to wait for something to turn up somehow; it is better, you tell yourself, not to rock the spaceship. Far in the distance, you see some sort of living creatures approaching; you don't know whether they are human, but they walk on two feet. *They*, you decide, will tell you what to do.

You are never heard from again.

This is fantasy, you say? You would not act like that and no astronaut ever would? Perhaps not. But this is the way most men live their lives, here, on earth.

Most men spend their days struggling to evade three questions, the answers to which underlie man's every thought, feeling and action, whether he is consciously aware of it or not: Where am I? How do I know it? What should I do?

By the time they are old enough to understand these questions, men believe that they know the answers. Where am I? Say, in New York City. How do I know it? It's self-evident. What should I do? Here, they are not too sure—but the usual answer is: whatever everybody does. The only trouble seems to be that they are not very active, not very confident, not very happy—and they experience, at times, a causeless fear and an undefined guilt, which they cannot explain or get rid of.

They have never discovered the fact that the trouble comes from the three unanswered questions—and that there is only one science that can answer them: *philosophy*.

Philosophy studies the *fundamental* nature of existence, of man, and of man's relationship to existence. As against the special sciences, which deal only with particular aspects, philosophy deals with those aspects of the universe which pertain to everything that exists. In the realm of cognition, the special sciences are the trees, but philosophy is the soil which makes the forest possible.

Philosophy would not tell you, for instance, whether you are in New York City or in Zanzibar (though it would give you the means to find out). But here is what it *would* tell you: Are you in a universe which is ruled by natural laws and, therefore, is stable, firm, absolute—and knowable? Or are you in an incomprehensible chaos, a realm of inexplicable miracles, an unpredictable, unknowable flux, which your mind is impotent to grasp? Are the things you see around you real—or are they only an illusion? Do they exist independent of any observer—or are they created by the observer? Are they the object or the subject of man's consciousness? Are they *what they are*—or can they be changed by a mere act of your consciousness, such as a wish?

The nature of your actions—and of your ambition—will be different, according to which set of answers you come to accept. These answers are the province of *metaphysics*—the study of existence as such or, in Aristotle's words, of "being qua being"—the basic branch of philosophy.

No matter what conclusions you reach, you will be confronted by the necessity to answer another, *corollary* question: How do I know it? Since man is not omniscient or infallible, you have to discover what you can claim as knowledge and how to *prove* the validity of your conclusions. Does man acquire knowledge by a process of reason—or by sudden revelation from a supernatural power? Is reason a faculty that identifies and integrates the material provided by man's senses—or is it fed by innate ideas, implanted in man's mind before he was born? Is reason competent to perceive reality—or does man possess some other cognitive faculty which is superior to reason? Can man achieve certainty—or is he doomed to perpetual doubt?

The extent of your self-confidence—and of your success—will be different, according to which set of answers you accept. These answers are the province of *epistemology*, the theory of knowledge, which studies man's means of cognition.

These two branches are the theoretical foundation of philosophy. The third branch—ethics—may be regarded as its technology. Ethics does not apply to everything that exists, only to man, but it applies to every aspect of man's life: his character, his actions, his values, his relationship to all of existence. Ethics, or morality, defines a code of values to guide man's choices and actions—the choices and actions that determine the course of his life.

Just as the astronaut in my story did not know what he should do, because he refused to know where he was and how to discover it, so you cannot know what you should do until you know the nature of the universe you deal with, the nature of your means of cognition—and your own nature. Before you come to ethics, you must answer the questions posed by metaphysics and epistemology: Is man a rational being, able to deal with reality—or is he a helplessly blind misfit, a chip buffeted by the universal flux? Are achievement and enjoyment possible to man on earth—or is he doomed to failure and disaster? Depending on the answers, you can proceed to consider the questions posed by ethics: What is good or evil for man—and why? Should man's primary concern be a quest for joy—or an escape from suffering? Should man hold self-fulfillment—or self-destruction—as the goal of his life? Should man pursue his values—or should he place the interests of others above his own? Should man seek happiness—or self-sacrifice?

I do not have to point out the different consequences of these two sets of answers. You can see them everywhere—within you and around you.

The answers given by ethics determine how man should treat other men, and this determines the fourth branch of philosophy: *politics*, which defines the principles of a proper social system. As an example of philosophy's function, political philosophy will not tell you how much rationed gas you should be given and on which day of the week—it will tell you whether the government has the right to impose any rationing on anything.

The fifth and last branch of philosophy is *esthetics*, the study of art, which is based on metaphysics, epistemology and ethics. Art deals with the needs—the refueling—of man's consciousness.

Now some of you might say, as many people do: "Aw, I never think in such abstract terms—I want to deal with concrete, particular, real-life problems—what do I need philosophy for?" My answer is: In order to be able to deal with concrete, particular, real-life problems—i.e., in order to be able to live on earth.

You might claim—as most people do—that you have never been influenced by philosophy. I will ask you to check that claim. Have you ever thought or said the following? "Don't be so sure—nobody can be certain of anything." You got that notion from David Hume (and many, many others), even though you might never have heard of him. Or: "This may be good in theory, but it doesn't work in practice." You got that from Plato. Or: "That was a rotten thing to do, but it's only human, nobody is perfect in this world." You got it from Augustine. Or: "It may be true for you, but it's not true for me." You got it from William James. Or: "I couldn't help it! Nobody can help anything he does." You got it from Hegel. Or: "I can't prove it, but I *feel* that it's true." You got it from Kant. Or: "It's logical, but logic has nothing to do with reality." You got it from Kant. Or: "It's evil, because it's selfish." You got it from Kant. Have you heard the modern activists say: "Act first, think afterward"? They got it from John Dewey.

Some people might answer: "Sure, I've said those things at different times, but I don't have to believe that stuff *all* of the time. It may have been true yesterday, but it's not true today." They got it from Hegel. They might say: "Consistency is the hobgoblin of little minds." They got it from a very little mind, Emerson. They might say: "But can't one compromise and borrow different ideas from different philosophies according to the expediency of the moment?" They got it from Richard Nixon—who got it from William James.

Now ask yourself: if you are not interested in abstract ideas, why do you (and all men) feel compelled to use them? The fact is that abstract ideas are conceptual integrations which subsume an incalculable number of concretes—and that without abstract ideas you would not be able to deal with concrete, particular, real-life problems. You would be in the position of a newborn infant, to whom every object is a unique, unprecedented phenomenon. The difference between his mental state and yours lies in the number of conceptual integrations your mind has performed.

You have no choice about the necessity to integrate your observations, your experiences, your knowledge into abstract ideas, i.e., into principles. Your only choice is whether these principles are true or false, whether they represent your conscious, rational convictions—or a grab-bag of notions snatched at random, whose sources, validity, context and consequences you do not know, notions which, more often than not, you would drop like a hot potato if you knew.

But the principles you accept (consciously or subconsciously) may clash with or contradict one another; they, too, have to be integrated. What integrates them? Philosophy. A philosophic system is an integrated view of existence. As a human being, you have no choice about the fact that you need a philosophy. Your only choice is whether you define your philosophy by a conscious, rational, disciplined process of thought and scrupulously logical deliberation—or let your subconscious accumulate a junk heap of unwarranted conclusions, false generalizations, undefined contradictions, undigested slogans, unidentified wishes, doubts and fears, thrown together by chance, but integrated by your subconscious into a kind of mongrel philosophy and fused into a single, solid weight: *self-doubt*, like a ball and chain in the place where your mind's wings should have grown.

You might say, as many people do, that it is not easy always to act on abstract principles. No, it is not easy. But how much harder is it, to have to act on them without knowing what they are? Your subconscious is like a computer—more complex a computer than men can build—and its main function is the integration of your ideas. Who programs it? Your conscious mind. If you default, if you don't reach any firm convictions, your subconscious is programmed by chance—and you deliver yourself into the power of ideas you do not know you have accepted. But one way or the other, your computer gives you print-outs, daily and hourly, in the form of *emotions*—which are lightning-like estimates of the things around you, calculated according to your values. If you programmed your computer by conscious thinking, you know the nature of your values and emotions. If you didn't, you don't.

Many people, particularly today, claim that man cannot live by logic alone, that there's the emotional element of his nature to consider, and that they rely on the guidance of their emotions. Well, so did the astronaut in my story. The joke is on him—and on them: man's values and emotions are determined by his fundamental view of life. The ultimate programmer of his subconscious is *philosophy*—the science which, according to the emotionalists, is impotent to affect or penetrate the murky mysteries of their feelings.

The quality of a computer's output is determined by the quality of its input. If your subconscious is programmed by chance, its output will have a corresponding character. You have probably heard the computer operators' eloquent term "gigo"—which means: "Garbage in, garbage out." The same formula applies to the relationship between a man's thinking and his emotions.

A man who is run by emotions is like a man who is run by a computer whose print-outs he cannot read. He does not know whether its programming is true or false, right or wrong, whether it's set to lead him to success or destruction, whether it serves his goals or those of some evil, unknowable power. He is blind on two fronts: blind to the world around him and to his own inner world, unable to grasp reality or his own motives, and he is in chronic terror of both. Emotions are not tools of cognition. The men who are not interested in philosophy need it most urgently: they are most helplessly in its power.

The men who are not interested in philosophy absorb its principles from the cultural atmosphere around them—from schools, colleges, books, magazines, newspapers, movies, television, etc. Who sets the tone of a culture? A small handful of men: the philosophers. Others follow their lead, either by conviction or by default. For some two hundred years, under the influence of Immanuel Kant, the dominant trend of philosophy has been directed to a single goal: the destruction of man's mind, of his confidence in the power of reason. Today, we are seeing the climax of that trend.

When men abandon reason, they find not only that their emotions cannot guide them, but that they can experience no emotions save one: terror. The spread of drug addiction among young people brought up on today's intellectual fashions demonstrates the unbearable inner state of men who are deprived of their means of cognition and who seek escape from reality—from the terror of their impotence to deal with existence. Observe these young people's dread of independence and their frantic desire to "belong," to attach themselves to some group, clique or gang. Most of them have never heard of philosophy, but they sense that they need some fundamental answers to questions they dare not ask—and they hope that the tribe will tell them *how to live.* They are ready to be taken over by any witch doctor, guru, or dictator. One of the most dangerous things a man can do is to surrender his *moral* autonomy to others: like the astronaut in my story, he does not know whether they are human, even though they walk on two feet.

Now you may ask: If philosophy can be that evil, why should one study it? Particularly, why should one study the philosophical theories which are blatantly false, make no sense, and bear no relation to real life?

My answer is: In self-protection—and in defense of truth, justice, freedom, and any value you ever held or may ever hold.

Not all philosophies are evil, though too many of them are, particularly in modern history. On the other hand, at the root of every civilized achievement, such as science, technology, progress, freedom—at the root of every value we enjoy today, including the birth of this country—you will find the achievement of *one man*, who lived over two thousand years ago: Aristotle.

If you feel nothing but boredom when reading the virtually unintelligible theories of *some* philosophers, you have my deepest sympathy. But if you brush them aside, saying: "Why should I study that stuff when I know it's nonsense?"—you are mistaken. It is nonsense, but you *don't* know it—not so long as you go on accepting all their conclusions, all the vicious catch phrases generated by those philosophers. And not so long as you are unable to *refute* them.

That nonsense deals with the most crucial, the life-or-death issues of man's existence. At the root of every significant philosophic theory, there is a legitimate issue—in the sense that there is an authentic need of man's consciousness, which some theories struggle to clarify and others struggle to obfuscate, to corrupt, to prevent man from ever discovering. The battle of philosophers is a battle for man's mind. If you do not understand their theories, you are vulnerable to the worst among them.

The best way to study philosophy is to approach it as one approaches a detective story: follow every trail, clue and implication, in order to discover who is a murderer and who is a hero. The criterion of detection is two questions: Why? and How? If a given tenet seems to be true—why? If another tenet seems to be false—why? and how is it being put over? You will not find all the answers immediately, but you will acquire an invaluable characteristic: the ability to think in terms of essentials.

Nothing is given to man automatically, neither knowledge, nor self-confidence, nor inner serenity, nor the right way to use his mind. Every value he needs or wants has to be discovered, learned and acquired—even the proper posture of his body. In this context, I want to say that I have always admired the posture of West Point graduates, a posture that projects man in proud, disciplined control of his body. Well, philosophical training gives man the proper *intellectual* posture—a proud, disciplined control of his mind.

In your own profession, in military science, you know the importance of keeping track of the enemy's weapons, strategy and tactics—and of being prepared to counter them. The same is true in philosophy: you have to understand the enemy's ideas and be prepared to refute them, you have to know his basic arguments and be able to blast them.

In physical warfare, you would not send your men into a booby trap: you would make every effort to discover its location. Well, Kant's system is the biggest and most intricate booby trap in the history of philosophy—but it's so full of holes that once you grasp its gimmick, you can defuse it without any trouble and walk forward over it in perfect safety. And, once it is defused, the lesser Kantians—the lower ranks of his army, the philosophical sergeants, buck privates, and mercenaries of today—will fall of their own weightlessness, by chain reaction.

There is a special reason why you, the future leaders of the United States Army, need to be philosophically armed today. You are the target of a special attack by the Kantian-Hegelian-collectivist establishment that dominates our cultural institutions at present. You are the army of the last semi-free country left on earth, yet you are accused of being a tool of imperialism—and "imperialism" is the name given to the foreign policy of this country, which has never engaged in military conquest and has never profited from the two world wars, which she did not initiate, but entered and won. (It was, incidentally, a foolishly overgenerous policy, which made this country waste her wealth on helping both her allies and her former enemies.) Something called "the military-industrial complex"—which is a myth or worse—is being blamed for all of this country's troubles. Bloody college hoodlums scream demands that R.O.T.C. units be banned from college campuses. Our defense budget is being attacked, denounced and undercut by people who claim that financial priority should be given to ecological rose gardens and to classes in esthetic self-expression for the residents of the slums.

Some of you may be bewildered by this campaign and may be wondering, in good faith, what errors you committed to bring it about. If so, it is urgently important for you to understand the nature of the enemy. You are attacked, not for any errors or flaws, but for your virtues. You are denounced, not for any weaknesses, but for your strength and your competence. You are penalized for being the protectors of the United States. On a lower level of the same issue, a similar kind of campaign is conducted against the police force. Those who seek to destroy this country, seek to disarm it—intellectually and physically. But it is not a mere political issue; politics is not the cause, but the last consequence of philosophical ideas. It is not a communist conspiracy, though some communists may be involved—as maggots cashing in on a disaster they had no power to originate. The motive of the destroyers is not love for communism, but hatred for America. Why hatred? Because America is the living refutation of a Kantian universe.

Today's mawkish concern with and compassion for the feeble, the flawed, the suffering, the guilty, is a cover for the profoundly Kantian hatred of the innocent, the strong, the able, the successful, the virtuous, the confident, the happy. A philosophy out to destroy man's mind is necessarily a philosophy of hatred for man, for man's life, and for every human value. Hatred of the good for being the good, is the hallmark of the twentieth century. *This* is the enemy you are facing.

A battle of this kind requires special weapons. It has to be fought with a full understanding of your cause, a full confidence in yourself, and the fullest certainty of the *moral* rightness of both. Only philosophy can provide you with these weapons.

The assignment I gave myself for tonight is not to sell you on my philosophy, but on philosophy as such. I have, however, been speaking implicitly of my philosophy in every sentence—since none of us and no statement can escape from philosophical premises. What is my *selfish* interest in the matter? I am confident enough to think that if you accept the importance of philosophy and the task of examining it critically, it is *my* philosophy that you will come to accept. Formally, I call it Objectivism, but informally I call it a philosophy for living on earth. You will find an explicit presentation of it in my books, particularly in *Atlas Shrugged*.

In conclusion, allow me to speak in personal terms. This evening means a great deal to me. I feel deeply honored by the opportunity to address you. I can say—not as a patriotic bromide, but with full knowledge of the necessary metaphysical, epistemological, ethical, political and esthetic roots—that the United States of America is the greatest, the noblest and, in its original founding principles, the *only* moral country in the history of the world. There is a kind of quiet radiance associated in my mind with the name West Point—because you have preserved the spirit of those original founding principles and you are their symbol. There were contradictions and omissions in those principles, and there may be in yours—but I am speaking of the essentials. There may be individuals in your history who did not live up to your highest standards— as there are in every institution—since no institution and no social system can guarantee the automatic perfection of all its members; this depends on an individual's free will. I am speaking of your standards. You have preserved three qualities of character which were typical at the time of America's birth, but are virtually nonexistent today: earnestness—dedication—a sense of honor. Honor is self-esteem made visible in action.

You have chosen to risk your lives for the defense of this country. I will not insult you by saying that you are dedicated to selfless service—it is not a virtue in *my* morality. In my morality, the defense of one's country means that a man is personally unwilling to live as the conquered slave of any enemy, foreign or domestic. *This* is an enormous virtue. Some of you may not be consciously aware of it. I want to help you to realize it.

The army of a free country has a great responsibility: the right to use force, but not as an instrument of compulsion and brute conquest—as the armies of other countries have done in their histories—only as an instrument of a free nation's self-defense, which means: the defense of a man's individual rights. The principle of using force only in retaliation against those who initiate its use is the principle of subordinating might to right. The highest integrity and sense of honor are required for such a task. No other army in the world has achieved it. You have.

West Point has given America a long line of heroes, known and unknown. You, this year's graduates, have a glorious tradition to carry on—which I admire profoundly, not because it is a tradition, but because it *is* glorious.

Since I came from a country guilty of the worst tyranny on earth, I am particularly able to appreciate the meaning, the greatness and the supreme value of that which you are defending. So, in my own name and in the name of many people who think as I do, I want to say, to all the men of West Point, past, present and future: Thank you.

APPENDIX B:

"Certainty"

It is the purpose of this paper to consider the question: "Can man ever be certain of the truth of any statement?"—or, as it is often phrased: "Is certain knowledge possible?"

I shall attempt to demonstrate the truth of my position on this issue, viz. that certain knowledge of reality *is* possible to man, by pointing out that any other position involves one in a contradiction. The position of those who maintain that no knowledge can be certain is most consistently stated by those who apply their position to the very statement of their case, those, that is, who maintain that they cannot even be certain that certainty is impossible. This type of advocate of uncertainty believes, and believes rightly, that he is the only noncontradictory upholder of universal uncertainty, for, he would say, if anyone maintained that he knew as a certainty that it was impossible to know anything as a certainty, he would be upholding a blatant contradiction. Consequently, the consistent statement of the belief in universal uncertainty is this: Man cannot be certain of anything, and he cannot be certain that he cannot be certain of anything, and he cannot be certain that he cannot be certain that he cannot be certain of anything . . . and so on to infinity. At no point can a state of certainty be reached, and consequently even uncertainty is uncertain, and uncertainty of uncertainty is uncertain, and so on back to infinity.

What I wish to demonstrate now is that this most consistent version of the belief in universal uncertainty is itself *not* an intellectual position, that nothing is being said when one asserts such a position, and consequently, that no refutation nor even consideration of the position is necessary, since nothing is being asserted that one could consider or refute. The truth of this derives from the Law of Excluded Middle, which states that anything (call it "x") about which men talk or think *either exists or does not exist*. It follows that in any discussion about "x" *only two positions are possible*: that x exists or that it does not exist. To say that one is uncertain of the existence of x is not an intellectual position *on the subject of x's existence*; it is the expression of a lack of knowledge about the existence or nonexistence of x. Consequently, the statement that one is uncertain of x's existence is irrelevant to the question of x's existence. One need not consider and one cannot refute a confession of a lack of knowledge. The advocates of universal uncertainty, however, are in this position with regard to any x whatever. Of no x can they say: It exists or it does not exist; their statement must always be that they are uncertain of x's existence. Even with regard to the x that stands for universal uncertainty, the advocates of universal uncertainty cannot assert its existence or nonexistence; they can state only that they are uncertain of its existence, and this process must, as has been pointed out, continue backward to infinity. It follows, therefore, that the believers in universal uncertainty cannot assert the existence or nonexistence of any x whatever, and that means that they cannot assert any intellectual position. The most that they can do is to confess ignorance or uncertainty about a subject, and even that they cannot do noncontradictorily without carrying the process of perpetual uncertainty back to infinity. Consequently, believers in universal uncertainty never say anything about existence, and, since there is nothing but existence about which to say things, they never say anything about anything, i.e., they say nothing. But saying nothing does not constitute an intellectual position; a confession of total ignorance is not an argument. Consequently, in any intellectual discussion, believers in perpetual and universal uncertainty must, of necessity, be ignored; one cannot consider nor refute that which has not been said.

Believers in perpetual uncertainty have attempted to save their position from the above consequences by asserting that there is one thing man can know as a certainty, and that is that he can never know anything else as a certainty. In this way, an escape from an infinite regress with its fatal consequences is afforded. However, believers in this viewpoint do not recognize that, in admitting the existence of even one certainty, they are giving up the case for otherwise universal uncertainty. Consider the number of truths about which a man must be certain before he could be *certain* that certainty was impossible. He must be certain that something exists *about* which he is uncertain; that he, who *is* uncertain, exists; that he, who is certain of uncertainty, is capable of being certain of (at least part of) that which exists; that the Law of Identity is true, for otherwise his position is and is not what it is, and under those conditions it could never be certain; that language has meaning, for otherwise his position is meaningless and consequently neither certain nor uncertain; that his position is capable of being communicated to other minds, for otherwise he is beyond the pale of intellectual discussion; and so on. But when all of these certainties are admitted, and all of them must be to enable the believer in the certainty of uncertainty to state his position intelligibly, what is left of the case for universal uncertainty? If a mind exists, capable of knowing for certain facts of reality and communicating them intelligibly to other minds, wherein lie the reasons for believing in universal uncertainty?

It is clear, then, that in the very statement of the position of universal uncertainty, one is either saying nothing at all or one is contradicting oneself. However, the contradictions become even more apparent when one considers the arguments advanced to support the position. All of the arguments, beneath their surface variations, have, of necessity, one point in common: viz. that the very conception of certainty is itself contradictory. There is no way of establishing the impossibility of the existence of anything except by showing that the thing in question is a contradiction, for contradictions are the only things that are necessarily incapable of existence. Consequently, if one wished to *demonstrate* that certainty could never exist (as opposed to merely stating it arbitrarily), one would have to resort to some form of argument proving that certainty is a contradictory conception. "Certainty" and "round squares" would have to be shown to be in the same class, for if certainty *were* a thoroughly consistent and noncontradictory conception, one could never establish the impossibility of its existence. As soon, however, as one does establish that certainty is contradictory and hence incapable of existence, it follows, since everything man thinks must be either certain or uncertain, that everything man thinks is uncertain and doubtful.

What the advocates of universal uncertainty do not realize is that in asserting that certainty is a contradictory conception, which they must do to establish their position, they are ipso facto rendering their own position—viz. that everything man thinks is uncertain and doubtful— meaningless. This can be shown as follows: Doubt and uncertainty are nothing more nor less than the *absence of certainty*. (This can be verified by an appeal to any standard dictionary.) Consequently, the meanings of "doubt" and "uncertainty" are dependent on the meaning of "certainty," for the "absence of x" means what it means only because x means what it does. However, if certainty is a contradictory conception, it is meaning- less, for all contradictory conceptions are, with reference to their mean- ing, in the same class as "round squares." Being contradictions, they stand for nonexistents, i.e., for nothing; i.e., they are meaningless. But if "certainty" is a meaningless conception, then the "absence of certainty" is a meaningless conception, for the absence of something meaningless is itself meaningless. In the same way in which "gribble," if it stood for the absence of round squares, would be meaningless, "uncertainty" or "doubt," if it stands for the absence of certainty, is meaningless. Conse- quently, when the conception of certainty is abandoned, the conception of uncertainty must also be abandoned. But, when this is done, the advocates of universal and perpetual doubt cannot even state their case, and a case that cannot even be stated certainly does not require refutation in order to be ignored. . . .

One of the apparent implications of the theory of universal uncertainty is that all statements are equally true or false, since all statements are equally uncertain. Believers in the theory of universal uncertainty attempt to save their position from this consequence by asserting that although *certainty* can never be achieved, uncertainty exists in varying *degrees*, and consequently, some statements, being *less* uncertain than others, have more value. (This position is also expressed by saying that certain statements are more *probable* than others.) If, however, the above arguments are accepted, it follows that, if certainty is impossible and hence meaningless, uncertainty is impossible and hence meaningless, and consequently that *degrees* of uncertainty or probability are impossible and hence meaningless, since "degrees of a meaningless conception" is itself a meaningless conception. This means that, if total certainty is not possible, degrees of probability are not possible, and consequently that all statements are equally probable or improbable, and that no differentiation between statements with reference to their truth value can be made. But that would mean that there is no difference in intellectual value between the assertion of a maniac that he is a sliced cucumber salad, and the theory of relativity advanced by Einstein as an explanation of the entire physical universe. And when this conclusion is endorsed, men have reached the final stage of intellectual bankruptcy.

"The Primacy of Consciousness: Some Manifestations"

"That drive was one where all sorts of thoughts went through my mind: one of complete disbelief that what had happened, happened; I remember looking out the window and *trying to hope* that I was going to see her walking down the road; as I miraculously had escaped that perhaps she had miraculously escaped as well. I really *willed* it in my mind that she survived and really *forced* myself to believe that she did. I had these false hopes that perhaps when I first saw the dawn of a new day, it would eliminate and eradicate the nightmare of the night before. I *prayed* that that would happen, that in the morning it would be past and that in some miraculous way, Mary Jo had returned to the cottage." (Emphasis added.)

In an attempt to defend actions that resulted in the death of a young woman in 1969, Senator Edward M. Kennedy made the above statements during a 1974 interview. Would *you* deal with a man who, when confronted with the facts of reality, had to "force himself" to believe otherwise?

Why would a man think this way? What is the cause, the basic philosophic principle involved that made possible such a course of action and thought? A clue to the answer can be found by identifying the assumptions that Kennedy's statements make about the relationship between man's mind and the external world, between consciousness and existence. First is that if existence is not what one wants it to be, one can try to change it; that the facts can be created by one's "will," by "trying to hope," or by "praying," i.e., by an act of consciousness. This means that existence is dependent upon consciousness. The second assumption is that one does not need to look *outward* in order to know existence but one can look *inward* at the thoughts in one's own mind and "force oneself to believe" that existence will be what one wants it to be.

This view of the relationship between existence and consciousness is called *the primacy of consciousness.* Metaphysically, it is "the notion that the universe has no independent existence, that it is a product of consciousness. . . . The epistemological corollary is the notion that man gains knowledge of reality by looking inward"* at consciousness. Thus, consciousness has metaphysical primacy.

This principle, I submit, dominates today's cultural atmosphere and is the cause of our cultural disintegration. This can be seen in the sphere of human action in which all human beings participate: the economy, and the controls imposed on it.

Consider the antitrust laws in the United States. One of the alleged main purposes of the Sherman Act of 1890 was to prevent individuals or companies from engaging in practices that would result in "restraint of trade" among the states of the United States. It did so by declaring that every contract that is found to be in restraint of trade is illegal. However, how does the judicial system define "restraint of trade"? In his analysis of antitrust laws, A. D. Neale points out that "unfortunately, no straightforward definition can be given, for 'restraint of trade' is a legal term of art, deriving its meaning from the current decisions and constructions making up the particular body of law in which it appears. . . . Thus, where antitrust is concerned, nothing less than the whole body of case law constitutes the definition of 'restraint of trade'; it can be given, if at all, at the end of the book but not at the beginning. . . .

---

* Ayn Rand, "The Metaphysical versus the Man-Made," *Philosophy: Who Needs It*, p. 24.

The courts in the United States have been engaged ever since 1890 in deciding case by case exactly what the law proscribes."*

How does a judge interpret and apply the provisions in the Sherman Act? Judge Learned Hand said of such a task that "the words he must construe are empty vessels into which he can put nearly anything he will."†

One government official, Emanuel Celler, an ex-chairman of the House Judiciary Committee, has stated, "I want to make it clear that I would vigorously oppose any antitrust laws that attempted to particularize violations, giving bills of particulars to replace general principles. The law must remain fluid, allowing for a dynamic society."‡ Thus, the government official wants *law*—the reality within which the businessman functions—to remain fluid, dependent on the government officials' minds' formulation and interpretation.

Try to imagine the mind of a businessman who would act within the context of the antitrust laws. He would have to follow *every* case and retain all the evidence of the "whole body of case law" in an attempt to define the concept of "restraint of trade." This would be necessary in order for him to know whether or not he was acting illegally. What would be the status of such a definition that, after *he* had been on trial, could be amended by the judge's "will"?

What possible courses of action and thought would such a businessman take? One possibility could be to simply accept the government officials' words because "the law must be obeyed." A second possibility is as follows. The businessman looks *inward* at his own consciousness and his desire to produce and trade goods. He also observes that reality depends on the officials' minds. He notices that, at times, the reality created by others clashes with his desire. To alleviate this, he uses the premises that reality depends on consciousness and that knowledge

---

* A. D. Neale, *The Antitrust Laws of the U.S.A.* (Cambridge University Press, 1966).
† Ibid.
‡ Harold Fleming, *Ten Thousand Commandments* (Prentice Publishing, 1951).

is acquired by looking *inward* to try to create the reality that is dependent on *his* consciousness: his desire to produce and trade goods. Thus, he resorts to techniques of influencing the minds of these "others" by what is commonly called bribery or lobbying, i.e., methods of determining what is in the minds of the government officials.

The primacy of consciousness can now be seen to be the dominant premise of the entire mixed economy, with all of the influence peddling by politicians who "create" reality by means of the laws they do or do not pass. In the field of energy, people want electricity and heat but tax the producers (those who have looked *outward* to discover the means and tools of production) for making "excessive" profits. What is "excessive" profit and who determines it? No answer; consult the minds of the legislators.

What is the fundamental error involved in the primacy of consciousness? The principle is incompatible with the Law of Identity, which holds that an entity is itself, that existence is what it is, that A is A. The primacy of consciousness holds that A can be non-A if consciousness decrees it: A dead woman can be alive if one forces oneself to believe so; businessmen should look outward when producing steel, but let's not define "restraint of trade" or "excessive" profits; there's no problem in never defining concepts or "putting nearly anything one wills" into a concept; consciousness decrees it to be so. The primacy of consciousness principle also evades the fact that consciousness can possess knowledge only *after* it has perceived existence; this is the prerequisite for it to identify itself as consciousness.

The dominance of the primacy of consciousness produced today's culture because of the fact that A is A. The function of the mind is to perceive reality. If one holds the mind as constituting the basis of reality, then one must engage in practices to acquire knowledge about the mind with no reference to existence. When one encounters other minds that are not readily amenable, one must use whatever means are available to influence these other minds to suit one's own mind. Hence, the spectacle of businessmen falling over each other in attempts to influence a senator's vote.

Today's cultural atmosphere will be reversed only when people reject the primacy of consciousness and uphold the opposite principle: the *primacy of existence*. Metaphysically, it is "the axiom that existence exists, i.e., that the universe exists independent of consciousness . . . that things are what they are, that they possess a specific nature, an identity. The epistemological corollary is the axiom that consciousness is the faculty of perceiving that which exists—and that man gains knowledge of reality by looking outward."*

It is on such a base that people will realize that reality cannot be created by their minds, that praying won't make it so, and that businessmen can't produce under conditions of existence that make it impossible to produce.

---

* Ayn Rand, "The Metaphysical Versus the Man-Made," p. 24.

APPENDIX D:

"Life, Liberty, and the Pursuit of Happiness"

Liberty. An American will put his life in jeopardy for it and declare the pursuit of happiness impossible without it. For us, the very sound of the word makes the heart beat a little faster, the shoulders square to support an incomparable value. There can be no doubt of our intention to support it—or of our resolve. And as for understanding it—we believe we understand it better than any other people. Why, we created the very model of liberty: the American Constitution and the Bill of Rights. And yet, we stand by, helplessly confused in the face of crisis after crisis: abroad—the issue of ownership of the Panama Canal, detente with the Russians versus military preparedness, the Iranian seizure of our embassy; at home—an inability to evaluate the merits of wage and price controls, gasoline rationing, and welfare programs. In the face of each issue we are unable to discern what action will support liberty and the political rights that implement it. Clearly the deficiency we must repair is in understanding; in order to know what action to take we must first gain a more thorough understanding of what liberty is, and as a consequence what it requires.

At the center of the idea of liberty is the idea of political rights: A man who is free has rights, and a man who does not have them cannot be free.

But here also there is confusion; should we respect the public's right to unbiased news or the publisher's right of free speech? Does a worker have the right to a job or does his employer have the right to fire him? Are rights always more important than other considerations—like providing for the poor?

We can evaluate political rights only by evaluating the underlying moral code of which they are the implementation. A physician evaluates a drug by its ability to implement his underlying professional code of ethics: to heal the sick. Without reference to this underlying code he would have no basis upon which to judge any particular drug. Americans are unable to judge between two radically different evaluations of political rights because most Americans believe in elements of two mutually exclusive moral codes.

The man who upholds the first of these two moral codes holds as his supreme value—as the primary value against which all else is measured as good or evil—his own life, its furtherance and fulfillment. The man who upholds this moral code, rational selfishness, *must* evaluate political rights as a necessity, for without political rights he does not have the right to take the actions necessary to support and further his life, nor the right to keep the products of his labor.

The second moral code is the only other possible alternative: If a man does not hold his own life as his highest value, then something else must occupy that position. But selection of a primary value (that is, a value standard) determines the value of all else by the criterion of how well it serves the primary value. If the primary value selected is the public good, then everything else including a man's life must be judged by how well it serves the public good. According to such a moral code, rights are a value only so long as they coincide with the public good—or with what a majority believes is the public good, or with what politicians declare it is. Regardless what is chosen as the primary value—whether a deity, the Aryan race, or the common good—if that value is anything other than man's life, his life *must* be held as potentially expendable. The physician who holds the advancement of medical knowledge as his *primary* professional ethic must sacrifice his patients to any experiment that may advance medical knowledge.

Nor is it possible to combine two moral codes that have differing primary values. The physician who holds medical progress as his primary value in patient care may argue that this is compatible with consistently beneficial patient care. But there will always be cases in which he must choose between the two values, and if he insists upon not choosing between them—not relegating one to a lesser position of value—he will lose the ability to make consistent decisions. He will sometimes act in the support of one and sometimes in the support of the other; sometimes he will experiment on his patients and sometimes not. The attempt to combine two value standards in a political system must fail for the same reason: Whenever two opposing actions in support of two differing value standards present themselves, it is necessary to choose between them. If the public good will be served by taxing the middle class to support the poor, and the individual's good by allowing him to spend his money as he sees fit, the political system can take the individual *or* the public good as its value standard. It cannot simultaneously do both. In America, it vacillates—sometimes recognizing the rights of the individual and sometimes sacrificing them to the "higher" value. In Russia, the value standard of the public good is far more consistently applied—with the inevitable consequence of the sacrifice of the individual and the rights that protect him.

The results of the moral code of altruism, regardless what value standard is chosen as "higher" than man's life and the rights that make his proper survival possible, have been demonstrated in China and Russia. The results of the attempt to mix altruism and rational selfishness are now apparent in our own country—the unstable mixed economy that results from a mixture of moral codes, the mixed concept of rights that attempts to keep the concept of rights and of liberty without holding man's life as a *consistent* value standard, the mixed foreign policy that is the result of the attempt to consistently defend liberty without first defining precisely what it is and what actions it requires. There is only one other alternative to be tried: a return to the political system that was inaugurated with the American Bill of Rights, a return to the economic system of laissez-faire capitalism, and a return to a foreign policy whose purpose is to protect our rights from dangers abroad—but this time with the full knowledge and acknowledgment of the moral code of which it is an expression: the moral code of rational selfishness. Let us examine whether a strict adherence to political rights as the implementation of such a moral code can provide us with a political ideology that will solve our present confusions.

The moral code of rational selfishness acknowledges that mankind's primary tool of survival is his mind; that the proper method of survival for a rational species is rational thought; and that his survival requires his freedom to act on the judgment of his mind. It is for the purpose of implementing this natural right of man that mankind invented political rights: "that all men are created equal . . . with certain unalienable Rights, that among these are Life, Liberty and the pursuit of Happiness. That to secure these rights, Governments are instituted among Men . . ." When an individual is faced with force by another man he calls the police and invokes the criminal law; when he is faced with force by the government he invokes the Bill of Rights.

A consistent definition of political rights as freedom from force by any man or group (including the government) results in a very specific concept of political rights. *The right to free speech* guarantees that no man will be silenced by force; it does not obligate him to speak nor to listen, to publish a newspaper nor to buy the one his neighbor publishes. It obligates him in only one way: not to use force to prevent anyone's free speech in any form. A man's right to freedom of speech is absolute; he doesn't lose it if no one listens to him, if he gains a very great following, or if he becomes a broadcaster or a publisher or businessman. This means that even if a town has only one newspaper, the publisher may not be compelled to reflect the views of his readers. Whether the readers themselves force him or whether a government bureaucrat does, the result is an infringement of his right to free speech. Government violation of the right to free speech is widely practiced today—particularly in broadcasting, where it is referred to as the public's "right" to unbiased programming. A legitimate right always protects against the use of force; a "right" that initiates force cannot be legitimate. *The right to act* preserves to the individual the widest possible choice of action. For this reason it cannot govern the *results* of his actions: The freedom to act guarantees that any individuals can interact in any way (except by using force); each can buy from, sell, or give to the other his labor or any possession. But it does not guarantee that any man *will* do any of these things; an individual has the right to offer his labor on the market but not a right to a job, which would compel another to hire him. Government violation of the right to act is widespread, especially in the economic sphere. For example, a company that succeeds in generating a large volume of sales (a *voluntary* transaction by each buyer) may be accused by the government of violating its competitors' "right" to a fair share of the market. The only way such a "right" can be implemented is by the use of force against the owners of the successful company and the customers who prefer their products. *The right to own property* guarantees the continued possession and right of disposal of whatever a man possesses by purchase, gift, or inheritance. Appropriation of privately owned wealth to "redistribute" it among others is an example of our government's violation of this right.

Only after acknowledging the nature of individual rights at home is it rationally possible to defend American property rights and lives abroad. Only by recognizing that government's only proper function is to protect man's rights will we come to an accurate evaluation of any foreign government that systematically denies the rights of its subjects.

Neither the intention nor the resolve to defend liberty was sufficient to create America. The bravery of the American revolutionaries could not have created it. Nor will good intentions, resolution, and courage save it. To save liberty requires the use of the same arduous faculty that created it—the clearest and most rigorous understanding of its nature.

APPENDIX E:

"The Moral and the Practical"

Most people would agree that our society has serious problems today. In politics and economics alone, these problems seem so serious as to threaten our ability to prosper and enjoy our lives. Inflation robs us of our savings and makes it difficult or impossible to plan for the future. The energy crisis is a damper on our high standard of living. Our government seems unable to protect its own representatives in foreign lands. Our economic well-being seems to be at the mercy of Arab dictators, and national and world security seem threatened by an increasingly dangerous Soviet Union.

These problems have existed for some years, and they have only been getting worse. Inflation approaches twenty percent. At the same time, the average citizen is giving an increasingly larger percentage of his income to government. Fuel for all purposes is becoming more dear and difficult to come by. War is becoming more and more of a possibility. Enslavement of young citizens in the military is becoming more likely, and yet our ability to defend our country seems to be fading.

Our government leaders tell us there are no easy solutions to these problems. (Whoever implied a statesman's job was supposed to be "easy"?) What they mean is, they don't know what to do. Or worse, they mean it's not their fault: No one could know what to do.

Suppose I were to state the following: One *can* know what to do. These problems do have solutions. And they are known, although not by our government leaders.

If I said that, the reader might be skeptical, but he probably would be intrigued enough to want to hear my solutions, and why I was so sure of them.

Suppose I then stated that the basis for my solutions was morality and the philosophical principles that underlie the proper moral code. Many of you might feel let down, as if you had been cheated. "Oh!" you might think, "I thought he meant *practical* solutions."

The purpose of this paper is not so much to convince the reader that my solutions are right. Rather, I want to show that if it is true that my solutions are the proper moral solutions, then they must be the only practical ones. In other words, the moral and the practical are identical. And therefore, the science of morality, or ethics, holds the answers to our society's fundamental practical problems.

To provide some motivation, let me for the record indicate the essentials of the solution to some of the problems mentioned.* To end inflation, the energy crisis, and a stagnant economy in general, the government should end its involvement in the economy. All regulations, including money-supply administration, price controls, licensing, and income-redistribution programs, should be eliminated. In other words, our economy should be based on capitalism, the "social system based on the recognition of individual rights, including property rights, in which all property is privately owned."† The only role of government should be to protect individuals from the initiation of the use of physical force, which is the only way an individual's rights can be violated. Moreover, underlying this solution, men should practice the highest moral virtue: the use of reason.

---

* For a full validation of this solution and its basis, the reader should consult the works of Ayn Rand, especially *Atlas Shrugged* and the essays "The Objectivist Ethics" and "Man's Rights" in *The Virtue of Selfishness*.

† Ayn Rand, "What Is Capitalism," in *Capitalism: The Unknown Ideal*, p. 19 (paperback).

Some readers might think, "The above solution might be moral, but it is impractical. It may be moral to have an economy free of all government controls, but it would not work. Big companies would raise their prices and would make it impossible for the common people to survive." Others would add, "Morality has nothing to do with the real world anyway."

Others would agree that morality and practicality are independent or even at odds, but they would have just the reverse view about what was moral and practical: "Of course, capitalism's free market would be very practical for satisfying material needs of greedy businessmen and even the needs of workers, but it is immoral. It does not recognize the needs of the poor and underprivileged, and it ignores everyone's spiritual duty to sacrifice personal desires for the common good." Even many people who think that a free-market economy is both moral and practical (or immoral and impractical) think the agreement is purely a coincidence.

The view that there is a dichotomy between the moral and the practical is more widespread than any particular moral or practical philosophy. What are the sources of this view?

One source is the mind-body dichotomy, which is the view that the mind and body belong to two different worlds or realms. The body is thought to be part of the physical world. But the mind is thought to be of some other spiritual or ideal world. The philosopher Plato, for example, thought the mind was part of a world he called the "world of Forms." He thought the physical world was an imperfect reflection of the perfect world of Forms.

Carrying this view further, the source of morality is thought to be some part of that spiritual world: either a god, or emotions, or the "soul" of each individual or of some group. The code of morality is thought to be applicable to the spiritual realm of the mind, which is higher, or nobler, than the crude physical world of the body. Adherence to the moral code usually is thought to be good for the spirit. For example, most Christian philosophers held that the moral man's spirit would be rewarded in the spiritual realm of heaven.

Now, these philosophers could not help noticing that when men followed these moral codes, their bodies—or, more generally, their existence on earth—suffered. (For example, religious missionaries renounced all personal ambitions in order to serve God.) But instead of changing their moral codes, these philosophers concluded that the physical world of man's body was at war with his spirit, constantly tempting him to break his moral code.

One now can see how the moral-practical dichotomy arose. "Practical" means something that works to achieve a specific goal. It implies a goal or a standard by which to judge if something works. This standard of practical action is usually meant to be the well-being of the individual man in the real world that our minds directly perceive, not in some mind-invented worlds of the above philosophers. And so, "practical" courses of action are in conflict with the mystical moral codes.

A moral code, however, can and should be based on the real world. What, then, is the proper relation between the moral and the practical?

A moral code is "a code of values to guide man's choices and actions.*" Just as practicality requires a standard, so does morality. According to the morality of rational self-interest, the proper moral standard is the individual man's life—in this world, the world that exists. In other words, the standard of morality and the standard of practicality are identical. The reason morality is necessary at all is that simply to want to be practical is not enough to be practical. Wanting food, shelter, clothing, luxuries, a successful career, self-esteem, a rewarding personal life and personal relations is not enough to obtain these things. One must know how to obtain them. Morality is the theory behind practicality's practice.

Now let us return to one problem I stated earlier, to see an example of how the moral and the practical go hand in hand.

I stated that capitalism is the moral social system because it recognizes each man's right to his own life and his right to act according to his own

---

* Ayn Rand, "The Objectivist Ethics," in *The Virtue of Selfishness*, p. 13 (paperback).

rational judgment. This principle is based on several more fundamental principles, stated briefly in the following argument.

Many alternate values and actions are possible to man. Some will further man's life; most will harm it. Man has the capacity to know which values will further his life. That capacity is his rational faculty, or reason, which he is free to use if he chooses. Therefore, reason is man's basic, practical means of survival. However, the only reason available to him is his own. The only way for him to know that his actions are good for his life is if they are the actions he himself chooses by his own rational judgment. Therefore, a political system should ensure that no one uses force against a man to prevent him from acting in accordance with his own rational judgment.

The principles stated in the above moral argument are very abstract. At the same time, they are profound and direct statements about practical reality. If they are true, then any political system that abridged individual freedom of action would be a disaster in practice.

The compelling practical importance of the above argument might be easier to grasp if the argument is examined in a less abstract light. The reader should try to personalize the statements, and ask himself if they apply to his own life. Such an exercise might proceed as follows:

What conditions do I need to be confident of my success in life? Can I live without government subsidies and welfare programs? Could I live if certain individuals or companies chose not to trade with me, or set their terms or prices in such a way that I could not deal with them? Could I survive anyway, just on the strength of my own mind and my ability to translate thought into action? Could I still produce what I need to live? Could I plan and save for the future? And could I not expect many other people to be able to survive on their own virtues as well? Could I not persuade at least some of them to trade their products for mine when it was to our mutual benefit? In short, could I not survive if the only issue to reckon with is my own ability and willingness to deal with reality?

But could I survive if I were not free to act according to my own judgment? Would a government handout today guarantee me more handouts forever? And what of all the handouts I may have to give to others in the future? What of the government regulators who one day may say my activities are legal and the next day say they are not, or the price I planned to charge for my labor is higher than the law allows? Can I save and plan for the future in such an unknowable environment, where the rules are set not by knowable reality or by agreement among men, but rather are set and reset by our "leaders"? In such an environment, can I plan a career, choose a place to live, plan a family life? Can I survive even in the present, when others decide what percentage of my production I may keep for myself, especially when that percentage is shrinking all the time?

And if I am no longer able to survive by my own effort, can I depend on the support of others? Can I decide for them to be rational, hardworking, and productive? Even if they wanted to, how productive could they be in an environment that is unfree and unpredictable? (How productive can the energy industry be today?) And if some of them were still able to be somewhat productive, how much of their production would be handed over to me and not to some others?

In short, is it more practical to live in a free country or a country that is becoming more and more like the Soviet Union?

From the construction of the above questions it should be clear how the author would answer them. However, the reader is not to infer that the answers are obvious or self-evident. It is the task of ethics to answer them. My point is that the answers hinge on the truth or falsehood of the principles stated in the abstract moral argument. In other words, the moral principles and practical conclusions are based on the same premises.

APPENDIX F:

"Racism"

Despite the pleas and demands of many of today's moral leaders that the phenomenon of racism be stopped, it still continues. Why is this so? What are the factors that allow and prompt men to hold and carry out racist policies? Can racism be stopped?

A good answer to these questions would begin with a clear, concise definition of racism, for as in the case of most persistent problems, clarity of the involved issues is usually lacking.

Racism is the judging of a man, an assessment of his very character, based upon some particular anatomical trait—usually skin color. It is a view of mankind that asserts that a person acts the way he does because the content of his mind is inherited, and that the nature of this content is reflected by an aspect of his body.

By definition racism is both a form of determinism and collectivism. Supposedly, a person does not decide his own character; his ancestors do this by acting in concert as a giant group, exerting their influence via genetics. Like tribalism, racism holds that a man is what he is, will live, and must be judged accordingly, because his ancestors were whoever they were and did whatever they did. This is the doctrine of innate ideas and leads to such things as "Negro thought," "the Asian mind," "white man's ways," "the Jew in him"—a host of characteristics all determined by the dead and mediated in the live via a man's chromosomes. A typical racist would assert the following: "It's in their genes for them to act like that. He's guilty by birth."

The question to answer now is whether or not this position is valid; does it, in fact, correctly describe man's nature; is he the collectivized product of his ancestors?

An emphatic *no* is the proper response! Man's nature is such that his defining attribute is the ability to reason—which means that his perceptions of existence may, through the process of thinking, be integrated into concepts. Concepts are the basis of knowledge. Since thinking is volitional, one must choose to have knowledge. Thus, the content of a man's mind is self-determined; it is not inherently derived, as claimed by the racists. Each person is responsible for acquiring his own knowledge and acting upon it. A man's character is self-made, and it is independent of his forefathers. Man is an independent entity and has certain fundamental rights by nature: the rights to life, to property, to be judged on the basis of his self-initiated actions.

Doctrines of determinism are irrational at their base; they stand contrary to man as he is known to be. Instead of reason, the racist believes that genes are his primary attribute. Hence, he negates the nature of both the mind and heredity. The evidence that chromosomes determine anatomy is conclusive, but any evidence that character is set by heredity is totally lacking. If it is irrational to stand against nature, then using the racist viewpoint as a basis for judging oneself and others, especially in the context of today's biological knowledge, is worse than irrational—it is immoral.

Irrationality breeds immorality. The results of the two can be seen in any history book or current newspaper. There are wars of racial extermination, such as World War II; there are battles between religious tribes, such as Catholic Ireland versus Protestant England; and as the latest headlines show, the Communist empire of the Soviet Union continues to expand and enslave more of humanity. Will such events ever stop happening? Can the doctrines of determinism be defeated?

Again an emphatic answer is given—but this time it is *yes*! Yes, that is, if more men will take the initiative to learn the full nature of the problems confronting society, the most urgent problems.

As stated earlier in this discussion, despite the pleas and urgings of today's moral leaders, racism still continues. Indeed, it would be difficult to find a current newspaper that did not have at least one report in it calling for an end to racial injustice. From the same paper, one can also learn the following: that it is in a man's best interest for the state to tax his salary—to pay for welfare, to subsidize big and small business, to finance mandatory education. Another interesting fact one can read is that the individual must make whatever sacrifice the state deems necessary, including even that of life. He must, via conscription, be prepared to die for the good of the state.

Obviously these duties are of great significance, and no serious person would take them lightly. Yet, what do they have in common with racism; why are such things mentioned now?

This list of alleged interests is included because the same moral leaders who cry for a cessation of racism also demand that a person sacrifice his life according to the needs of the state. They assert that one's moral duty is to support the goals of the state; it is immoral to do otherwise. But what is the state?

It is, unfortunately, the same thing as discussed before—the race, the tribe, only now these things are clothed in the trappings of government.

To understand this point, remember that man is an independent entity, with the right to life, to property, and to be judged on the basis of his self-initiated action. Remember, too, that governments exist in order to secure these rights. Thus, individualism is the guiding principle of a free society. Bearing this in mind, consider the contrary: a slave society.

In a slave society, the guiding principle is collectivism, and in this society the individual has no rights. Man becomes a slave because collectivism negates the very source and purpose of right—man's nature and life. Collectivism, showing its deterministic essence, asserts that a person is primarily genes and innate knowledge expressed in the anatomical form. Since determinism dispenses with the significance of the mind, and since there is no such thing as innate knowledge, collectivism is left with nothing but whim, wish, and mysticism upon which to base a government.

Several questions immediately arise: Whose whim will rule the collectivist society? Whose wish will dictate orders? Whose God will prevail? The answer to all three is—whichever tribe, race, or group can command the sharpest spear or knife. What will this society be called? Depending upon the group in power, it will be called many different things, names such as kingdom, empire, the Third Reich, the welfare state. In all cases, the position of individual rights will not change.

Statism, then, is just another deadly variation of determinism; it is a political expression of collectivism. Therefore, when the moral leaders of today call for sacrifice to the state, to any group or anyone, they are, in effect, calling for racism. That is why racism still continues.

A man's chief attribute is his mind, and how he chooses to use it will determine his character. What are the factors in the psychology of the racist that prompt his irrational views? Briefly stated, his main desire is for the unearned. In terms of psychology, the racist seeks a strong self-esteem. However, since he is unable to deal successfully with reality, instead of feeling competent, he feels inferior. Therefore, to gain the much-needed self-esteem, the racist clings to a group identity. Within his race he finds much to be proud of but it still is not his own. He is content to fake a high level of esteem by substituting group identity for the psychological reward of personal achievement.

In terms of material wealth, the same is true. However, due to the nature of material goods, unless earned, they have to be stolen. At the lowest level of society, common sneak thieves commit these acts. At the highest level, statist government is the criminal.

To close this presentation, a final point remains to be said on government.

The mind, the faculty of reason, does not work automatically; a man must choose to think. A thought is implemented via action, and in order to be moral, an act has to comply with three criteria: It must be consistent with a man's knowledge of reality; it must sustain or further his life; it cannot violate the rights of other men. In terms of politics, this means establishing a political system that allows man to live as man. Because he has fundamental, inalienable rights—of life and property—it follows that man's government, if it is to be moral, cannot violate these rights. The only political system that follows from man's rights is laissez-faire capitalism.